THE CRITICAL WRITINGS *of* OSCAR WILDE

THE CRITICAL WRITINGS
of OSCAR WILDE

AN ANNOTATED SELECTION

EDITED BY **NICHOLAS FRANKEL**

HARVARD UNIVERSITY PRESS

Cambridge, Massachusetts, and London, England

2022

FIRST PRINTING

Publication of this book has been supported through the
generous provisions of the Maurice and Lula Bradley Smith Memorial Fund.

Library of Congress Cataloging-in-Publication Data

Names: Wilde, Oscar, 1854–1900, author. | Frankel, Nicholas, 1962– editor.
Title: The critical writings of Oscar Wilde : an annotated selection /
Oscar Wilde ; edited by Nicholas Frankel.
Description: Cambridge, Massachusetts : Harvard University Press, 2022. |
Includes bibliographical references.
Identifiers: LCCN 2022010857 | ISBN 9780674271821 (cloth)
Subjects: LCSH: Criticism. | Literature—History and criticism. |
England—Social life and customs—19th century.
Classification: LCC PR5811 .C75 2022 | DDC 824/.8—dc23/eng/20220425
LC record available at https://lccn.loc.gov/2022010857

CONTENTS

CONTENTS

THE CRITICAL WRITINGS *of* OSCAR WILDE

Photoportrait of Wilde, by Napoleon Sarony, 1882.

INTRODUCTION

Not by wrath does one kill but by laughter—Nietzsche

Although chiefly known today as the paragon of wit and style, a pathbreaking sexual dissident, and the Victorian era's greatest playwright, Oscar Wilde was also Victorian Britain's most provocative, entertaining, and forward-thinking critic. For a period of roughly seven years leading up to his career as a successful playwright in the early 1890s, he published literary and cultural criticism in an array of periodicals, including articles in the leading monthlies *The Nineteenth Century* and *The Fortnightly Review* and over eighty book reviews in London's *Pall Mall Gazette* alone. His only published book of criticism, the aptly named *Intentions,* is regarded by many as among the finest of his writings—the poet W. B. Yeats called it "a wonderful book" and the American essayist Agnes Repplier judged it the best book published in 1891, while the *New York Times* described it as Wilde's "finest prose work"—and three years after its publication Wilde himself remarked, "I simply love that book!"[1] (Wilde's friend Ada Leverson had just presented him with a specially bound copy as a birthday present.)[2]

As with everything he did, Wilde approached the writing of criticism with wit, irony, and a consummate sense of style, so much so that his critical writing is often hardly recognizable as *criticism.* Like Plato's *Symposium*—called by Wilde "of all the Platonic dialogues perhaps the most perfect"—Wilde's major critical expositions, "The Decay of Lying" and "The Critic as Artist," are written in the form of conversations or dialogues, the first of them between characters who are named for Wilde's children, Vivian and Cyril, who were two and three years old, respectively, at the time of publication; and they eloquently demonstrate Wilde's notions that "recreation, not instruction, is the aim of conversation" and that conversation is seriously undermined by "a permanent gravity of demeanour and a general dulness of mind." Even Wilde's most sophisticated and trenchant criticism is inflected by the rhythms and intonations of his speaking voice—the "only . . . essential" for a "good conversationalist," Wilde once remarked, "is the possession of a musical voice"—and, as Wilde observed of another erudite and witty talker, reading his critical writings is like entertaining "Aristotle at afternoon tea."

Together with its conversational character, perhaps the most striking and surprising feature of Wilde's criticism is its wit. The epigrams with which some of his earliest published pieces begin— "Mr. Whistler made his first public appearance as a lecturer on art, and spoke . . . with really marvellous eloquence on the absolute uselessness of all lectures of the kind"; "A man can live for three days without bread, but no man can live for one day without poetry"; "Who, . . . in these degenerate days, would hesitate between an ode and an omelette, a sonnet and a salmis?"—set the tone in this regard. Reviewing *Intentions* in *The Academy,* Richard

Le Gallienne observed that "there will be many who . . . take him seriously; but let me assure them that Mr. Wilde is not of the number,"[3] and Wilde himself remarked that, while art is the only serious thing in the world, "the artist is never serious." Wilde would certainly have wanted his criticism to be understood with a smile and as an extension or expression of his "art"—"Criticism is itself an art," he declares in "The Critic as Artist," for like the artist, the critic "works with materials, and puts them into a form that is at once new and delightful"—and it is much to the point that many of the epigrams sprinkled throughout Wilde's criticism anticipate those to be found in his fiction and his plays. Given this epigram-maticism, it is not surprising that Wilde's career as a critic culmi-nated in "Phrases and Philosophies for the Use of the Young" and "A Few Maxims for the Instruction of the Over-Educated," just months before his criminal conviction. In these astonishing dis-plays of epigrammatic wit and wisdom, Wilde elevated the epigram into a distinctive literary form in its own right.

If he was right to highlight Wilde's absence of seriousness, how-ever, Le Gallienne was surely wrong to write that "Mr. Wilde [is] essentially a humorist who has taken art-criticism for his medium" and "his intricate tracery of thought and elaborate jewel-work of expression is simply built-up to make a casket for one or two clever homeless paradoxes."[4] The witty epigram and the paradox were not ends in themselves, for Wilde, but rather expressions of a distinctly provocative intellectual intent. If "gravity of demeanour and . . . dulness of mind" were the enemy, sharpness of mind was Wilde's object as well as his medium. Wilde himself states at the end of "The Truth of Masks" that "just as it is only in art-criticism, and through it, that we can apprehend the Platonic theory of ideas, so it is only in art-criticism, and through it, that we can realize Hegel's system of contraries. The truths of metaphysics are the truths of masks." Humor and paradox were expressions of what we might term, after Bakhtin, Wilde's "dialogic imagination," for they encapsulated not merely Wilde's drive to provoke and destabilize the staid formulas of sound judgment and earnest belief, but also a dialectical understanding of truth, built on the notion that any utterance contains and even presupposes its opposite. As Wilde puts it in "The Critic as Artist," "to know the truth one must imagine myriads of falsehoods." "Verbal discourse is a social phenomenon," Bakhtin explains, no matter how individual or unitary a given author's personal style may seem, and partly for this reason "the word is born in a dialogue as a living rejoinder with it, . . . shaped in dialogic interaction with an alien word that is already in the object. . . . [E]very word is directed toward an *answer* and cannot escape the profound influence of the answering word that it anticipates."[5] The verbal cut-and-thrust of Wilde's social comedies— in which the young waste no time in contradicting their elders—is the keynote of Wilde's critical writings, too, even those among them not explicitly written in the form of the dialogue. Perhaps the most straightforward and seemingly earnest of his essays, "The Truth of Masks," for instance, ends tongue-in-cheek with the essayist declaring, "not that I agree with everything I have said in this essay. There is much with which I entirely disagree. The essay simply represents an artistic standpoint, and in aesthetic criticism attitude is everything." Conversation "implies differences in opinion," Wilde insists elsewhere, and while "the well-bred contradict other people," only "the wise contradict themselves." "Diversity of opinion," Wilde insists in the Preface to *The Picture of Dorian Gray,* "shows that the work is new, complex, and vital."

If Wilde's criticism begs to be contradicted, it is also willfully ironic, subordinating what is "said" to what remains unsaid or merely implied. ("Only the great masters of style ever succeed in being obscure," Wilde declares in "Phrases and Philosophies for the Use of the Young.") Wilde's backhanded compliment about Whistler's "really marvellous eloquence on the absolute uselessness of all lectures" is typical in this regard, not merely because it subtly sets the stage for the serious intellectual disagreements that Wilde goes on to express in the course of his review of Whistler's important "Ten O'Clock" lecture, but also because it punctures Whistler's vaingloriousness and hubris in venturing into a field, the public lecture on art, that Wilde had in recent years made more or less his own. (In this regard, Wilde's review of Whistler's lecture anticipates his short story "The Remarkable Rocket," published three years later, in which Wilde parodies Whistler allegorically as a "remarkable" firework that, after failing to go off properly, gets thrown into a ditch, where it eventually explodes unseen.) Similarly, the joy with which Wilde delights in classifying the various kinds of artist's models, in "London Models," gives a clue that the essay, like Wilde's "Philosophy of Dress," extends far beyond its ostensible subject to embrace the liberation of the body and of gender from the rigid constraints imposed upon them by Wilde's fellow Victorians. The essay's wit is decidedly risqué. When Wilde remarks that artists' models "usually marry well, and sometimes they marry the artist," that while such models are philistines intellectually, "physically they are perfect—at least some are," and that "though they cannot appreciate the artist as artist, they are quite ready to appreciate the artist as a man," the unspoken eroticism and sly sexual provocativeness of the essay rise briefly to the surface, underscoring Wilde's aphorism in the Preface to *Dorian Gray* that "all art is at once surface and symbol."

In its embrace of an ironic tone, we might say, Wilde's criticism is designed not so much to express Wilde's own ideas as to activate independent critical judgment on its reader's part. As the literary theorist Linda Hutcheon has observed, irony always "has an edge" and "is a 'weighted' mode of discourse in the sense that it is asymmetrical, unbalanced in favor of the silent and the unsaid."[6] In setting up "a differential relationship between the said and the unsaid," Hutcheon explains, "irony seems to invite inference, not only of meaning, but of attitude and judgment."[7] In its irony, then, Wilde's criticism not only makes us better readers, particularly when it comes to inferring Wilde's own attitudes and beliefs—which as the title of his collection *Intentions* cheekily implies, are at best only ever indirectly expressed—but also better thinkers. We question appearances and arrive at judgments often far from those overtly expressed. Does Wilde truly believe that "there is no essential incongruity between crime and culture," as he puts it near the end of "Pen Pencil and Poison," or that "the fact of a man being a poisoner is nothing against his prose"? The question is perhaps less relevant than the diverse reactions these controversial assertions evoke. To some readers the militant aestheticism of these epigrams is the sign of a haughty, even elitist, amorality or indifference, while to others such aestheticism demonstrates a welcome subversiveness, a freewheeling playfulness, and a necessary corrective to the ethical impulse latent beneath the surface of much criticism. In this regard, "the fact of a man being a poisoner is nothing against his prose" is twin to Edgar Allan Poe's notorious pronouncement that "the death of a beautiful woman is, unquestionably, the most poetical topic in the world."

It will be clear then that, far from being mere exhibitions of splendid humor and wit, Wilde's criticism is a distinct expression of "mind" no less than that of the overtly sage-like Victorians Thomas Carlyle, John Ruskin, and Matthew Arnold who inspired him. Earlier in the Victorian period, each of these great thinkers had done much to cement the figure of "the critic" in the public mind, and Wilde's admiration for each of them is well documented. But Wilde takes issue with Arnold in "The Critic as Artist" just as he does with Ruskin in "The Decay of Lying" and with Carlyle in "Pen Pencil and Poison." In "The Function of Criticism at the Present Time" (1865), Arnold had defined the critic's task as "to see the object as in itself it really is" while accepting "as a general proposition, that the critical faculty is lower than the inventive."[8] In "The Critic As Artist," by contrast, extending ideas that by his own admission he had absorbed from Walter Pater's *Studies in the History of the Renaissance* (1873), a work he revered as "the golden book of spirit and sense,"[9] Wilde argues that the critical capacity is ineluctably bound up with the creative, that "the antithesis between them is entirely arbitrary"—since "all fine imaginative work is self-conscious and deliberate" and "without the critical faculty, there is no artistic creation at all"—and that "the primary aim of the critic is to see the object as in itself it really is not." Similarly in *Modern Painters* (vol. 1, 1843), John Ruskin had asserted that "the representation of facts . . . is the foundation of all art" and "nothing can atone for the want of truth."[10] Ruskin had enjoined young artists to "go to Nature . . . rejecting nothing, selecting nothing, and scorning nothing," while Ruskin's entire critical oeuvre is governed by what has been called a "moral aesthetic," encapsulated in his contention that one of art's principal functions is "that of perfecting the morality, or ethical state, of men."[11] By contrast, Wilde insists in "The Decay of Lying" that "two touches of Nature will destroy any work of art," that "Nature hates mind," and that "the telling of beautiful untrue things is the proper aim of art," while in the Preface to *Dorian Gray* he says that "no artist has ethical sympathies," that "the morality of art consists in the perfect use of an imperfect medium," and that "all art is quite useless." Finally, with its rigorous, disquieting insistence on the broad "artistic temperament" of the murderer and forger Thomas Griffiths Wainewright—who was equally "powerful with pen, pencil, and poison," Wilde cheekily asserts—"Pen Pencil and Poison" invites us to embrace a more expansive definition of artistic *greatness* or *heroism* than that underpinning Carlyle's influential *On Heroes, Hero-Worship, and the Heroic in History* (1841), in which Dante and Shakespeare jostle with Cromwell, Napoleon, and Martin Luther, among others, as historic examples of great men.

As these instances imply, much of Wilde's criticism is directly concerned with creative practice, as well as with the spirit in which art should be received. His early friendship and later enmity with the outspoken painter James McNeill Whistler were critical in this regard. Whistler had turned to a court of law in 1878 in order to defend the freedoms and rights of the artist, having long before this date bemoaned in print what he deemed the pernicious influence of critics.[12] After viewing Whistler's *Nocturne in Black and Gold: The Falling Rocket* on display at London's Grosvenor Gallery (a gallery where "we are enabled to see the highest development of the modern artistic spirit," according to Wilde), the critic John Ruskin had written that he "never expected to hear a coxcomb ask two hundred guineas for flinging a pot of paint in the public's face" and that "the ill-educated conceit of the artist . . . approached the aspect of willful imposture."[13] Despite securing a legal verdict against Ruskin in the highly publicized libel case that followed, Whistler won only a farthing in damages from the jury, who took a dim view of his bringing the case to court. He had struck an important blow for the prerogatives of the artist, and successfully challenged the hitherto unquestioned authority of the critic (in resigning the prestigious Slade Professorship of Art in the wake of Whistler's libel suit, Ruskin complained, "I cannot hold a Chair from which I have no power of expressing judgment without being

Oil portrait of the painter James McNeill Whistler, by
William Merritt Chase, 1885. At first a friend and mentor to
Wilde, Whistler later became Wilde's intellectual nemesis.

James McNeill Whistler, *Nocturne in Black and Gold: The Falling Rocket,*
c. 1875. Whistler's revolutionary oil painting created a firestorm when it was
first exhibited at London's Grosvenor Gallery in 1877. The critic John Ruskin
remarked that he "never expected to hear a coxcomb ask two hundred
guineas for flinging a pot of paint in the public's face." For the artist himself
at least, Whistler's victory over Ruskin in the highly publicized libel trial
that followed represented the triumph of art over criticism.

taxed for it by British Law"),[14] but he had bankrupted himself in the process and was forced to sell his beloved Godwin-designed house and home studio ("White House") on Chelsea's Tite Street. It was soon after this that Wilde befriended Whistler, whom he praised in a review of the 1879 Grosvenor Gallery exhibition as a "wonderful and eccentric genius . . . better appreciated in France than in England."[15] Within months of Whistler's legal victory and ensuing bankruptcy, Wilde had moved to Tite Street too.

At first Wilde was held in sway by Whistler's ideas and example. But as Wilde acquired international fame in the early 1880s and started lecturing on art in his own right, he began to differentiate his views forcefully from those of Whistler, as the witty and increasingly malicious review of Whistler's "Ten O'Clock" lecture that begins this selection indicates. "An artist is not an isolated fact," Wilde declares, "he is the resultant of a certain milieu and a certain entourage, and can no more be born of a nation that is devoid of any sense of beauty than a fig can grow from a thorn or a rose blossom from a thistle." Further, Wilde could not "accept the dictum that only a painter is a judge of painting. I say that only an artist is a judge of art; there is a wide difference. As long as a painter is a painter merely, he should not be allowed to talk of anything but mediums and megilp, and on those subjects should be compelled to hold his tongue; it is only when he becomes an artist that the secret laws of artistic creation are revealed to him."

In the notion that "only an artist is a judge of art," we find the seed of Wilde's argument, as expressed later in "The Critic as Artist," that the creative and critical roles are interdependent, as well as Wilde's expansive, Platonic notion of art as something that transcends its medium or physical instantiation. For as Wilde explains, "there are not many arts, but one art merely: poem, picture and Parthenon, sonnet and statue–all are in their essence the same, and he who knows one knows all." Perhaps most importantly of all, Wilde recognized that Whistler's successful suit against Ruskin represented a dangerous assault on the power of the written word in favor of the nonverbal image, and a questionable elevation of the artistic claims of the painter over those of the writer. More personally, he understood that Whistler's attack on "the unattached writer [who] has become the middleman in this matter of Art" was a thinly veiled attack on himself. Not till 1890, when he published both "Mr. Pater's Last Volume" and the serial version of "The Critic as Artist," would Wilde answer Whistler's attack by expressly arguing for the critic's own incomparable "artistry." Five years before this, when he reviewed Whistler's lecture, Wilde viewed himself principally as a poet (his wide-selling poetry collection *Poems* had appeared in 1881) so it is perhaps unsurprising that at this date Wilde answered Whistler's attack by asserting that "the poet is the supreme artist, for he is the master of colour and of form, and the real musician besides, and is lord over all life and all arts; and so to the poet beyond all others are these mysteries known." The publication of Wilde's synesthetic poem "The Harlot's House" six weeks after his review of Whistler's lecture was, it has been argued, an effort to drive home the point.[16]

While his review of Whistler's "Ten O'Clock" represents one of his earliest meditations on the spirit in which art is produced and received, Wilde's most extensive treatment of the topic comes in the essays and dialogues which make up his 1891 collection *Intentions.* All four of these pieces had been published previously in leading monthly magazines, one of them as early as 1885. As detailed in the annotations below, Wilde made extensive revisions for their republication in *Intentions,* in two cases giving the piece an entirely new title, in three cases adding a witty and ironic subtitle, and in one case giving the essay an entirely new, willfully paradoxical, ending. The subtitle given to "The Truth of Masks" ("A Note on Illusion") is especially telling, since it underscores Wilde's repeated incorporation of the word *illusion* into the 1891 version of the essay so as to stress art's *construction* or *artifice,* rather than its imitation of life. Thus, a movement in the staging of Shakespeare that in 1885 "has Truth for its aim, and Beauty for its result" six years later "has the illusion of truth for its method, and the illusion of beauty for its result." Even beauty is a self-conscious and deliberate *effect,* as Vivian explains in "The Decay of Lying":

> Art begins with abstract decoration, with purely imaginative and pleasurable work dealing with what is unreal and non-existent. This is the first stage. Then Life becomes fascinated with this new wonder, and asks to be admitted into the charmed circle. [So] Art takes life as part of her rough material, recreates it, and refashions it in fresh forms, is absolutely indifferent to fact, invents, imagines, dreams, and keeps between herself and reality the impenetrable barrier of beautiful style, of decorative or ideal treatment. The third stage is when Life gets the upper hand, and drives Art out into the wilderness.

As Vivian recognizes here, beauty can be discomfiting to some, and even Shakespeare, in his late plays, suffers from being "too fond of going directly to life, and borrowing life's natural utterance . . . [forgetting] that when Art surrenders her imaginative medium she surrenders everything." Moreover, to prioritize artistic creativity and invention over moral or social aims for art is to court controversy, if not social expulsion, from those who insist that art be a mirror or "glass" in which their own face is reflected. "The nineteenth century dislike of Romanticism," Wilde proclaims in his Preface to *Dorian Gray,* "is the rage of Caliban not seeing his own face in a glass." "The highest Criticism deals with art not as expressive but as impressive purely," Gilbert explains in "The Critic as Artist": "Beauty . . . makes the critic a creator in his turn" and "the work of art is simply a suggestion for a new work of [the critic's] own." In fact the true critic "does not even require for the perfection of his art the finest materials," and as Wilde's hugely enjoyable reviews of unpromising-sounding guidebooks to cookery and marriage indicate, "from subjects of little or of no importance, . . . the true critic can, if it be his pleasure so to direct or waste his faculty of contemplation, produce work that will be flawless in style and instinct with intellectual subtlety" (see "Dinners and Dishes" and "A Handbook to Marriage," below). Where "those who find beautiful meanings in beautiful things are the cultivated," however, a different class of readers finds only "ugly meanings" and calls down moral judgment on the artist as a result. As Wilde explains in "The Soul of Man Under Socialism," when critics misapprehend art they frequently try to exercise over it "an authority that is as immoral as it is ridiculous, and as corrupting as it is contemptible. . . . They are continually asking Art to be popular, to please their want to taste, to flatter their absurd vanity, to tell them what they have been told before." Nonetheless even popular and purportedly realist artworks succeed or fail according to their makers' judicious care and craft, Wilde reminds us, and "the work that seems to us to be the most natural and simple product of its time is always the result of the most self-conscious effort."

Perhaps the most important idea running through *Intentions* is Wilde's principled rejection of art's mimetic and representational functions, with its accompanying insistence that, as Wilde puts it in "The Decay of Lying," "art finds her own perfection within, and not outside of, herself. She is not to be judged by any external standard of resemblance. She is a veil, rather than a mirror." The idea is the basis of Wilde's argument for art's freedom and independence from life, as well as the foundation of his insistence that, as Vivian puts it in "The Decay of Lying," "Life imitates Art far more than Art imitates Life." For if art "never expresses anything but itself . . . and develops purely on its own lines," as Vivian explains, the "basis of life" is nonetheless "the desire for expression." In consequence life "holds the mirror up to Art," searching for "forms through which this expression can be attained," and ultimately life "either reproduces some strange type imagined by painter or sculptor, or realizes in fact what has been dreamed in fiction."

As a number of recent commentators have pointed out, Wilde here anticipates late-twentieth-century notions that language is the parent, not the servant, of thought, and that reality is a *construction,* inseparable from the values and traditions that shape our thoughts and beliefs. "It is in our brain" that the world "quickens to life," asserts Vivian: "things are because we see them, and what we see, and how we see it, depends on the Arts that have influenced us." Yosemite Valley and the English Lake District are now inseparable from their representation in the photographs of Ansel Adams and the poetry of William Wordsworth respectively. Similarly, "people see fogs, not because there are fogs," declares Vivian, "but because poets and painters have taught them the mysterious loveliness of such effects." Wilde was perhaps thinking here of the "crepuscular impressionism" on display in some of his own early poems, such as "Impression du Matin" and "La Mer," as well as the painted nocturnes of James McNeill Whistler and the early Thames paintings of Claude Monet, who once declared that "without fog London would not be beautiful."

Many of these ideas recur in condensed epigrammatic form in Wilde's Preface to *Dorian Gray*, first published over Wilde's signature in the influential *Fortnightly Review* independently from his only novel, two months before the appearance of *Intentions*. "The artist is the creator of beautiful things" and "[t]o reveal art and conceal the artist is art's aim," Wilde declares, while "the critic is he who can translate into another manner or a new material his impression of beautiful things." The Preface remains Wilde's quintessential statement on art, as well as a classic example of what the French literary theorist Gérard Genette calls a "delayed preface," whereby an author responds in a "compensatory" fashion "to the first reactions of the first public and the critics."[17] But if it reads ultimately like a Preface to *Intentions* as much as to Wilde's novel, there is a crucial difference in the Preface's manner and tone. As the annotations below detail, some of the epigrams it contains had been rehearsed the previous year in letters defending Wilde's novel from the attacks made upon it in the papers shortly after its appearance in periodical form, and there is a new militancy to Wilde's ideas ("those who find ugly meanings in beautiful things are corrupt without being charming," "books are well written, or badly written. That is all," "an ethical sympathy in an artist is an unpardonable mannerism of style," "when critics disagree, the artist is in accord with himself") that is lacking in the more playful and speculative dialogues. In utilizing the form of the dialogue, Gilbert remarks in "The Critic as Artist," the thinker "can both reveal and conceal himself, and give form to every fancy, and reality to every mood. By its means he can exhibit the object from each point of view, and show it to us in the round." By contrast, the epigrams of the Preface have something of the doctrinal air of the "new aesthetics" with which Vivian concludes his peroration in "The Decay of Lying" so that his interlocutor may "avoid making any error." And if "The Truth of Masks" ends with Wilde asserting "[n]ot that I agree with everything that I have said" and "in art there is no such thing as a universal truth," Wilde's signature beneath his Preface to *Dorian Gray* makes it clear exactly where he stands. If "the artist is the creator of beautiful things," that artist is Oscar Wilde, the author of *The Picture of Dorian Gray,* and the Preface has been understood ever since its first publication as Wilde's personal artistic manifesto.

This note of militancy carries over to Wilde's essay "The Soul of Man Under Socialism" too, published one month before the Preface in the same prominent monthly magazine.[18] Like the Preface, the essay was composed in the wake of the controversy surrounding *Dorian Gray*'s publication in *Lippincott's,* in the course of which more than one reviewer had hinted that Wilde ought to be prosecuted for presenting "matters only fitted for the Criminal Investigation Department or a hearing *in camera.*"[19] As we will shortly see, much of the essay consists of broad political theory laced with characteristic paradoxes and epigrams, but it turns in its second half to the rights of the artist, freedom of artistic expression, the power of the press, and the despotism of public opinion. "*Art is the most intense mode of Individualism that the world has known,*" Wilde boldly declares—indeed, "I am inclined to say that it is the only real mode of Individualism that the world has known." But "the public try to exercise over it an authority that is as immoral as it is ridiculous, and as corrupting as it is contemptible." Society no longer insists that the philosopher and the scientist constrain their speculations so as to fit with popular belief and prejudice, Wilde observes, and "we have to a very great extent got rid of any attempt on the part of the community, or the Church, or the Government, to interfere with the individualism of speculative thought, but the attempt to interfere with the individualism of imaginative art still lingers. In fact, it does more than linger; it is aggressive, offensive, and brutalising."

Wilde was probably thinking here of the dual threat of prosecution and censorship hovering over *Dorian Gray* in the period leading up to the publication of "The Soul of Man Under Socialism"—and more specifically still, of the despotic power of the National Vigilance Association, founded in 1885 "for the enforcement and improvement of the laws for the repression of criminal vice and public immorality." The Association had been directly invoked by one reviewer of *Dorian Gray*, who had remarked "whether the Treasury or the Vigilance Society will think it worth while to prosecute Mr. Oscar Wilde or Messrs. Ward, Lock & Co. [English publisher of Wilde's novel], we do not know"; and in 1889 it had succeeded in having Emile Zola's English publisher Henry Vizetelly prosecuted—twice—for obscenity, with the result that Vizetelly spent three months in jail and was fined a total of £300, while a number of Zola's most important works remained unpublished in Britain for many years. Perhaps Wilde was thinking, too, of timorous publishers, editors, booksellers, libraries, and licensing bodies, whose pernicious interference he had already experienced at first hand in the case of *Dorian Gray*, and was to experience again in 1892 when his play *Salomé* was denied a performance license. Nonetheless he insists finally that "an artist in England gains something by being attacked. His individuality is intensified. He becomes more completely himself." For Wilde, the artist is an avant-garde figure opposed to all convention, prejudice, and the force of public opinion. As Wilde puts it in the Preface, "When critics disagree the artist is in accord with himself."

While "The Soul of Man Under Socialism" demands to be understood partly in tandem with the Preface to *Dorian Gray* as Wilde's declaration of the artist's freedom from control and authority, it also demands to be understood—as its title makes abundantly clear—as a political treatise, deeply concerned with systems of government and the rights of the individual. Besides Wilde's own recent experiences as a writer, it reflects his longstanding interest in both socialist and anarchist thought, as well as the influence of John Stuart Mill's epochal treatise *On Liberty* (1859). The essay begins with a vehement critique of the capitalist system of Victorian Britain, based on property rights and a hierarchy of social and economic classes. This system only reifies large-scale inequality, Wilde argues, aggravating rather than solving the problem of mass poverty, for instance, through its sentimental recourse to institutionalized charity and questionable acts of philanthropy. ("Charity creates a multitude of sins," Wilde quips, wittily adapting the First Epistle of Peter, in part since it "is immoral to use private property in order to alleviate the horrible evils that result from the institution of private property.") "The proper aim is to try and reconstruct society on such a basis that poverty will be impossible," he argues: "Socialism, Communism, or whatever one chooses to call it, by converting private property into public wealth, and substituting co-operation for competition, will restore society to its proper condition of a thoroughly healthy organism, and insure the material well-being of each member of the community. It will, in fact, give Life its proper basis and its proper environment."

But although Wilde had attended socialist lectures and was a paid-up subscriber to *The Commonweal,* the official organ of the recently founded Socialist League, his essay is hardly an orthodox expression of early socialist thought, as Wilde himself acknowledges. It reflects the influence of the anarchist Peter Kropotkin and the Darwinian sociologist Herbert Spencer as much as the ideas expounded by William Morris, George Bernard Shaw, and other early socialists. "With the abolition of private property," Wilde declares, "we shall have true, beautiful, healthy Individualism. Nobody will waste his life in accumulating things, and the symbols for things. One will live. To live is the rarest thing in the world. Most people exist, that is all." Liberated from their enslavement to a capitalist economy, property owners and workers alike will be free to "develop what is wonderful and fascinating and delightful" in themselves, Wilde contends, thereby realizing more fully "the true pleasure and joy of living." Moreover, nobody will answer to any authority external to themselves.[20] For it is not merely authority over the artist to which Wilde objects. "All authority is quite degrading," he insists: "it degrades those who exercise it, and degrades those over whom it is exercised." Consequently "the State must give up all idea of government, because, as a wise man once said many centuries before Christ, there is such a thing as leaving mankind alone; there is no such thing as governing mankind. *All modes of government are failures.*"

On the surface, "The Soul of Man Under Socialism" appears the most sincere of Wilde's essays and the very antithesis of "The Truth of Masks," with its closing assertions that "in aesthetic criticism, attitude is everything" and that "the essay simply represents an artistic standpoint." But the later essay is built around a typical Wildean paradox—that the "establishment of socialism . . . would relieve us from that sordid necessity of living for others"—and on closer inspection it becomes clear that Wilde adopts an "attitude" and means to provoke dissent no less than with his more obviously ironic criticism. "It will, of course, be said that such a scheme as is set forth here is quite unpractical, and goes against human nature," he writes towards the essay's conclusion. "This is perfectly true," he explains: "It is unpractical, and it goes against human nature. This is why it is worth carrying out, and that is why one proposes it." Similarly, "Is this Utopian?" he asks about his own vision of how "there will be great storages of force for every city, and for every house if required, and this force man will convert into heat, light, or motion, according to his needs."[21] "A map of the world that does not include Utopia is not worth even glancing at," he says in answer to the anticipated objection, in one of the essay's most famous and frequently quoted epigrams, "for it leaves out the one country at which Humanity is always landing. And when Humanity lands there, it looks out, and, seeing a better country, sets sail. Progress is the realisation of Utopias."

Wilde himself thought highly of "The Soul of Man Under Socialism," and although it was composed too late for inclusion in *Intentions,* he wanted it to replace "The Truth of Masks" in the authorized French translation (as it duly did when this translation finally appeared in 1914). The essay "contient une partie de mon esthétique" (*contains a part of my aesthetics),* he told his French translator.[22] His considered opinion of the much lighter and shorter "Fashions in Dress," published virtually simultaneously at the beginning of February 1891, is not recorded, but no less than "The Soul of Man" it, too, contains a valuable part of Wilde's aesthetics. "Freedom in . . . selection of colour is a necessary condition of variety and individualism of costume, and the uniform black that is worn now, though valuable at a dinner-party, where it serves to isolate and separate women's dresses . . . is dull and tedious and depressing," Wilde proclaims:

Another important point . . . is that the decorative value of buttons is recognised. . . . Now, when a thing is useless it should be made beautiful, otherwise it has no reason for existing at all. Buttons should be either gilt . . . or of paste, or enamel, or inlaid metals, or any other material that is capable of being artistically treated. The handsome effect produced by servants' liveries is almost entirely due to the buttons they wear. . . .

The coat . . . of next season will be an exquisite colour-note, and have also a great psychological value. It will emphasize the serious and thoughtful side of a man's character. One will be able to discern a man's views of life by the colour he selects. The colour of the coat will be symbolic. It will be part of the wonderful symbolist movement in modern art. The imagination will concentrate itself upon the waistcoat. Waistcoats will show whether a man can admire poetry or not.

If "The Decay of Lying" is an expression of *aesthetic theory,* and "The Soul of Man" a treatise on the *politics* of aestheticism, "Fashions in Dress" is an exercise in what we might call *practical aestheticism* or *dandyism.* With an obvious relation to Wilde's obsession with his personal couture, it shows how life might be made more beautiful and enjoyable through a revolution in men's clothing; and it puts flesh, so to speak, on some of the witty aphorisms ("the first duty of life is to be as artificial as possible," "style, not sincerity, is the essential," "only the shallow know themselves," "the only way to atone for being occasionally a little over-dressed is by being always absolutely over-educated," "one should either be a work of art, or wear a work of art," "it is only the superficial qualities that last") that Wilde will later express in "Phrases and Philosophies for the Use of the Young." Once again Wilde writes in part to court controversy and dissent,[23] and it is tempting to read this short essay as wholly ironic, especially when Wilde writes wittily, "How the change is to be brought about is not difficult to see. . . . Nothing but a resolution on the subject passed by the House of Commons will do. . . . Surely there are some amongst our legislators who are capable of taking a serious interest in serious things? They cannot all be absorbed in the county-court collection of tithes." Nonetheless the tone is sober, and the essay has obvious connections to Wilde's earlier writings on dress as well as to "Shakespeare and Stage Costume" (as "The Truth of Masks" was titled in its unrevised earlier published version).

When he wrote "Fashions in Dress," Wilde had long since established himself as one of Britain's foremost critics of fashion. Fashion "is the great enemy of art," he writes in "The Philosophy of Dress," since it "rests upon folly" and "is ephemeral," whereas "Art rests upon law" and "is eternal." Since the early 1880s Wilde had called for greater artistry, originality, color, and above all freedom in dress. He drew in part upon the ideas of female dress reformers such as Mary Eliza Haweis and Emily King, authors respectively of *The Art of Dress* (1879) and *Rational Dress* (1882), and in some respects Wilde's ideas are consistent with those of the Rational Dress Society, which Haweis and King cofounded with Florence Pomeroy, Viscountess Harberton, in 1881.[24] (In the years following her 1884 marriage, Wilde's wife Constance was an active member— and briefly an officer—of the Society, while Viscountess Harberton later contributed to the *Woman's World* during Wilde's two-year editorship of that magazine in the late 1880s. See pp. 93–95, headnote.) But in other respects, Wilde went beyond purely "rational" dress reform: in "Shakespeare and Stage Costume," he had highlighted dress's artistic importance, arguing without irony that "even small details of dress . . . become in Shakespeare's hands points of actual dramatic importance, and by some of them the action of the play in question is conditioned absolutely." Implicitly, the later "Fashions in Dress" pursues a more political and social argument, as its historical coincidence with the publication of "The Soul of Man Under Socialism" perhaps indicates. Where the latter argues that "we shall have true, beautiful, healthy Individualism" only through the abolition of private property, "Fashions in Dress" effectively argues that the necessary social transformation could come also via subtler, less revolutionary means. The "suggested changes [would not] be in any way violent, or abrupt, or revolutionary, or calculated to excite terror in the timid, or rage in the dull, or fury in the honest Philistine," Wilde writes with irony. In his review of Whistler's "Ten O'Clock," he had referred in passing to "a nation that is devoid of any sense of beauty." In "Fashions of Dress," the self-appointed Professor of Aesthetics addresses precisely such a nation, determined on teaching "the value of beautiful costume in creating an artistic temperament."

As his exclusive concern with masculine dress in "Fashions in Dress" implies, Wilde's desired social transformation is grounded, finally, in the politics of gender. And like his essays "The American Invasion" and "The American Man," "Fashions in Dress" demands to be understood in part as a critique of Victorian gender stereotypes as much as one concerned with purely sartorial matters. "Most women are so artificial that they have no sense of Art," Wilde writes maliciously in "A Few Maxims for the Instruction of the Over-Educated," while "most men are so natural that they have no sense of Beauty." If "Fashions in Dress" is not exactly dedicated to inculcating a sense of art, it is nonetheless committed to creating a missing sense of beauty or artifice in men. This would be a form of liberation, Wilde implies, since the life of men dressed in "uniform black" is "monotonous and uninteresting" and "if one is to behave badly, it is better to be bad in a becoming dress than in one that is unbecoming." Both remarks anticipate the close association between masculine sartorial elegance and the secret life of "Bunburying" to be found in Wilde's *Importance of Being Earnest,* particularly where that play concerns Algernon, a male protagonist proud of his neckties and shirtcuffs and whose neglect of Victorian masculine norms makes him at once "attractive" and "painfully effeminate." That Wilde's principal instance in "Fashions in Dress" of a man behaving badly in a becoming dress is his friend, the actor Charles Wyndham, who was later briefly slated to play Algernon and to produce the first theatrical staging of *The Importance of Being Earnest,* gives a clue that the essay shares in some of the play's complex, modern sexual politics.

Similarly, Wilde's 1887 essays "The American Invasion" and "The American Man," published close upon the heels of one another in the short-lived London weekly *The Court and Society Review,* are at least implicitly concerned with the politics of gender and sexuality too, notwithstanding their more obvious concern with the social behavior of wealthy Americans in Europe. As the first of these witty essays makes abundantly clear, what Wilde terms "the American invasion" was really an invasion of women, and it "has done English society a great deal of good." In broad brushstrokes, Wilde sharply distinguishes young unmarried American women ("the American girl") from "women of other countries" and from "the American mother." Where the latter is "a tedious person," usually "dull, dowdy, or dyspeptic," American "girls" are "always welcome," and despite their "lack [of] repose" and "voices [that] are somewhat harsh and strident, . . . one grows to love these pretty whirlwinds in petticoats that sweep so recklessly through society and are so agitating to all duchesses who have daughters." In Wilde's characterization of her, the American "girl" is effectively a representative of the so-called New Woman—literate, sexually self-possessed, independent, and outspoken—and a forerunner of the fearless, indomitable young women who will later feature in *The Importance of Being Earnest.*

While "The American Invasion" is essentially a witty celebration of a new kind of femininity, "The American Man," as its title implies, is a critique of conventional masculinity, and it follows from Wilde's comment towards the end of "The American Invasion" that "the American father is . . . never seen in London. He passes his life entirely in Wall Street, and communicates with his family once a month by means of a telegram in cipher." Although less commonly seen and less comfortable in Europe than American women, the American man is for Wilde the architype of the modern businessman, who treats the world "as if it were a Broadway store, and each city a counter for the sampling of shoddy goods. For him Art has no marvel, and Beauty no meaning, and the Past no message." American women "shine in our *salons* and delight our dinner-parties," says Wilde, but in Europe at least "the poor American man remains permanently in the background, and never rises beyond the level of the tourist. . . . he always looks *deplacé,* and feels depressed. Indeed, he would die of weariness if he were not in constant telegraphic communication with Wall Street; and the only thing that can console him for having wasted a day in a picture-gallery is a copy of the *New York Herald* or the *Boston Times.*"

Wilde had spent nearly a full year traveling and lecturing in America in 1882, however, so he concludes his essay by confidently declaring that "at home, the American man is the best of companions, as he is the most hospitable of hosts. The young men are especially pleasant, with their bright, handsome eyes, their unwearying energy, their amusing shrewdness." One reason for the American man's urbanity in his own home, Wilde suggests, is the power and confidence of the American woman: "from childhood, the husband has been brought up on the most elaborate fetch-and-carry system, and his reverence for the sex has a touch of compulsory chivalry about it; while the wife exercises an absolute despotism, based upon female assertion, and tempered by womanly charm." In consequence, Wilde declares in one of his most famous witticisms, "the American man marries early, and the American woman marries often; and they get on extremely well together." Marriage in America, Wilde implies, is driven not by love, sexual passion, or misguided ideas of romance, but rather by a strict, practical demarcation between the sexes that allows each to pursue their own interests unchallenged: "the great success of marriage in the States is due partly to the fact that no American man is ever idle, and partly to the fact that no American wife is considered responsible for the quality of her husband's dinners. In America, the horrors of domesticity are almost entirely unknown . . . and as, by a clause inserted in every marriage settlement, the husband solemnly binds himself to use studs and not buttons for his shirts, one of the chief sources of disagreement in ordinary middle-class life is absolutely removed. The habit also of residing in hotels and boarding-houses does away with any necessity for those tedious *têtes-à-têtes* that are the dream of engaged couples, and the despair of married men." Wilde does not specify why American husbands enjoy residing in hotels and boarding houses, or why they should be so keen to avoid *têtes-à-têtes* with their own wives. But the independence of husband and wife makes marriage "one of [America's] most popular institutions," he says, and "even the American freedom of divorce, questionable though it undoubtedly is on many grounds, has at least the merit of bringing into marriage a new element of romantic uncertainty."

With their witty, satiric comments on contemporary ideas of gender, "The American Invasion" and "The American Man," like

Wilde's writings on dress, make for a striking contrast with the sometimes more rarified treatments of art, politics, literature, individualism—and indeed criticism itself—that run through Wilde's critical writings. In many ways, these two essays anticipate the criticisms of gender stereotypes and of marriage found in Wilde's social comedies. Yet they also highlight how matters of gender and sexuality are nearly always lurking close beneath the surface of even Wilde's self-consciously "aesthetic" criticism. They provide an important perspective from which to consider more closely the intimate all-male environments in which Wilde's dialogues on art and criticism take place; and as with "Fashions in Dress" and "London Models," they help us see that when Wilde is most self-consciously "artistic" and ironic, matters of sexual behavior, embodiment, and gender are never far behind. To be sure, Wilde does not characterize the dreamy "tired hedonists" who populate his dialogues on art and criticism as expressly sexual or even especially masculine beings. And yet they end their conversations "tired of thought," fascinated by the moon, longing for cigarettes, sunset, and the "subtle influence" of fine wine and food.[25] For Wilde, the critic is an artist, to be sure, but he is also a corporeal creature, whose thoughts and ideas are extensions of his physical life, not a repudiation of it. "Who could say where the fleshly impulse ceased, or the psychical impulse began?" reflects Lord Henry Wotton in Wilde's epochal novel *The Picture of Dorian Gray.* Taken as a whole, Wilde's critical writings constitute an implicit endorsement of Wotton's question, for they demonstrate that, as Walter Pater puts it, "the objects with which aesthetic criticism deals—music, poetry, artistic and accomplished forms of human life—are indeed receptacles of so many powers or forces." "The textual and sensual qualities of books are interwoven" in Wilde's reviews, remarks the scholar Nazia Parveen, with Wilde consciously "appealing to the reader's senses" and simultaneously "disclaim[ing] the view that 'verbal art, especially narrative, is almost bereft of any sensuous content.'"[26] Art's power lies in its command of the body, Wilde implies, not merely its command of the imagination. Criticism might well be "the record of one's own soul," as Gilbert remarks in "The Critic as Artist," but Wilde's own criticism repeatedly suggests that mind and body are inseparable, that speculative thought sits comfortably with the "fleshly impulse," and that, as Wilde wittily puts it in "Phrases and Philosophies for the Use of the Young," "those who see any difference between soul and body have neither."

1. *The Collected Letters of W. B. Yeats, Vol. 1: 1865–1895,* ed. John Kelly and Eric Domville (Oxford: Clarendon Press, 1986), 252; "Agnes Repplier on *Intentions,*" in *Oscar Wilde: The Critical Heritage,* ed. Karl Beckson (London: Routledge & Kegan Paul, 1970), 103–106; *New York Times,* Dec. 1, 1900, repr. in *Oscar Wilde: The Critical Heritage,* ed. Beckson, 225; *The Complete Letters of Oscar Wilde,* ed. Merlin Holland and Rupert Hart-Davis (New York: Henry Holt, 2000), 616. Other notable books published in 1891 include Thomas Hardy's *Tess of the D'Urbervilles,* George Gissing's *New Grub Street,* Mary Wilkins Freeman's *A New England Nun,* George Bernard Shaw's *Quintessence of Ibsenism,* Emily Dickinson's *Poems (Second Series),* and Wilde's own *The Picture of Dorian Gray* and *A House of Pomegranates.*

2. Wilde acknowledged receipt of the gift on October 27, 1894, saying "it is more green that the original even" (*Complete Letters,* 616, n.2). Three weeks earlier, he had asked Leverson "Is your birthday really the 10th? Mine is the 16th!" (*Complete Letters,* 618). These facts suggest that the letter in which Wilde tells Leverson "How sweet of you to have *Intentions* bound for me for your birthday" (*Complete Letters,* 616), speculatively dated "?23 September 1894" by its recent editors, has been misdated and in fact derives from October 1894. "Bound for me for your birthday" is, of course, Wilde's generous and witty way of sharing Leverson's birthday gift with her, given the very close proximity of their birthdays.

3. Richard Le Gallienne, signed rev. of *Intentions,* in *The Academy* (July 4, 1891), repr. in *Oscar Wilde: The Critical Heritage,* ed. Beckson, 99.

4. Le Gallienne, signed rev. of *Intentions,* 97.

5. "Discourse in the Novel," in *The Dialogic Imagination: Four Essays by M. M. Bakhtin,* ed. Michael Holquist, tr. Caryl Emerson and Michael Holquist (Austin: Univ. of Texas Press, 1981), 259, 279–280.

6. Linda Hutcheon, *Irony's Edge: The Theory and Politics of Irony* (London & NY: Routledge, 1995), 37.

7. Hutcheon, *Irony's Edge,* 39.

8. Matthew Arnold, "The Function of Criticism at the Present Time" (1865), in *Lectures and Essays in Criticism: Vol. 3 of The Complete Works of Matthew Arnold,* ed. R. H. Super (Ann Arbor, MI.: Univ. of Michigan Press, 1962), 158.

9. In the preface to his *Studies in the History of The Renaissance* (1873; rev. 1877 as *The Renaissance: Studies in Art and Poetry),* Pater had written "in aesthetic criticism the first step towards seeing one's object as it really is, is to know one's own impression as it really is. . . . What is this song or picture, this engaging personality presented in life or in a book, to *me*? What effect does it really produce on me? Does it give me pleasure? . . . How is my nature modified by its presence, and under its influence?" (Pater, *The Renaissance: Studies in Art and Poetry: The 1893 Text,* ed. Donald L. Hill [Berkeley: Univ. of California Press, 1980], xix–xx). For Wilde's frank acknowledgement of the influence *The Renaissance* had upon his own life, thought, and prose style, see "Mr. Pater's Last Volume," below.

10. *Modern Painters, Volume 1* (1843), vol. 3 of *The Works of John Ruskin,* ed. E. T. Cook and Alexander Wedderburn (London: George Allen, 1903–12), 136–137.

11. *Modern Painters, Vol. 1,* 624; Jerome H. Buckley, *The Victorian Temper* (1951; New York: Vintage, 1964), 143–160; *Lectures on Art and Aratra Pentelici* (1870), vol. 20 of *The Works of John Ruskin,* ed. Cook and Wedderburn, 73.

12. See "The Critic's Mind Considered" (1867) in James McNeill Whistler, *The Gentle Art of Making Enemies* (Heinemann, 1890), 45; also p. 126, n.10 below.

13. Oscar Wilde, "Grosvenor Gallery (first notice)" (1879), in *Journalism: Part One,* ed. John Stokes and Mark Turner (Oxford: Oxford Univ. Press, 2016), vol. 6 of *The Complete Works of Oscar Wilde,* 16; Ruskin, *Fors Clavigera, Letters 73–96,* vol. 29 of *The Works of John Ruskin,* ed. Cook and Wedderburn, 160.

14. Ruskin, Letter to H. G. Liddell, Nov. 28, 1878, quoted in introduction to *Fors Clavigera, Letters 73–96,* xxv. For detailed commentary on the libel trial, see Linda Merrill, *A Pot of Paint: Aesthetics on Trial in Whistler v. Ruskin* (Washington, DC: Smithsonian, 1992) and Nicholas Frankel, "On the Whistler-Ruskin Trial, 1878," http://www.branchcollective.org/?ps_articles=nicholas-frankel-on-the-whistler-ruskin-trial-1878.

15. Wilde, "Grosvenor Gallery (first notice)," 17.

16. See J. D. Thomas, "The Composition of Wilde's 'The Harlot's House,'" *Modern Language Notes* 65, no.7 (Nov. 1950), 486.

17. Gérard Genette, *Paratexts: Thresholds of Interpretation,* tr. Jane E. Lewin (Cambridge: Cambridge Univ. Press, 1997), 240. Genette cites Wordsworth's preface (1800) to *Lyrical Ballads* (1798) and Tolstoy's preface (1890) to *The Kreutzer Sonata* (1889) as classic examples of delayed prefaces. However, Genette (who was unaware or uninterested in the circumstances surrounding the publication of *The Picture of Dorian Gray*) does not cite Wilde's Preface as another example. Instead he sees it, not incorrectly, as exemplifying the "preface-manifesto" (*Paratexts*, 228) whereby an author seeks to redefine or overthrow existing artistic conventions. In the breadth of its aims, says Genette, Wilde's Preface is comparable not merely to Gautier's preface to *Mademoiselle de Maupin,* but also to Conrad's preface to *The Nigger of the Narcissus* and Victor Hugo's never-completed "philosophical preface" to *Les Misérables.*

18. *The Fortnightly* had been a monthly magazine since a year after its inception in 1865. For its iconoclastic editor, Wilde's fellow Irishman and friend Frank Harris, see headnote, p. 358, below.

19. Unsigned review of *The Picture of Dorian Gray, St James's Gazette,* June 20, 1890, quoted in general introduction to *The Picture of Dorian Gray: An Annotated, Uncensored Edition,* ed. Frankel (Cambridge, MA: Harvard Univ. Press, 2011), 7.

20. "Nothing should be able to harm a man except himself," Wilde argues: "What is outside of him should be a matter of no importance."

21. Wilde's vision here, indebted to Edward Bellamy's important Utopian novel *Looking Backward,* is in effect a prediction of the modern electrical grid.

22. *Complete Letters,* 487.

23. "I have been sometimes accused of setting too high an importance on dress," he remarked drily in "The Philosophy of Dress."

24. In its founding manifesto, the Rational Dress Society issued a strong "protest against the introduction of any fashion in dress that either deforms the figure, impedes the movements of the body, or in any way tends to injure the health. It protests against the wearing of tightly-fitting corsets; of high-heeled shoes; of heavily-weighted skirts, as rendering healthy exercise almost impossible; and of all tie-down cloaks or other garments impeding on the movements of the arms. It protests against crinolines or crinolettes of any kind as ugly and deforming. . . . [It] requires all to be dressed healthily, comfortably, and beautifully, to seek what conduces to birth, comfort and beauty in our dress as a duty

to ourselves and each other" (quoted in *Clothing, Society and Culture in Nineteenth Century Britain: Abuses and Reforms,* ed. Clare Rose [2011; London: Routledge, 2016], 237).

25. The "Tired Hedonists . . . is a club to which I belong," remarks Vivian in "The Decay of Lying." "The Decay of Lying" ends with Vivian saying "We have talked long enough" and inviting Cyril to accompany him out on the twilit terrace. Similarly, Gilbert ends part two of "The Critic as Artist" by saying "I am tired of thought" and it is "too late to sleep," while part one ends with him praising the "subtle influence" of supper.

26. Parveen, "The body-mind of Oscar Wilde's reviews for the *Pall Mall Gazette," European Review of History* 17, no.2 (2010), 311. Parveen is quoting the book historian Leah Price.

A NOTE ON THE TEXTS

Selections from Wilde's critical writings are divided here into four categories, each organized chronologically by date of publication, so that readers can more easily appreciate both the diversity and genesis of Wilde's achievement as a critic. Before he was a successful playwright, Wilde was fundamentally a man of the press, as the editors of his journalism remark, and apart from some early lectures (not selected for inclusion here) that remained unpublished in his lifetime, all of his critical writings appeared originally in the pages of Victorian periodicals and magazines.[1] With two important exceptions, they were not republished or revised in Wilde's own lifetime. With the same two exceptions, they are presented here, either in full or by a representative extract, in the form in which they originally appeared in the Victorian press. Original spellings have been retained, except for two small, obvious misprints.[2] Dates and venues of original publication are given in the annotations.

The first exception concerns Wilde's epigrammatic preface to his novel *The Picture of Dorian Gray*, first published under the title "A Preface to *Dorian Gray*" in March 1891—independently from the novel—as a series of twenty-three aphorisms in the magazine *The Fortnightly Review,* which had published "The Soul of Man Under Socialism" the previous month and "Pen Pencil and Poison" two years before that. Wilde retitled it "The Preface" when including it in the first book edition of *Dorian Gray,* published by Ward, Lock, and Co. the following month, in April 1891, but more importantly he expanded the number of aphorisms to twenty-five by splitting the ninth aphorism in two and adding the entirely new aphorism "No artist is ever morbid. The artist can express everything." The later, revised version of the Preface is given here, with significant variants from the earlier *Fortnightly Review* version noted in the annotations.

The second and larger exception concerns the four essays and dialogues that Wilde gathered into his important 1891 collection *Intentions.* All four of these had appeared previously in leading Victorian monthly magazines, one of them as early as 1885. Wilde revised these pieces extensively for republication in *Intentions,* changing them significantly in the process, in two cases giving the pieces entirely new titles. *Intentions* was surprisingly well received and went into a second edition in 1894. A few months after its first publication, Wilde was already making plans for the publication of an authorized French translation (which duly appeared in 1914). Selections from the essays and dialogues of *Intentions* are presented here in their revised 1891 versions, with significant variants from the earlier serial versions noted in the annotations. Wilde's provocative subtitles have here been prefaced with a colon rather than being printed on a separate line, in a smaller font, as they were in 1891.[3]

While the bulk of Wilde's critical writings first appeared over their author's signature or under his byline and were quickly associated with Wilde personally, many of the earliest and most enjoyable of them, particularly reviews, were published anonymously in Wilde's own lifetime. (My annotations record where this was the case.) Anonymous reviews, like modern-day editorials, were the norm for the *Pall Mall Gazette* and other Victorian dailies, as well as for many weekly magazines, and while the former's editor courted Wilde personally to write his very first review for the paper (Wilde's review of Whistler's "Ten O'Clock" lecture, which begins this selection, was published under Wilde's personal byline, with the paper clearly hoping to capitalize on the well-publicized friendship—and increasing enmity—between Wilde and Whistler), the practice of reviewing anonymously allowed experienced and inexperienced journalists alike a remarkable degree of both intellectual and stylistic freedom.[4] The biting satire and "no holds barred" style of "Dinners and Dishes" and "Aristotle at Afternoon Tea," for instance, owe much to the fact that these reviews were published anonymously, with no fear of recrimination. (This was especially important in the case of "Aristotle at Afternoon Tea," since the author of the book under review was Wilde's onetime college tutor J. P. Mahaffy, whom Wilde once called "my first and my best teacher."). But the practice is important, too, because it allowed Wilde quickly to develop his self-assurance as a critic and to nurture that highly personal, sometimes acidic, style that he later came to employ in much of his other writing as well. Both stylistically and intellectually, there is a direct line running from "Dinners and Dishes" and "A Handbook to Marriage"—via "The Decay of Lying" and "Pen Pencil and Poison"—to "Phrases and Philosophies for the Use of the Young," one of two extraordinary compilations of witty epigrams and paradoxes with which Wilde effectively signed off as a critic, a mere five months before his criminal conviction and imprisonment.

If many of Wilde's critical writings were published anonymously, others presumed his personal fame and reputation for controversy. The sets of epigrams that end this selection were signed in bold large capitals, and I have already mentioned that the *Pall Mall Gazette* hoped to capitalize on Wilde's friendship with Whistler when they commissioned him to review the controversial painter's 1885 "Ten O'Clock" lecture. (The magazine courted Wilde again the following year to supply book recommendations for its "Hundred Best Books" feature [see p. 330 below]). The intersection between Wilde's fame and criticism is still clearer in the recently discovered essay "The Philosophy of Dress," first published under Wilde's personal byline in *The New-York Daily Tribune* in 1885, nearly three years after he had lectured throughout North America on subjects related to the decorative arts. The essay, which builds on lectures concerning modern dress that Wilde had delivered more recently in Britain, clearly presupposes Wilde's transatlantic fame as a tastemaker. The excerpt selected here retains the Americanized spellings of the original.

Wilde was engaged with the Victorian press as a reader as well as a writer, and included in this selection are four letters to periodical editors on topics of importance to Wilde. These were always intended by their author for publication and were duly published by their recipients upon receipt, three of them under short, catchy titles of their editors' invention.[5] Wilde frequently employed letters for critical ends, especially when defending his work in the press, and while a wider selection of such letters could easily have been made, particularly from Wilde's oft-quoted and oft-reprinted letters in defense of his novel *Dorian Gray,* the consistency and relevance of the letters reprinted here will be evident to my readers. They overlap considerably with Wilde's other critical writings in both subject and style.

As my inclusion of these letters indicates, there may be something arbitrary, finally, about designating or categorizing the present selection as Wilde's *critical* writings, and some readers will object that a few selections don't meet the criteria of *criticism* at all, at least if that term is understood narrowly to describe only writing that employs the traditional earnest genres of the essay, the review, the lecture, or the treatise. Certainly, Wilde extended criticism into forms—the dialogue, the epigram, the personal letter—which aren't generally associated today with critical thought (although there exist important historical precedents for Wilde's choice in each case). By a similar token, many important writings by Wilde that are not included here—his short stories "The Portrait of Mr. W. H." and "The Happy Prince," his poem "The Ballad of Reading Gaol," his lengthy prison letter *De Profundis,* or the two letters on the justice system that he published shortly after his release from prison—can by some lights be considered writings of social or literary *criticism.* But what the present selections have in common is a fierce engagement with the narrow mores and conventions of Victorian Britain, whether they be the mores of fashion, politics, literature, art, gender, courtship, marriage, or even cookery. Indeed, they continue to challenge suppositions and expectations about these topics, while disarming us with their wit and bewitching us with their style. They are masterpieces of paradox and provocation, and they exemplify perfectly the poet Alexander Pope's notion that, if most "authors are partial to their wit," and critics to their judgments too, nothing quite compares to the "censure" of those like Wilde "who themselves excell, / And . . . have written well."[6]

1. Insofar as Wilde's American publications are concerned, a further exception must be made for "L'Envoi," Wilde's gushing, hastily written introduction to a little-known book of poems, *Rose-Leaf and Apple-Leaf,* by his college friend Rennell Rodd, that appeared in Philadelphia during Wilde's lecture tour of America in 1882. In the midst of his other tour commitments, Wilde personally oversaw—and likely financed—the production of Rodd's volume. "L'Envoi" did not appear in Britain in Wilde's lifetime.

2. In "Mr. Whistler's Ten O'Clock," the *Pall Mall Gazette* misprinted "Corot" as *Carot* (p. 46 below); and in "The Philosophy of Dress," *The New-York Daily Tribune* misprinted "too high an importance" (p. 95 below) as "too high tan importance."

3. For Wilde's subtitles and their debts to the paintings of Whistler, see Nicholas Frankel, *Oscar Wilde's Decorated Books* (Ann Arbor: Univ. of Michigan Press, 2000), 99.

4. As John Stokes and Mark Turner point out, the monthly magazines for which Wilde wrote made a virtue of identifying their contributors by name, whereas daily papers such as the *Pall Mall Gazette*—and even some weeklies—kept reviews and even short essays anonymous ("Oscar Wilde: New Journalist," in *Journalism and The Periodical Press in Nineteenth-Century Britain*, ed. Joanne Shattock [Cambridge: Cambridge Univ. Press, 2017], 374–376).

5. "To Read, or Not to Read" was solicited for publication by its editor. See p. 330 below.

6. Alexander Pope, *An Essay on Criticism* (1711).

REVIEWS

Self-designed, engraved invitation for Whistler's "Ten O'Clock," Prince's Hall, Piccadilly, February 1885. Whistler didn't publicly advertise his lecture, but instead issued private invitations using this specially engraved card, as if the lecture were a fashionable gallery opening. In his subtly acidic review, Wilde remarked that Whistler's audience was doubtless used to receiving "many charming invitations to wonderful private views."

Mr. Whistler's Ten O'Clock*

Last night, at Prince's Hall, Mr. Whistler made his first public appearance as a lecturer on art, and spoke for more than an hour with really marvellous eloquence on the absolute uselessness of all

* Published under Wilde's personal byline in the *Pall Mall Gazette,* February 21, 1885. On the previous evening, at the unusual hour of 10 p.m.—an hour calculated to appeal to an elite after-dinner audience—the painter James McNeill Whistler gave a carefully written public lecture at Prince's Hall, a prominent auditorium in London's Piccadilly where Wilde himself had lectured two years earlier. In his lecture, Whistler articulated many important tenets of aestheticism, while simultaneously attacking the broader "Aesthetic Movement" in which Wilde had lately played a leading role. Whistler subsequently delivered the lecture again in Oxford and Cambridge—the seats of the prestigious Slade Professorships of Art, along with London—before publishing it, first in 1888 as a pamphlet titled *Mr. Whistler's Ten O'Clock,* then again in 1890 as part of his artistic and personal manifesto *The Gentle Art of Making Enemies.* The lecture is now regarded as a central document of Victorian aestheticism and an important precursor to Wilde's Preface to *The Picture of Dorian Gray* as well as "The Decay of Lying."

Hitherto Wilde and Whistler had been close friends and neighbors, and Whistler helped shape Wilde's early views about art. But Whistler's lecture marked the beginning of a painful breach between the two men, whose differences were to play out in print with increasing animosity over the ensuing five years, culminating in Wilde's forceful rebuke, in "The Critic as Artist," to Whistler's elevation of the artist over the critic.

lectures of the kind.[1] Mr. Whistler began his lecture with a very pretty *aria* on pre-historic history, describing how in earlier times hunter and warrior would go forth to chase and foray, while the artist sat at home making cup and bowl for their service. Rude imitations of nature they were first, like the gourd bottle, till the sense of beauty and form developed and, in all its exquisite proportions, the first vase was fashioned. Then came a higher civilization of architecture and armchairs, and with exquisite design, and dainty diaper, the useful things of life were made lovely; and the hunter and the warrior lay on the couch when they were tired, and, when they were thirsty, drank from the bowl, and never cared to lose the exquisite proportion of the one, or the delightful ornament of the other; and this attitude of the primitive anthropoph-

---

1. Wilde's opening sentence would have irked Whistler personally: Wilde had himself been publicly lecturing on art for over three years by this date; and Whistler had reportedly been jealous when Wilde had lectured art students at the Royal Academy in 1883. See Geoff Dibb, *A Vagabond With a Mission: The Story of Oscar Wilde's Lecture Tours of Britain and Ireland* (London: The Oscar Wilde Society, 2013), 21–29. Wilde was to puncture Whistler's vanity and parody his "marvellous eloquence" again in the story "The Remarkable Rocket," published three years after Whistler's "Ten O'Clock." Here Wilde would parody Whistler allegorically as a self-important and "remarkable" rocket that, after failing to go off properly as expected in public, finally explodes unseen and unheard in a ditch. "I like hearing myself talk," declares Wilde's haughty rocket: "it is one of my greatest pleasures. I often have long conversations all by myself, and I am so clever that sometimes I don't understand a single word of what I am saying." ("The Remarkable Rocket," in Wilde, *The Happy Prince and Other Tales* [London: David Nutt, 1888], 110.)

agous Philistine[2] formed the text of the lecture and was the attitude which Mr. Whistler entreated his audience to adopt towards
art. Remembering, no doubt, many charming invitations to wonderful private views, this fashionable assemblage seemed somewhat
aghast, and not a little amused, at being told that the slightest appearance among a civilized people of any joy in beautiful things is
a grave impertinence to all painters; but Mr. Whistler was relent-
less, and, with charming ease, and much grace of manner, explained
to the public that the only thing they should cultivate was ugliness, and that on their permanent stupidity rested all the hopes of
art in the future.[3]

2. "Anthropophagous" means *cannibalistic.* The Biblical Philistines
were a warlike people who came into conflict with the children of Israel.
In Wilde's day, *Philistines* referred euphemistically to the unenlightened
and materialistic wealthy classes of England. In *De Profundis,* Wilde defines the Philistine as one "who upholds and aids the heavy, cumbrous,
blind mechanical forces of Society, and who does not recognise the dy-
namic force when he meets it either in a man or a movement," adding
that *Philistinism* is "that side of man's nature that is not illumined by the
imagination" (*The Annotated Prison Writings of Oscar Wilde*, ed. Nicholas
Frankel [Cambridge, MA: Harvard Univ. Press, 2018], 239, 223).

3. A mischievous and reductionist paraphrase of Whistler's argument
that art had been compromised through the efforts of educators and reformers to popularize it. Whistler had written "The people have been
harassed with Art in every guise, and vexed with many methods as to
its endurance. They have been told how they shall love Art, and live
with it. Their homes have been invaded . . . until roused at last, bewildered and filled with the doubts and discomforts of senseless suggestion, they resent such intrusion, and cast forth the false prophets, who
have brought the very name of the beautiful into disrepute, and derision
upon themselves. Alas! ladies and gentlemen, Art has been maligned.
She has nought in common with such practices. She is a goddess of
dainty thought—reticent of habit, abjuring all obtrusiveness. . . . selfishly

The scene was in every way delightful; he stood there, a miniature Mephistopheles,[4] mocking the majority! He was like a brilliant surgeon lecturing to a class composed of subjects destined ultimately for dissection, and solemnly assuring them how valuable to science their maladies were, and how absolutely uninteresting the slightest symptoms of health on their part would be. In fairness to the audience, however, I must say that they seemed extremely gratified at being rid of the dreadful responsibility of admiring anything, and nothing could have exceeded their enthusiasm when they were told by Mr. Whistler that no matter how vulgar their dresses were, or how hideous their surroundings at home, still it was possible that a great painter, if there was such a thing, could, by contemplating them in the twilight and half closing his eyes, see them under really picturesque conditions, and produce a picture which they were not to attempt to understand, much less dare to enjoy.[5] Then there were some arrows, barbed and brilliant, shot off, with all the speed and splendour of fireworks,[6] at the archaeologists, who spend their lives in verifying the birthplaces of nobodies, and

occupied with her own perfection only. . . . Art seeks the Artist alone" (Whistler, "Ten O'Clock," repr. in his *The Gentle Art of Making Enemies,* 136–157).

4. In the German legend of Faust, Mephistopheles is a corrupting demon. Whistler was short and slight of build, so this may be a personal insult.

5. Another mischievous reduction of Whistler, who had written that art "seek[s] and find[s] the beautiful in all conditions and in all times, as did her high priest Rembrandt, when he saw picturesque grandeur and noble dignity in the Jews' quarter of Amsterdam. . . . As did Tintoret and Paul Veronese, among the Venetians" (Whistler, "Ten O'Clock," 136–137).

6. An allusion to Whistler's controversial painting "Nocturne in Black and Gold: The Falling Rocket" (see p. 10 above), as well as a prefigurement of Wilde's 1888 story "The Remarkable Rocket." See n.1 above.

estimate the value of a work of art by its date or its decay; at the art critics who always treat a picture as if it were a novel, and try and find out the plot; at dilettanti in general and amateurs in particular; and (*O mea culpa!*) at dress reformers most of all.[7] "Did not Velasquez paint crinolines? What more do you want?"[8]

Having thus made a holocaust of humanity, Mr. Whistler turned to Nature, and in a few moments convicted her of the Crystal Palace, Bank holidays, and a general overcrowding of detail, both in omnibuses and in landscapes,[9] and then, in a passage of singular

7. Besides being a self-professed apostle of art, Wilde was one of Britain's leading dress reformers: over the previous six months Wilde had lectured and published widely on the subject of dress reform. See "From 'The Philosophy of Dress'" and "From 'Woman's Dress'" below; also Dibb, *A Vagabond With a Mission,* 262–283. As Wilde's *mea culpa* acknowledges, Whistler had more or less openly attacked Wilde without naming him, much as he'd done by writing elsewhere in "Ten O'Clock": "the Dilettante walks abroad. The amateur is loosed. The voice of the aesthete is heard in the land, and catastrophe is upon us. . . . . Shall this gaunt, ill-at-ease, distressed, abashed mixture of *mauvaise honte* [false modesty] and desperate assertion call itself artistic, and claim cousinship with the artist" (Whistler, "Ten O'Clock," 152–153).

8. Whistler had remarked that Velasquez created "works of Art of the same quality as the Elgin marbles" by depicting "Infantas clad in inaesthetic hoops," adding that "No reformers were these great men [Rembrandt, Tintoretto, Veronese, Velasquez]—no improvers of the way of others" (Whistler, "Ten O'Clock," 137).

9. The Crystal Palace was a giant pavilion of glass and steel, designed by Joseph Paxton for London's Great Exhibition of 1851. *Bank holidays* (originally weekdays on which financial institutions were closed) are public holidays, as first mandated in The Bank Holidays Act of 1871. With typical mischief, Wilde reduces and disparages Whistler's argument that "Nature contains the elements, in colour and form, of all pictures, as the keyboard contains the notes of all music. But the artist is

beauty, not unlike one that occurs in Corot's letters, spoke of the artistic value of dim dawns and dusks, when the mean facts of life are lost in exquisite and evanescent effects, when common things are touched with mystery and transfigured with beauty, when the warehouses become as palaces, and the tall chimneys of the factory seem like campaniles in the silver air.[10]

Finally, after making a strong protest against anybody but a painter judging of painting, and a pathetic appeal to the audience not to be lured by the aesthetic movement into having beautiful things about them, Mr. Whistler concluded his lecture with a

---

born to pick, and choose, and group with science, these elements, that the result may be beautiful. . . . . To say to the painter, that Nature is to be taken as she is, is to say to the player that he may sit on the piano. That Nature is always right, is an assertion, artistically, as untrue as it is one whose truth is universally taken for granted. Nature is very rarely right, to such an extent even, that it might almost be said that Nature is usually wrong: that is to say, the condition of things that shall bring about the perfection of harmony worthy a picture, is rare, and not common at all" (Whistler, "Ten O'Clock," 142–143). Four years later, in "The Decay of Lying," Wilde would closely echo Whistler's ideas about Nature.

10. See Whistler, "Ten O'Clock," 144–145. The landscape painter Jean Baptiste Corot (1796–1875) purportedly remarked in a letter that "The sun has disappeared. . . . All that remains in the softened sky is a hazy shade of pale yellow . . . which melts into the dark blue of the night . . . with a fluid and ungraspable delicacy . . . One begins no longer to see. . . . The illusion is being created. . . . When the sun goes down, the interior of the soul, the sun of art rises up" (quoted and translated from the French in *Journalism: Part One*, ed. John Stokes and Mark Turner [Oxford: Oxford Univ. Press, 2016], vol. 6 of *The Complete Works of Oscar Wilde,* 235). Wilde's allusion to Corot (misprinted as *Carot* by the *Pall Mall Gazette*) would have irked Whistler, who had once dismissed the French painter as an imitator.

pretty passage about Fusiyama on a fan,[11] and made his bow to an audience which he had succeeded in completely fascinating by his wit, his brilliant paradoxes, and, at times, his real eloquence. Of course, with regard to the value of beautiful surroundings I differ entirely from Mr. Whistler. An artist is not an isolated fact; he is the resultant of a certain milieu and a certain entourage, and can no more be born of a nation that is devoid of any sense of beauty than a fig can grow from a thorn or a rose blossom from a this-tle.[12] That an artist will find beauty in ugliness, *le beau dans*

11. "even were [an artist] never to appear [again], the story of the beau-tiful is already complete—hewn in the marbles of the Parthenon—and broidered, with the birds, upon the fan of Hokusai—at the foot of Fusi-yama" (Whistler, "Ten O'Clock," 159). For Hokusai, see p. 235, n.136 below. Fusiyama is Japanese for Mt. Fuji, the subject of some of Hoku-sai's most famous woodblock prints and fan paintings.

12. Wilde alludes here to Whistler's contention that "The master stands in no relation to the moment at which he occurs—a monument of isolation—hinting at sadness—having no part in the progress of his fellow men. He is also no more the product of civilisation than is the scientific truth asserted dependent upon the wisdom of a period. The assertion itself requires the *man* to make it. The truth was from the be-ginning" (Whistler, "Ten O'Clock," 154–155). Wilde had not always dif-fered so entirely from Whistler on this point. In his 1883 lecture "Modern Art Training," purportedly written with Whistler's assistance, Wilde had argued that "such an expression as English art is a meaningless expression. . . . Nor is there any such thing as a school of art even. There are merely artists, that is all. . . . Never talk of an artistic people; there has never been such a thing" (" Modern Art Training" [1883], printed as appendix A in Dibb, *A Vagabond With a Mission,* 225–226).

Wilde's notion that an artist "can no more be born. . . . than a fig can grow from a thorn, etc" is a deliberate echo of Matthew 7:16: "Ye shall know them by their fruits. Do men gather grapes of thorns, or figs of thistles?" See p. 299, n.287 below.

l'horrible,[13] is now a commonplace of the schools, the argot of the atelier,[14] but I strongly deny that charming people should be condemned to live with magenta ottomans and Albert-blue curtains in their rooms in order that some painter may observe the sidelights on the one and the values of the other. Nor do I accept the dictum that only a painter is a judge of painting. I say that only an artist is a judge of art; there is a wide difference. As long as a painter is a painter merely, he should not be allowed to talk of anything but mediums and megilp,[15] and on those subjects should be compelled to hold his tongue; it is only when he becomes an artist that the secret laws of artistic creation are revealed to him. For there are not many arts, but one art merely: poem, picture and Parthenon, sonnet and statue—all are in their essence the same, and he who knows one knows all. But the poet is the supreme artist, for he is the master of colour and of form, and the real musician besides, and is lord over all life and all arts;[16] and so to the poet

13. beauty in ugliness, a direct quotation from Charles Baudelaire, "The Painter of Modern Life."

14. The language of the studio. Wilde would reuse this phrase in "London Models" (see p. 125 below).

15. *megilp* is a liquid used to make oil paints thin, glossy, and easy to work with.

16. "[I]n its special mode of handling its given material, each art may be observed to pass into the condition of some other art," Walter Pater had observed previously: "by . . . a partial alienation from [their] own limitations . . . the arts are able not indeed to supply the place of each other, but reciprocally to lend each other new forces" (*The Renaissance: Studies in Art and Poetry: The 1893 Text*, ed. Donald L. Hill [Berkeley: Univ. of California Press, 1980], 105). For Wilde's notion that "the type of all the arts is the art of the musician," with its nod to Pater's idea that "all art constantly aspires to the condition of music," see p. 356, n.7 below.

William Powell Frith, *A Private View at the Royal Academy, 1881*. Photogravure engraving based on Frith's 1883 oil painting. Top-hatted and clean-shaven, Wilde features prominently in Frith's panorama of a fashionable private view: he is virtually the only person who is admiring the art on the gallery walls. In his review of Whistler's equally fashionable "Ten O'Clock" lecture, Wilde remarked that Whistler's audience "seemed somewhat aghast . . . at being told that the slightest appearance . . . of any joy in beautiful things is a grave impertinence to all painters." But Wilde could not "accept the dictum that only a painter is a judge of painting" and maintained instead that "only an artist is a judge of art."

beyond all others are these mysteries known; to Edgar Allan Poe and to Baudelaire, not to Benjamin West and Paul Delaroche.[17]

17. Whistler responded to Wilde's review with a hostile telegram, simultaneously published in the gossipy society magazine *The World*, in which he belittled Wilde's allusions to the painters Delaroche and West as follows: "Oscar, I have read your exquisite article in the *Pall Mall*. Nothing is more delicate, in the flattery of 'the poet' to 'the painter,' than the naiveté of 'the poet' in the choice of his painters—Benjamin West and Paul Delaroche! You have pointed out that 'the painter's' mission

However, I should not enjoy anybody else's lectures unless in a few points I disagreed with them, and Mr. Whistler's lecture last night was, like everything that he does, a masterpiece. Not merely for its clever satire and amusing jests will it be remembered, but for the pure and perfect beauty of many of its passages—passages delivered with an earnestness which seemed to amaze those who had looked on Mr. Whistler as a master of persiflage merely, and had not known him as we do, as a master of painting also. For that he is indeed one of the very greatest masters of painting is my opinion. And I may add that in this opinion Mr. Whistler himself entirely concurs.

---

is to find '*le beau dans l'horrible,*' and have left to 'the poet' the discovery of '*l'horrible' dans 'le beau'?*' To this attack, Wilde replied (also in the pages of *The World*): "Dear Butterfly, by the aid of a biographical dictionary, I made the discovery that there were once two painters, called Benjamin West and Paul Delaroche, who rashly lectured upon Art. As of their works nothing at all remains, I conclude that they explained themselves away. Be warned in time, James; and remain, as I do, incomprehensible. To be great is to be misunderstood" (both Whistler's telegram and Wilde's reply are repr. in Whistler, *The Gentle Art,* 162–163).

Dinners and Dishes*

A man can live for three days without bread, but no man can live for one day without poetry, was an aphorism of Baudelaire's:[1] you can live without pictures and music, but you can't live without eating, says the author of *Dinners and Dishes;* and this latter view is, no doubt, the more popular. Who, indeed, in these degenerate days, would hesitate between an ode and an omelette, a sonnet and a salmis?[2] Yet the position is not entirely Philistine;[3] cookery is an art; are not its principles the subject of South Kensington

---

* Unsigned (i.e., anonymous) review of *Dinners and Dishes,* by "Wanderer" (pseud.), published in *Pall Mall Gazette,* March 7, 1885. Stokes and Turner identify "Wanderer" as the pseudonym of Elim Henry d'Avigdor, the author of *Across Country* (1882), *Hunt-room Stories* (1885) and *Whims* (1889), among other books. Like the slightly later "A Handbook to Marriage," "Dinners and Dishes" exemplifies Wilde's notion that the critic "does not . . . require for the perfection of his art the finest materials" and "from subjects of little or of no importance, . . . the true critic can, if it be his pleasure so to direct or waste his faculty of contemplation, produce work that will be flawless in style and instinct with intellectual subtlety" (pp. 304–305 below).

1. This is probably Wilde's own translation of Charles Baudelaire's aphorism *Vous pouvez vivre trois jours sans pain—sans poésie, jamais* (Baudelaire, *Salon de 1846* [Paris: Michel Levy, 1846], vi).

2. A highly spiced dish consisting of duck or other game bird stewed in wine.

3. See p. 43, n.2 above.

lectures,[4] and does not the Royal Academy give a banquet once a year? Besides, as the coming democracy will,[5] no doubt, insist on feeding us all on penny dinners, it is well that the laws of cookery should be explained: for were the national meal burned, or badly seasoned, or served up with the wrong sauce, a dreadful revolution might follow.

Under these circumstances we strongly recommend *Dinners and Dishes* to every one: it is brief, and concise, and makes no attempt at eloquence, which is extremely fortunate. For even on ortolans[6] who could endure oratory? It also has the advantage of not being illustrated. The subject of a work of art has of course nothing to

4. The National School of Cookery, in Exhibition Road, South Kensington, was established in 1873 to promote the science of fine cuisine. South Kensington was the official center of artistic inquiry and comparative cultural study in Victorian Britain: the Great Exhibition of 1851 had been held there, and the cookery school was located in premises that had previously housed the International Exhibition of 1873.

5. Universal suffrage would take another forty-three years to arrive in Britain, but Wilde must have felt that it was imminent. "Dinners and Dishes" appeared three months after passage of the 1884 Representation of the People Act (the so-called Third Reform Act), which doubled the size of the franchise in Britain to over five million adult males; and three months later, in June 1885, Parliament would pass the Redistribution Act, which established the principle of equally populated parliamentary constituencies.

6. The ortolan is a small songbird. Long considered the pinnacle of gastronomic delight in France, eating ortolans is now outlawed there owing to the small number of birds remaining. Part two of Wilde's dialogue "The Critic as Artist" begins with its two interlocutors, Ernest and Gilbert, having just dined on ortolans accompanied by Chambertin (a Grand Cru Burgundy wine).

do with its beauty, but still there is always something depressing about the coloured lithograph of a leg of mutton.

As regards the author's particular views, we entirely agree with him on the important question of macaroni. "Never," he says, "ask me to back a bill for a man who has given me a macaroni pudding." Macaroni is essentially a savoury dish, and may be served with cheese or tomatoes, but never with sugar and milk. There is also a useful description of how to cook risotto, a delightful dish too rarely seen in England; an excellent chapter on the different kinds of salads, which should be carefully studied by those many hostesses whose imaginations never pass beyond lettuce and beetroot; and actually a recipe for making Brussels sprouts eatable. The last is of course a masterpiece.

The real difficulty, however, that we all have to face in life is not so much the science of cookery as the stupidity of cooks. And in this little handbook to practical Epicureanism,[7] the tyrant of the English kitchen is shown in her proper light. Her entire ignorance of herbs, her passion for extracts and essences, her total inability to make a soup which is anything more than a combination of pepper and gravy, her inveterate habit of sending up bread poultices with pheasants,—all these sins, and many others, are ruthlessly unmasked by the author. Ruthlessly and rightly. For the British cook is a foolish woman who should be turned, for her iniquities, into a pillar of that salt which she never knows how to use.[8]

---

7. A philosophy, named after the Greek philosopher Epicurus, which advocates living so as to derive the greatest pleasure from life.

8. An allusion to the biblical story of Lot's wife (Genesis 19:26), who was turned into a pillar of salt upon looking back at the city of Sodom.

But our author is not local merely. He has been in many lands; he has eaten back-hendl[9] at Vienna and kulibatsch[10] at St. Petersburg; he has had the courage to face the buffalo veal of Roumania, and to dine with a German family at one o'clock;[11] he has serious views on the right method of cooking those famous white truffles of Turin, of which Alexandre Dumas was so fond, and, in the face of the Oriental Club,[12] declares that Bombay curry is better than the curry of Bengal. In fact he seems to have had experience of almost every kind of meal, except the "square meal" of the Americans. This he should study at once; there is a great field for the philosophic epicure in the United States. Boston beans may be dismissed at once as delusions, but soft-shell crabs, terrapin, canvas-back ducks, blue fish and the pompono of New Orleans are all wonderful delicacies, particularly when one gets them at Delmonico's.[13] Indeed, the two most remarkable bits of scenery in the States are undoubtedly Delmonico's and the Yosemite Valley; and the former place has done more to promote a good feeling between England and America than anything else has in this century.

9. Viennese dish, consisting of fried chicken.

10. A Russian fish pie.

11. Germans traditionally enjoy their main cooked meal for lunch rather than dinner.

12. Exclusive gentleman's club, founded in 1824, originally for retired members of the East India Company.

13. Reputedly the first American restaurant to allow patrons to order from a menu *à la carte*. In Wilde's day, Delmonico's operated at four different south Manhattan locations.

We hope that "Wanderer" will go there soon and add a chapter to *Dinners and Dishes,* and that his book will have in England the influence it deserves. There are twenty ways of cooking a potato, and three hundred and sixty-five ways of cooking an egg, yet the British cook up to the present moment knows only three methods of sending up either one or the other.[14]

14. In a culinary context, to "send up" means to serve.

A Handbook to Marriage*

In spite of its somewhat alarming title this book may be highly recommended to every one. As for the authorities the author quotes, they are almost numberless, and range from Socrates down to Artemus Ward.[1] He tells us of the wicked bachelor who spoke of marriage as "a very harmless amusement" and advised a young friend of his to "marry early and marry often";[2] of Dr. Johnson, who proposed that marriage should be arranged by the Lord Chancellor, without the parties concerned having any choice in the matter; of the Sussex labourer who asked, "Why should I give a woman half my victuals for cooking the other half?" and of Lord Verulam, who thought that unmarried men did the best public

---

* Unsigned (i.e., anonymous) review of *How to be Happy though Married* by "a Graduate in the University of Matrimony," published in *Pall Mall Gazette*, November 18, 1885. The unnamed author of *How to be Happy* was the Rev. E. J. Hardy, a cousin of Wilde's by marriage, and also a fellow graduate of Trinity College, Dublin. In 1889, in his capacity as editor of the magazine *Woman's World,* Wilde published a short essay by Hardy titled "Being Married, and Afterwards."

1. "Artemus Ward" (Charles Farrar Browne [1834–1867]), the favourite author of Abraham Lincoln, was an American humor writer.

2. A joke repeated by Wilde in *The Importance of Being Earnest,* as well as in "The American Invasion."

work.[3] And, indeed, marriage is the one subject on which all women agree and all men disagree. Our author, however, is clearly of the same opinion as the Scotch lassie who, on her father warning her what a solemn thing it was to get married, answered, "I ken that, father, but it's a great deal solemner to be single." He may be regarded as the champion of the married life. Indeed, he has a most interesting chapter on marriage-made men, and though he dissents, and we think rightly, from the view recently put forward by a lady or two on the woman's rights platform, that Solomon owed all his wisdom to the number of his wives,[4] still he appeals to Bismarck, John Stuart Mill, Mahommed and Lord Beaconsfield, as instances of men whose success can be traced to the influence of the women they married. Archbishop Whately[5] once defined woman as "a creature that does not reason and pokes the fire from the top," but since his day the higher education of women has considerably altered their position. Women have always had an emotional sympathy with those they love; Girton and Newnham have rendered intellectual sympathy also possible.[6] In our day it is best for a man to be married,[7] and men must give up the tyranny in married life

3. Francis Bacon (1561–1626), the British philosopher and statesman, given the title Lord Verulam in 1618.

4. The movement for women's emancipation, extremely active in Wilde's day, often went hand in hand with a critique of traditional marriage.

5. Richard Whately (1787–1863), Anglican Archbishop of Dublin.

6. Girton College and Newnham College at Cambridge, founded in 1869 and 1871 respectively, were two of the first colleges for the higher education of women in England. They were not fully accredited as colleges of Cambridge University until 1948, when women were first fully admitted to the university.

7. A line that is heavily ironic given the later implosion in Wilde's own marriage as well as the critique of marriage that takes center stage in many of Wilde's plays and fictions in the period 1887–1895.

which was once so dear to them, and which, we are afraid, lingers still, here and there. "Do you wish to be my wife, Mabel?" said a little boy. "Yes," incautiously answered Mabel. "Then pull off my boots."

On marriage vows our author has, too, very sensible views and very amusing stories. He tells of a nervous bridegroom who, confusing the baptismal and marriage ceremonies, replied, when asked if he consented to take the bride for his wife: "I renounce them all"; of a Hampshire rustic who, when giving the ring, said solemnly to the bride: "With my body I thee wash up, and with all my hurdle goods I thee and thou"; of another who, when asked whether he would take his partner to be his wedded wife, replied, with shameful indecision: "Yes, I'm willin'; but I'd a much sight rather have her sister"; and of a Scotch lady who, on the occasion of her daughter's wedding, was asked by an old friend whether she might congratulate her on the event, and answered: "Yes, yes, upon the whole it is very satisfactory; it is true Jeannie hates her good man, but then there's always a something!" Indeed, the good stories contained in this book are quite endless and make it very pleasant reading, while the good advice is on all points admirable. Most young married people nowadays start in life with a dreadful collection of ormolu inkstands covered with sham onyxes, or with a perfect museum of salt-cellars. We strongly recommend this book as one of the best of wedding presents. It is a complete handbook to an earthly Paradise, and its author may be regarded as the Murray of matrimony and the Baedeker of bliss.[8]

8. Like Frommer's and Fodor's guidebooks today, guidebooks published by John Murray and Karl Baedeker were so popular with travelers in the nineteenth century that they became synonymous with their publishers' names.

Great Writers by Little Men*

In an introductory note prefixed to the initial volume of "Great Writers," a series of literary monographs now being issued by Mr. Walter Scott, the publisher himself comes forward in the kindest manner possible to give his authors the requisite "puff preliminary," and ventures to express the modest opinion that such original and valuable works "have never before been produced in any part of the world at a price so low as a shilling a volume."[1] Far

---

* Unsigned (i.e., anonymous) review of Eric S. Robertson, *Life of Henry Wadsworth Longfellow* (London: Walter Scott, 1887) and Hall Caine, *Life of Samuel Taylor Coleridge* (London: Walter Scott, 1887), published in *Pall Mall Gazette,* March 28, 1887.

1. Wilde alludes to the enterprising English publisher Walter Scott (1826–1910), not his earlier namesake the famous Scottish writer. The former had made his fortune as a builder and had only entered publishing as recently as 1883, quickly establishing a name for publishing inexpensive books—especially books of and about literature—in series. "Puff preliminary" is a quotation from Richard Brinsley Sheridan's timeless burlesque *The Critic* (1779), while "have never before been produced . . . at a price so low as a shilling a volume" is a direct quotation from Walter Scott's "Introductory Note" (situated, as Wilde indicates, at the front of Robertson's *Life of Longfellow,* the "initial volume" in Scott's "Great Writers" series). The print historian Richard D. Altick writes of such late-Victorian cost-cutting ventures as Scott's: "The serious reader with only pennies to spend was served as he had never been served before. Inevitably, price-cutting was accompanied by corner-cutting. In many

be it from us to make any heartless allusion to the fact that Shakespeare's *Sonnets* were brought out at fivepence, or that for fourpence-halfpenny one could have bought a Martial in ancient Rome. Every man, a cynical American tells us, has the right to beat a drum before his booth.[2] Still, we must acknowledge that Mr. Walter Scott would have been much better employed in correcting some of the more obvious errors that appear in his series. When, for instance, we come across such a phrase as "the brotherly liberality of the brothers Wedgewood," the awkwardness of the expression is hardly atoned for by the fact that the name of the great potter is misspelt;[3] Longfellow is so essentially poor in rhymes that it is unfair to rob him even of one, and the misquotation on page 77 is absolutely unkind;[4] the joke Coleridge himself made upon the subject should have been sufficient to remind any one that "Comberbach" (*sic*) was not the name under which he enlisted, and no real beauty is added to the first line of his pathetic *Work*

---

cases, cheapness was a synonym for shoddiness" (*The English Common Reader: A Social History of the Mass Reading Public, 1800–1900* [1957; 2nd. ed. Columbus, Ohio: Ohio State Univ. Press, 1998], 309).

2. Stokes and Turner identify the "cynical American" as the showman P. T. Barnum, who in his autobiography insisted on the need for self-advertisement in business.

3. Wilde alludes to the great English potter Sir Josiah Wedgwood (1730–1795), who initially served as apprentice to his older brother Thomas Wedgwood (died 1739). The quotation "the brotherly liberality of the brothers Wedgewood" appears on p. 73 of Caine's *Life of Coleridge.*

4. On p. 77 of his *Life of Longfellow,* Robertson misquotes the fourth stanza of Longfellow's "Psalm of Life" and gives "our hearts, though stout and *true,* / Still, like muffled drums, are beating" instead of "our hearts, though stout and *brave,* / Still, like muffled drums, are beating" (my emphasis).

Without Hope by printing "lare" (*sic*) instead of "lair."[5] The truth is that all premature panegyrics bring their own punishment upon themselves and, in the present case, though the series has only just entered upon existence, already a great deal of the work done is careless, disappointing, unequal and tedious.

Mr. Eric Robertson's *Longfellow* is a most depressing book. No one survives being over-estimated, nor is there any surer way of destroying an author's reputation than to glorify him without judgment and to praise him without tact. Henry Wadsworth Longfellow was one of the first true men of letters America produced, and as such deserves a high place in any history of American civilisation. To a land out of breath in its greed for gain he showed the example of a life devoted entirely to the study of literature; his lectures, though not by any means brilliant, were still productive of much good; he had a most charming and gracious personality, and he wrote some pretty poems. But his poems are not of the kind that call for intellectual analysis or for elaborate description or, indeed, for any serious discussion at all. They are as unsuited for panegyric as they are unworthy of censure, and it is difficult to help smiling when Mr. Robertson gravely tells us that few modern poets have given utterance to a faith so comprehensive as that expressed

5. In December 1793, at the age of 21, Coleridge abandoned his university studies and briefly enlisted in the 15th (The King's) Light Dragoons using the false name Silas Tomkyn Comberbache. His brothers arranged for his discharge a few months later. Of the false name that he assumed when enlisting, Coleridge later quipped "being at a loss when suddenly asked my name, I answered *Cumberback,* and verily my habits were so little equestrian that my horse, I doubt not, was of that opinion." The opening line of Coleridge's 1825 poem "Work Without Hope"—misquoted on p. 143 of Caine's *Life of Coleridge*—runs "All Nature seems at work. Slugs leave their lair."

in the *Psalm of Life,* or that *Evangeline* should confer on Longfellow the title of "Golden-mouthed" and that the style of metre adopted "carries the ear back to times in the world's history when grand simplicities were sung." Surely Mr. Robertson does not believe that there is any connection at all between Longfellow's unrhymed dactylics and the hexameter of Greece and Rome, or that any one reading *Evangeline* would be reminded of Homer's or Virgil's line? Where also lies the advantage of confusing popularity with poetic power? Though the *Psalm of Life* be shouted from Maine to California, that would not make it true poetry. Why call upon us to admire a bad misquotation from the *Midnight Mass for the Dying Year,* and why talk of Longfellow's "hundreds of imitators"? Longfellow has no imitators, for of echoes themselves there are no echoes and it is only style that makes a school.

Now and then, however, Mr. Robertson considers it necessary to assume a critical attitude. He tells us, for instance, that whether or not Longfellow was a genius of the first order, it must be admitted that he loved social pleasures and was a good eater and judge of wines, admiring "Bass's ale" more than anything else he had seen in England! The remarks on *Excelsior* are even still more amazing. *Excelsior,* says Mr. Robertson, is not a ballad because a ballad deals either with real or with supernatural people, and the hero of the poem cannot be brought under either category. For, "were he of human flesh, his madcap notion of scaling a mountain with the purpose of getting to the sky would be simply drivelling lunacy," to say nothing of the fact that the peak in question is much frequented by tourists, while, on the other hand, "it would be absurd to suppose him a spirit . . . for no spirit would be so silly as climb a snowy mountain for nothing"! It is really painful to have to read such preposterous nonsense, and if Mr. Walter Scott imagines that work of this kind is "original and valuable" he has much to learn. Nor are Mr. Robertson's criticisms upon other poets at all more felicitous. The casual allusion to Herrick's "confectioneries of verse" is, of course, quite explicable, coming as it does from an editor who excluded Herrick from an anthology of the child-poems of our literature in favour of Mr. Ashby-Sterry and Mr. William Sharp,[6] but when Mr. Robertson tells us that Poe's "loftiest flights of imagination in verse . . . rise into no more empyreal realm than the fantastic," we can only recommend him to read as soon as possible the marvellous lines *To Helen,* a poem as beautiful as a Greek gem and as musical as Apollo's lute.[7] The remarks, too, on Poe's

6. Wilde alludes here to *The Children of the Poets: An Anthology from English and American Writers of Three Centuries,* ed. and intro. Eric Robertson (London: Walter Scott, 1886), which Wilde had previously reviewed in the *Pall Mall Gazette* in October 1886. In his review of Robertson's anthology, Wilde had objected to Herrick's omission much as he does here, writing that "no English poet has written of children with more love and grace and delicacy." As importantly, Wilde had also warned Robertson to "take care when he publishes a poem to publish it correctly," adding that "a poet can survive everything but a misprint."

7. For Apollo, see p. 206, n.69 below. Poe's "poem as beautiful as a Greek gem" runs as follows:

Helen, thy beauty is to me
Like those Nicéan barks of yore,
That gently, o'er a perfumed sea,
The weary, way-worn wanderer bore
To his own native shore.

On desperate seas long wont to roam,
Thy hyacinth hair, thy classic face,
Thy Naiad airs have brought me home
To the glory that was Greece,
And the grandeur that was Rome.

critical estimate of his own work show that Mr. Robertson has never really studied the poet on whom he pronounces such glib and shallow judgments, and exemplify very clearly the fact that even dogmatism is no excuse for ignorance.

After reading Mr. Hall Caine's *Coleridge* we are irresistibly reminded of what Wordsworth once said about a bust that had been done of himself. After contemplating it for some time, he remarked, "It is not a bad Wordsworth, but it is not the real Wordsworth; it is not Wordsworth the poet, it is the sort of Wordsworth who might be Chancellor of the Exchequer."[8] Mr. Caine's Coleridge is certainly not the sort of Coleridge who might have been Chancellor of the Exchequer, for the author of *Christabel* was not by any means remarkable as a financier; but, for all that, it is not the real Coleridge, it is not Coleridge the poet. The incidents of the life are duly recounted; the gunpowder plot at Cambridge, the egg-hot and oronokoo at

Lo! in yon brilliant window-niche
How statue-like I see thee stand,
The agate lamp within thy hand!
Ah, Psyche, from the regions which
Are Holy-Land!
　(Poe, "To Helen")

8. This is Wilde's version of an anecdote first told about Wordsworth rather differently in *The Autobiography of Henry Taylor 1800–1875:* "I once discussing with him the merits of a picture of himself hanging on the wall in Lockhart's house in London. Some one had said it was like: 'Yes,' he replied, 'I cannot deny that there is a likeness; such a likeness as the artist could produce; it is like me so far as *he* could go in me; it is like if you suppose all the finer faculties of the mind to be withdrawn: that, I should say, is Wordsworth, a Chancellor of the Exchequer,—Wordsworth, the Speaker of the House of Commons.'"

the little tavern in Newgate Street, the blue coat and white waist-coat that so amazed the worthy Unitarians, and the terrible smoking experiment at Birmingham are all carefully chronicled, as no doubt they should be in every popular biography; but of the spiritual progress of the man's soul we hear absolutely nothing. Never for one single instant are we brought near to Coleridge; the magic of that wonderful personality is hidden from us by a cloud of mean details, an unholy jungle of facts, and the "critical history" promised to us by Mr. Walter Scott in his unfortunate preface is conspicuous only by its absence.

Carlyle once proposed in jest to write a life of Michael Angelo without making any reference to his art, and Mr. Caine has shown that such a project is perfectly feasible. He has written the life of a great peripatetic philosopher and chronicled only the peripatetics. He has tried to tell us about a poet, and his book might be the biography of the famous tallow-chandler who would not appreciate the *Watchman*. The real events of Coleridge's life are not his gig excursions and his walking tours; they are his thoughts, dreams and passions, his moments of creative impulse, their source and secret, his moods of imaginative joy, their marvel and their meaning, and not his moods merely but the music and the melancholy that they brought him; the lyric loveliness of his voice when he sang, the sterile sorrow of the years when he was silent. It is said that every man's life is a Soul's Tragedy. Coleridge's certainly was so, and though we may not be able to pluck out the heart of his mystery, still let us recognise that mystery is there; and that the goings-out and comings-in of a man, his places of sojourn and his roads of travel are but idle things to chronicle, if that which is the man be left unrecorded. So mediocre is Mr. Caine's book that even accuracy could not make it better.

On the whole, then, Mr. Walter Scott cannot be congratulated on the success of his venture so far. The one really admirable feature of the series is the bibliography that is appended to each volume. These bibliographies are compiled by Mr. Anderson, of the British Museum, and are so valuable to the student, as well as interesting in themselves, that it is much to be regretted that they should be accompanied by such tedious letterpress.

Aristotle At Afternoon Tea*

In society, says Mr. Mahaffy, every civilized man and woman ought to feel it their duty to say something, even when there is hardly anything to be said, and in order to encourage this delightful art of brilliant chatter he has published a social guide without which no *débutante* or dandy should ever dream of going out to dine. Not that Mr. Mahaffy's book can be said to be, in any sense of the word, popular. In discussing this important subject of conversation, he has not merely followed the scientific method of Aristotle, which is perhaps excusable, but he has adopted the literary style of Aristotle, for which no excuse is possible. There is, also, hardly a single anecdote, hardly a single illustration, and the reader is left to put

---

* Unsigned (i.e., anonymous) review of John Pentland Mahaffy, *The Principles of the Art of Conversation: A Social Essay,* published in *Pall Mall Gazette,* December 16, 1887. Mahaffy had been Wilde's tutor at Trinity College, Dublin, from 1871–1874. Wilde twice traveled to Italy and Greece with Mahaffy, in 1875 and again in 1877, and also contributed in a modest way to Mahaffy's *Social Life in Greece* (1874). In 1893 Wilde was to call Mahaffy "a man of high and distinguished culture . . . my first and best teacher . . . the scholar who showed me how to love Greek things" (*The Complete Letters of Oscar Wilde,* ed. Merlin Holland and Rupert Hart-Davis [New York: Henry Holt, 2000], 562). Mahaffy in turn boasted that Wilde had learned the art of conversation from himself. Upon Wilde's receipt of a Classics Demyship to Magdalen College, Oxford, in 1874, Mahaffy purportedly quipped, "You're not clever enough for us here, Oscar. Better run up to Oxford."

the Professor's abstract rules into practice, without either the examples or the warnings of history to encourage or to dissuade him in his reckless career. Still, the book can be warmly recommended to all who propose to substitute the vice of verbosity for the stupidity of silence. It fascinates in spite of its form, and pleases in spite of its pedantry, and is the nearest approach that we know of in modern literature to meeting Aristotle at an afternoon tea.

As regards physical conditions, the only one that is considered by Mr. Mahaffy as being absolutely essential to a good conversationalist, is the possession of a musical voice. Some learned writers have been of opinion that a slight stammer often gives peculiar zest to conversation, but Mr. Mahaffy rejects this view and is extremely severe on every eccentricity, from a native brogue to an artificial catchword. With his remarks on the latter point, the meaningless repetition of phrases, we entirely agree. Nothing can be more irritating than the scientific person who is always saying *Exactly so,* or the commonplace person who ends every sentence with *Don't you know,* or the pseudo-artistic person who murmurs *Charming, charming,* on the smallest provocation. It is, however, with the mental and moral qualifications for conversation that Mr. Mahaffy specially deals. Knowledge he naturally regards as an absolute essential, for as he most justly observes, "an ignorant man is seldom agreeable, except as a butt." Upon the other hand, strict accuracy should be avoided. "Even a consummate liar," says Mr. Mahaffy, is a better ingredient in a company than "the scrupulously truthful man, who weighs every statement, questions every fact, and corrects every inaccuracy." The liar at any rate recognizes that recreation, not instruction, is the aim of conversation, and is a far more civilized being than the blockhead who loudly expresses his disbelief in a story which is told simply for the amusement of the company. Mr. Mahaffy, however, makes an exception in favour of the eminent specialist, and tells us that intelligent questions addressed to an astronomer, or a pure mathematician, will elicit many curious facts which will pleasantly beguile the time. Here, in the interest of society, we feel bound to enter a formal protest. Nobody, even in the provinces, should ever be allowed to ask an intelligent question about pure mathematics across a dinner-table. A question of this kind is quite as bad as inquiring suddenly about the state of a man's soul, a sort of *coup* which, as Mr. Mahaffy remarks elsewhere, "many pious people have actually thought a decent introduction to a conversation."[1]

As for the moral qualifications of a good talker, Mr. Mahaffy, following the example of his great master, warns us against any disproportionate excess of virtue.[2] Modesty, for instance, may easily become a social vice, and to be continually apologising for one's ignorance or stupidity is a grave injury to conversation, for "what we want to learn from each member is his free opinion on the subject in hand, not his own estimate of the value of that opinion." Simplicity, too, is not without its dangers. The *enfant terrible,* with his shameless love of truth, the raw country-bred girl, who always says what she means, and the plain, blunt man who makes a point

1. Wilde's quotation should properly begin earlier. Mahaffy writes: "there can be no greater blunder than to inquire suddenly about the state of a man's soul, a sort of *coup* which many pious people have actually thought a decent introduction to a conversation." *Coup* is French for "blow."

2. Mahaffy's "great master," according to the witty logic of the opening paragraph, is Aristotle. Wilde appears to be thinking here of Aristotle's *Nicomachian Ethics,* Book 2, Sec. 7, in which Aristotle says that during conversation, any pretension to truth "in the form of exaggeration is Boastfulness," while "wittiness" is indispensable to "Pleasantness and social amusement" (2.7.12–14).

of speaking his mind on every possible occasion, without ever considering whether he has a mind at all, are the fatal examples of what simplicity leads to. Shyness may be a form of vanity, and reserve a development of pride, and as for sympathy, what can be more detestable than the man, or woman, who insists on agreeing with everybody, and so makes "a discussion, which implies differences in opinion," absolutely impossible? Even the unselfish listener is apt to become a bore. "These silent people," says Mr. Mahaffy, "not only take all they can get in society for nothing, but they take it without the smallest gratitude, and have the audacity afterwards to censure those who have laboured for their amusement." Tact, which is an exquisite sense of the symmetry of things, is, according to Mr. Mahaffy, the highest and best of all the moral conditions for conversation. The man of tact, he most wisely remarks, "will instinctively avoid jokes about Bluebeard" in the company of a woman who is a man's third wife; he will never be guilty of talking like a book, but will rather avoid too careful an attention to grammar and the rounding of periods; he will cultivate the art of graceful interruption, so as to prevent a subject being worn threadbare by the aged or the inexperienced; and should he be desirous of telling a story, he will look round and consider each member of the party, and if there be a single stranger present will forgo the pleasure of anecdotage rather than make the social mistake of hurting even one of the guests. As for prepared or premeditated art, Mr. Mahaffy has a great contempt for it and tells us of a certain college Don (let us hope not at Oxford or Cambridge) who always carried a jest-book in his pocket and had to refer to it when he wished to make a repartee. Great wits, too, are often very cruel, and great humorists often very vulgar, so it will be better to try and "make good conversation without any large help from these brilliant but dangerous gifts." In a tête-à-tête one should talk about persons, and in general society about things. The state of the weather is always an excusable exordium, but it is convenient to have a paradox or heresy on the subject always ready so as to direct the conversation into other channels. Really domestic people are almost invariably bad talkers as their very virtues in home life have dulled their interest in outer things. The very best mothers will insist on chattering of their babies and prattling about infant education. In fact, most women do not take sufficient interest in politics, just as most men are deficient in general reading. Still, anybody can be made to talk, except the very obstinate, and even a commercial traveller may be drawn out and become quite interesting. As for society small talk, it is impossible, Mr. Mahaffy tells us, for any sound theory of conversation to depreciate gossip, "which is perhaps the main factor in agreeable talk throughout society." The retailing of small personal points about great people always gives pleasure, and if one is not fortunate enough to be an Arctic traveller or an escaped Nihilist, the best thing one can do is to relate some anecdote of "Prince Bismarck, or King Victor Emmanuel, or Mr. Gladstone." In the case of meeting a genius and a Duke at dinner, the good talker will try to raise himself to the level of the former and to bring the latter down to his own level. To succeed amongst one's social superiors one must have no hesitation in contradicting them. Indeed, one should make bold criticisms, and try and introduce a bright and free tone into a society whose grandeur and extreme respectability make it, Mr. Mahaffy remarks as pathetically as inaccurately, "perhaps somewhat dull." The best conversationalists are those whose ancestors have been bilingual,[3]

3. Wilde was himself bilingual: at various points in his life, he self-identified as an Irishman, an Englishman, and a Frenchman. When the Censor banned theatrical productions of *Salomé* (written in French) in

like the French and Irish, but the art of conversation is really within the reach of almost every one, except those who are morbidly truthful, or whose high moral worth requires to be sustained by a permanent gravity of demeanour and a general dulness of mind.

These are the broad principles contained in Mr. Mahaffy's clever little book, and many of them will, no doubt, commend themselves to our readers. The maxim, "If you find the company dull, blame yourself," seems to us somewhat optimistic, and we have no sympathy at all with the professional storyteller who is really a great bore at a dinner-table; but Mr. Mahaffy is quite right in insisting that no bright social intercourse is possible without equality, and it is no objection to his book to say that it will not teach people how to talk cleverly. It is not logic that makes men reasonable, nor the science of ethics that makes men good, but it is always useful to analyse, to formularize, and to investigate. The only thing to be regretted in the volume is the arid and jejune character of the style. If Mr. Mahaffy would only write as he talks his book would be much pleasanter reading.

_____

1892, Wilde threatened to "leave England to settle in France, where I shall take out letters of naturalization. I will not consent to call myself a citizen of a country that shows such narrowness in artistic judgement. I am not English. I am Irish, which is quite another thing."

From "A Chinese Sage"*

An eminent Oxford theologian once remarked that his only objection to modern progress was that it progressed forward instead of backward—a view that so fascinated a certain artistic undergraduate that he promptly wrote an essay upon some unnoticed analogies between the development of ideas and the movements of the common sea-crab.[1] I feel sure *The Speaker* will not be suspected of

* Signed review of *Chuang Tzŭ: Mystic, Moralist and Social Reformer,* intro. and tr. Herbert A. Giles (London: Bernard Quaritch, 1889), published in *The Speaker* 1, no.6 (February 8, 1890). Chuang Tzŭ, also known as Zhuang Zhou or Zhuangzi, was an influential Chinese philosopher who lived around the fourth century BCE. He is credited with writing the *Zhuangzi,* one of the foundational texts of Taoism. Perhaps to underscore Wilde's point that the "name must carefully be pronounced as it is not written," *Tzŭ* is printed as "Tsŭ" throughout Wilde's review, including in the citation of the title of Giles's book.

1. Kimberley Stern speculates that "eminent Oxford theologian" is a playful allusion to the Oxford philologist Max Müller, who challenged Hegel's notion that history progressed dialectically, on the grounds that it was unsupported by historical reality. Müller was hardly a theologian, however, and it seems more likely that Wilde was thinking of one of the theologians of the Oxford Movement, otherwise known as "Tractarians," such as Edward Pusey (1800–1882), Regius Professor of Hebrew, who was still active at Oxford when Wilde was an undergraduate there in the 1870s. The identity of the "certain artistic undergraduate" is unknown, although it might well have been Wilde himself.

holding this dangerous heresy of retrogression even by its most enthusiastic friends. But I must candidly admit that I have come to the conclusion that the most caustic criticism of modern life I have met with for some time is that contained in the writings of the learned Chuang Tsŭ, recently translated into the vulgar tongue by Mr. Herbert Giles, Her Majesty's Consul at Tamsui.

The spread of popular education has no doubt made the name of this great thinker quite familiar to the general public,[2] but, for the sake of the few and the over-cultured, I feel it my duty to state definitely who he was, and to give a brief outline of the character of his philosophy.

Chuang Tsŭ, whose name must carefully be pronounced as it is not written, was born in the fourth century before Christ, by the banks of the Yellow River, in the Flowery Land; and portraits of the wonderful sage seated on the flying dragon of contemplation may still be found on the simple tea-trays and pleasing screens of many of our most respectable suburban households.[3] The honest

2. The "spread of popular education" dates from 1870, when the so-called Forster Act mandated the creation of local School Boards across England to ensure secular elementary education for all. As his irony here suggests, Wilde was skeptical about such democratic education reforms, which continued on into the early 1900s.

3. Wilde is alluding to the cult-like collecting of *chinoiserie* (French term to describe artifacts and decorative objects reflecting or simulating a distinct Chinese influence) in the early decades of the nineteenth century. By Wilde's day, the collecting of chinoiserie had been eclipsed by the cult of *Japonisme* (French term to describe the cultivation of Japanese styles and artifacts), at least among the artistic avant-garde, but Wilde implies that it lingers on past its time ("may still be found") among the respectable Victorian middle classes. At nearly 3,400 miles long, the Yellow River is the second-longest river in China. The *Flowery Land,* from the Chinese *hwa kwo,* meaning "flower of the world," is a

Portrait of Zhuang Zhou (Chuang Tzǔ), artist and date unknown.

ratepayer and his healthy family have no doubt often mocked at the dome-like forehead of the philosopher, and laughed over the strange perspective of the landscape that lies beneath him. If they really knew who he was, they would tremble. For Chuang Tsŭ spent his life in preaching the great creed of Inaction, and in pointing out the uselessness of all useful things. "Do nothing, and everything will be done,"[4] was the doctrine which he inherited from his great master Lao Tsŭ. To resolve action into thought, and thought into abstraction, was his wicked transcendental aim. Like the obscure philosopher of early Greek speculation, he believed in the identity of contraries;[5] like Plato, he was an idealist, and had all the idealist's contempt for utilitarian systems; he was a mystic like Dionysius, and Scotus Erigena, and Jacob Böhme, and held, with them and with Philo, that the object of life was to get rid of self-consciousness, and to become the unconscious vehicle of a higher illumination.[6] In fact, Chuang Tsŭ may be said to have

---

name traditionally employed by many Chinese to designate their own country.

4. Lao Tzŭ, quoted in Giles, Introduction to *Chuang Tzŭ*, viii.

5. An allusion to the pre-Socratic philosopher Heraclitus, who declared that "All is, and is not. For though it comes into being, yet it ceases to be." Chuang Tzŭ's similarities to Heraclitus had been spelt out in "A Note on the Philosophy of Chuang Tzŭ," by Canon Aubrey Moore, which prefaced the book that Wilde is reviewing. Similarly, Wilde draws his allusions to mystics and Neoplatonists elsewhere in this paragraph from Moore's prefatory note.

6. Dionysius, or "Pseudo-Dionysius" as he has come to be known, was a Christian Neoplatonist who wrote in the late fifth or early sixth century CE; John Scotus Erigena was an Irish Neoplatonist of the ninth century CE, best known for his translations of, and commentaries upon, the work of Pseudo-Dionysius; Jacob Böhme (1575–1624) was a German Christian mystic and theologian. Philo (20 BCE–50 CE), known also as

summed up in himself almost every mood of European metaphysical or mystical thought, from Herakleitus down to Hegel. There
was something in him of the Quietist also; and in his worship of
Nothing he may be said to have in some measure anticipated those
strange dreamers of mediaeval days who, like Tauler and Master
Eckhart, adored the *purum nihil* and the Abyss.[7] The great middle
classes of this country, to whom, as we all know, our prosperity, if
not our civilisation, is entirely due, may shrug their shoulders over
all this, and ask, with a certain amount of reason, what is the identity of contraries to them, and why they should get rid of that
self-consciousness which is their chief characteristic. But Chuang
Tsŭ was something more than a metaphysician and an illuminist.
He sought to destroy society, as we know it, as the middle classes
know it; and the sad thing is that he combines with the passionate
eloquence of a Rousseau the scientific reasoning of a Herbert
Spencer.[8] There is nothing of the sentimentalist in him. He pities
the rich more than the poor, if he ever pities at all, and prosperity

Philo of Alexandria, was a Hellenistic Jewish philosopher who, in recon-
ciling ancient Greek philosophy with Biblical truth, held that God was
the only efficient cause and the body was a source of evil.

7. Eckhart von Hochheim (c. 1260–c. 1327), commonly known as
Master (or "Meister") Eckhart, was a German mystic theologian and philosopher; the theologian Johannes (or "John") Tauler (c. 1300–1361) was
his student. Both believed that all living creatures are "unum purum nihil"
(one pure nothing).

8. Wilde is thinking of the autobiographical *Confessions* (1782) of the
Enlightenment philosopher Jean-Jacques Rousseau (1712–1778), about
whom he was to write in "The Critic as Artist": "Humanity will always
love Rousseau for having confessed his sins, not to a priest, but to the
world." Whilst an undergraduate, Wilde had greatly admired the work of
the pioneering sociologist Herbert Spencer, and Spencer's ideas continued
to shape Wilde's thinking. See p. 216, n.90 below. However, by 1889

seems to him as tragic a thing as suffering. He has nothing of the modern sympathy with failures, nor does he propose that the prizes should always be given on moral grounds to those who come in last in the race. It is the race itself that he objects to; and as for active sympathy, which has become the profession of so many worthy people in our own day, he thinks that trying to make others good is as silly an occupation as "beating a drum in a forest in order to find a fugitive."[9] It is a mere waste of energy. That is all. While as for a thoroughly sympathetic man, he is, in the eyes of Chuang Tsŭ, simply a man who is always trying to be somebody else, and so misses the only possible excuse for his own existence.

Yes; incredible as it may seem, this curious thinker looked back with a sigh of regret to a certain Golden Age when there were no competitive examinations, no wearisome educational systems, no missionaries, no penny dinners for the people, no Established Churches, no Humanitarian Societies, no dull lectures about one's duty to one's neighbour, and no tedious sermons about any subject at all. In those ideal days, he tells us, people loved each other without being conscious of charity, or writing to the newspapers about it. They were upright, and yet they never published books upon Altruism. As every man kept his knowledge to himself, the world escaped the curse of scepticism; and as every man kept his virtues to himself, nobody meddled in other people's business. They lived simple and peaceful lives, and were contented with such food and raiment as they could get. Neighbouring districts were in sight,

---

Wilde classed Spencer with "scientific historians, and the compilers of statistics in general" (p. 216 below), as one of those opposed to art and truth.

9. Wilde's own reformulation of Giles's translation of Chuang Tzŭ: "Why . . . these vain struggles after charity and duty to one's neighbour, as though beating a drum in search of a fugitive?" (167)

and "the cocks and dogs of one could be heard in the other,"[10] yet the people grew old and died without ever interchanging visits. There was no chattering about clever men, and no laudation of good men. The intolerable sense of obligation was unknown. The deeds of humanity left no trace, and their affairs were not made a burden for posterity by foolish historians.

In an evil moment the Philanthropist made his appearance, and brought with him the mischievous idea of Government. "There is such a thing," says Chuang Tsŭ, "as leaving mankind alone: there has never been such a thing as governing mankind."[11] All modes of government are wrong. They are unscientific, because they seek to alter the natural environment of man; they are immoral, because, by interfering with the individual, they produce the most aggressive forms of egotism; they are ignorant, because they try to spread education; they are self-destructive, because they engender anarchy. . . .

The economic question, also, is discussed by this almond-eyed sage at great length, and he writes about the curse of capital as eloquently as Mr. Hyndman.[12] The accumulation of wealth is to him the origin of evil. It makes the strong violent, and the weak dishonest. It creates the petty thief, and puts him in a bamboo cage. It creates the big thief, and sets him on a throne of white jade. It is the father of competition, and competition is the waste, as well as the destruction, of energy. The order of nature is rest, repetition, and peace. Weariness and war are the results of an artificial society based

10. *Chuang Tzŭ*, 117.

11. *Chuang Tzŭ*, 119.

12. As well as founding England's first Socialist party, Henry Mayers Hyndman (1842–1921) translated and popularized Karl Marx's ideas through articles and books such as *England For All* (1881) and *Socialism Made Plain* (1883).

upon capital; and the richer this society gets, the more thoroughly bankrupt it really is, for it has neither sufficient rewards for the good nor sufficient punishments for the wicked. There is also this to be remembered—that the prizes of the world degrade a man as much as the world's punishments. The age is rotten with its worship of success. As for education, true wisdom can neither be learnt nor taught. It is a spiritual state, to which he who lives in harmony with nature attains. Knowledge is shallow if we compare it with the extent of the unknown, and only the unknowable is of value. Society produces rogues, and education makes one rogue cleverer than another. That is the only result of School Boards. . . . [13]

Who, then, according to Chuang Tsǔ, is the perfect man? And what is his manner of life? The perfect man does nothing beyond gazing at the universe. He adopts no absolute position. "In motion, he is like water. At rest, he is like a mirror. And, like Echo, he only answers when he is called upon."[14] He lets externals take care of themselves. Nothing material injures him; nothing spiritual punishes him. His mental equilibrium gives him the empire of the world. He is never the slave of objective existences. He knows that, "just as the best language is that which is never spoken, so the best action is that which is never done."[15] He is passive, and accepts the laws of life. He rests in inactivity, and sees the world become virtuous of itself. He does not try to "bring about his own good deeds."[16] He never wastes himself on effort. He is not troubled about moral distinctions. He knows that things are what they

13. For School Boards, see n.2 above.

14. *Chuang Tzǔ*, 447, slightly reformulated: Wilde has merged Chuang Tzǔ's text ("Respond, like the echo") with Giles's running commentary ("Only when called upon").

15. Wilde's slight reformulation of *Chuang Tzǔ*, 293.

16. *Chuang Tzǔ*, 401.

are, and that their consequences will be what they will be. His mind is the "speculum of creation,"[17] and he is ever at peace.

All this is of course excessively dangerous, but we must remember that Chuang Tsŭ lived more than two thousand years ago, and never had the opportunity of seeing our unrivalled civilisation. And yet it is possible that, were he to come back to earth and visit us, he might have something to say to Mr. Balfour about his coercion and active misgovernment in Ireland;[18] he might smile at some of our philanthropic ardours, and shake his head over many of our organised charities; the School Board might not impress him,[19] nor our race for wealth stir his admiration; he might wonder at our ideals, and grow sad over what we have realised. Perhaps it is well that Chuang Tsŭ cannot return.

Meanwhile, thanks to Mr. Giles and Mr. Quaritch,[20] we have his book to console us, and certainly it is a most fascinating and delightful volume. Chuang Tsŭ is one of the Darwinians before Darwin. He traces man from the germ, and sees his unity with nature. As an anthropologist he is excessively interesting, and he describes our primitive arboreal ancestor living in trees through his terror of animals stronger than himself, and knowing only one

17. *Chuang Tzŭ*, 158.

18. As Chief Secretary for Ireland since 1887 (he relinquished the post upon becoming First Lord of the Treasury and Leader of the House of Commons late in 1891), Arthur James Balfour (1848–1930) had by this time gained a reputation for the ruthless suppression of Irish unrest, earning him the nickname "Bloody Balfour." He authored and enforced the Perpetual Crimes Act of 1887, termed the "Coercion Act" in the Nationalist press, outlawing the use of boycotting and unlawful assembly among Irish tenant farmers.

19. See n.2 above.

20. See headnote, p. 73 above.

parent, the mother, with all the accuracy of a lecturer at the Royal Society. Like Plato, he adopts the dialogue as his mode of expression, "putting words into other people's mouths," he tells us, "in order to gain breadth of view."[21] As a story-teller he is charming. The account of the visit of the respectable Confucius to the great Robber Chê is most vivid and brilliant, and it is impossible not to laugh over the ultimate discomfiture of the sage, the barrenness of whose moral platitudes is ruthlessly exposed by the successful brigand.[22] Even in his metaphysics, Chuang Tsŭ is intensely humorous. He personifies his abstractions, and makes them act plays before us. The Spirit of the Clouds, when passing eastward through the expanse of air, happened to fall in with the Vital Principle.[23] The latter was slapping his ribs and hopping about: whereupon the Spirit of the Clouds said, "Who are you, old man, and what are you doing?" "Strolling!" replied the Vital Principle, without stopping, for all activities are ceaseless. "I want to *know* something," continued the Spirit of the Clouds. "Ah!" cried the Vital Principle, in a tone of disapprobation, and a marvellous conversation follows, that is not unlike the dialogue between the Sphynx and the Chimaera in Flaubert's curious drama.[24] Talking animals, also, have their place in Chuang Tsŭ's parables and stories, and through myth and poetry and fancy his strange philosophy finds musical utterance.

21. *Chuang Tzŭ*, 449, slightly reformulated; Giles is here summarizing the judgments of early Chinese commentators, not quoting Chuang Tzŭ himself.

22. See *Chuang Tzŭ*, 387–406.

23. The details and dialogue of this anecdote are taken from *Chuang Tzŭ*, 129.

24. An allusion to Flaubert's *La Tentation de Saint Antoine* (The Temptation of St. Anthony). See p. 242, n.155 below.

Of course it is sad to be told that it is immoral to be consciously good, and that doing anything is the worst form of idleness. Thousands of excellent and really earnest philanthropists would be absolutely thrown upon the rates if we adopted the view that nobody should be allowed to meddle in what does not concern them.[25] The doctrine of the uselessness of all useful things would not merely endanger our commercial supremacy as a nation, but might bring discredit upon many prosperous and serious-minded members of the shop-keeping classes. What would become of our popular preachers, our Exeter Hall orators,[26] our drawing-room evangelists, if we said to them, in the words of Chuang Tsǔ, "Mosquitoes will keep a man awake all night with their biting, and just in the same way this talk of charity and duty to one's neighbour drives us nearly crazy. Sirs, strive to keep the world to its own original simplicity, and, as the wind bloweth where it listeth, so let Virtue establish itself. Wherefore this undue energy?"[27] And what would be the fate of governments and professional politicians if we came to the conclusion that there is no such thing as governing mankind at all? It is clear that Chuang Tsǔ is a very dangerous writer, and the publication of his book in English, two thousand years after his death, is obviously premature, and may cause a great deal of pain to many thoroughly respectable and industrious persons.

25. In Victorian Britain, the *rates* were local property taxes, which in turn funded elementary public welfare programs. To go *on the rates* was to go on public welfare.

26. Exeter Hall, located on the north side of The Strand, was a large auditorium, seating 5000 people, much favored by evangelists and reform-minded audiences and orators (the Anti-Slavery Society had met there in the 1830s). "The building . . . is dedicated to piety and virtue," quipped the satirical magazine *Punch* in 1842.

27. *Chuang Tzǔ*, 184.

It may be true that the ideal of self-culture and self-development, which is the aim of his scheme of life, and the basis of his scheme of philosophy, is an ideal somewhat needed by an age like ours, in which most people are so anxious to educate their neighbours that they have actually no time left in which to educate themselves. But would it be wise to say so? It seems to me that if we once admitted the force of any one of Chuang Tsǔ's destructive criticisms we should have to put some check on our national habit of self-glorification; and the only thing that ever consoles man for the stupid things he does is the praise he always gives himself for doing them. There may, however, be a few who have grown wearied of that strange modern tendency that sets enthusiasm to do the work of the intellect. To these, and such as these, Chuang Tsǔ will be welcome. But let them only read him. Let them not talk about him. He would be disturbing at dinner-parties, and impossible at afternoon teas, and his whole life was a protest against platform speaking. "The perfect man ignores self; the divine man ignores action; the true sage ignores reputation."[28] These are the principles of Chuang Tsǔ.

28. *Chuang Tzǔ*, 5.

From "Mr. Pater's Last Volume"*

When I first had the privilege—and I count it a very high one—of meeting Mr. Walter Pater, he said to me, smiling, "Why do you always write poetry? Why do you not write prose? Prose is so much more difficult."

It was during my undergraduate days at Oxford; days of lyrical ardours and of studious sonnet-writing; days when one loved the exquisite intricacy and musical repetitions of the ballade, and the villanelle with its linked long-drawn echoes and its curious completeness; days when one solemnly sought to discover the proper temper in which a triolet should be written; delightful days, in which, I am glad to say, there was far more rhyme than reason.

I may frankly confess now that at the time I did not quite comprehend what Mr. Pater really meant; and it was not till I had

* Signed review of Walter Pater, *Appreciations, with an Essay on Style* (London: Macmillan, 1889), published in *The Speaker,* March 22, 1890. A key figure in the rise of Victorian aestheticism, and arguably the single greatest influence on Wilde's thought, Pater was the first English-speaking exponent of art for art's sake. *Appreciations* was not the first book by Pater that Wilde reviewed. Three years previously, in the *Pall Mall Gazette,* in the course of reviewing Pater's *Imaginary Portraits,* Wilde had called Pater "if . . . not among the greatest prose writers of our literature . . . , at least, our greatest artist in prose." Like all "those who are artists as well as thinkers," Wilde added, Pater always strove "to convey ideas through the medium of images" and "to give a sensuous environment to intellectual concepts."

carefully studied his beautiful and suggestive essays on the Renaissance that I fully realised what a wonderful self-conscious art the art of English prose-writing really is, or may be made to be.[1] Carlyle's stormy rhetoric, Ruskin's winged and passionate eloquence, had seemed to me to spring from enthusiasm rather than from art. I do not think I knew then that even prophets correct their proofs. As for Jacobean prose, I thought it too exuberant; and Queen Anne prose appeared to me terribly bald, and irritatingly rational. But Mr. Pater's essays became to me the golden book of spirit and sense, the holy writ of beauty.[2] They are still this to me. It is possible, of course, that I may exaggerate about them. I certainly hope that I do; for where there is no exaggeration there is no love, and where there is no love there is no understanding. It is only about things that do not interest one, that one can give a really unbiassed opinion; and this is no doubt the reason why an unbiassed opinion is always valueless.

But I must not allow this brief notice of Mr. Pater's new volume to degenerate into an autobiography. I remember being told in America that whenever Margaret Fuller wrote an essay upon Emerson the printers had always to send out to borrow some addi-

1. Wilde refers to Pater's controversial *Studies in the History of the Renaissance* (1873), which in *De Profundis* he calls "that book which has had such a strange influence over my life" (*The Annotated Prison Writings of Oscar Wilde,* ed. Nicholas Frankel [Cambridge, MA: Harvard Univ. Press, 2018], 181).

2. An unacknowledged quotation from the poet Algernon Swinburne, who had said, in a sonnet written to accompany Théophile Gautier's novel *Mademoiselle de Maupin,* "This is the golden book of spirit and sense, / The holy writ of beauty." As Stokes and Turner observe, Wilde redirects Swinburne's tribute from Gautier to Pater.

tional capital "I"s, and I feel it right to accept this transatlantic warning.

"Appreciations," in the fine Latin sense of the word, is the title given by Mr. Pater to his book, which is an exquisite collection of exquisite essays, of delicately wrought works of art—some of them being almost Greek in their purity of outline and perfection of form, others mediæval in their strangeness of colour and passionate suggestion, and all of them absolutely modern, in the true meaning of the term modernity. For he to whom the present is the only thing that is present, knows nothing of the age in which he lives. To realise the nineteenth century one must realise every century that has preceded it, and that has contributed to its making. To know anything about oneself, one must know all about others. There must be no mood with which one cannot sympathise, no dead mode of life that one cannot make alive. The legacies of heredity may make us alter our views of moral responsibility, but they cannot but intensify our sense of the value of Criticism; for the true critic is he who bears within himself the dreams and ideas and feelings of myriad generations, and to whom no form of thought is alien, no emotional impulse obscure.

Perhaps the most interesting, and certainly the least successful, of the essays contained in the present volume is that on Style. It is the most interesting because it is the work of one who speaks with the high authority that comes from the noble realisation of things nobly conceived. It is the least successful, because the subject is too abstract. A true artist like Mr. Pater is most felicitous when he deals with the concrete, whose very limitations give him finer freedom, while they necessitate more intense vision. And yet what a high ideal is contained in these few pages! How good it is for us, in these days of popular education and facile journalism, to be reminded of the real scholarship that is essential to the perfect writer, who, "being a true lover of words for their own sake, a minute and constant observer of their physiognomy," will avoid what is mere rhetoric, or ostentatious ornament, or negligent misuse of terms, or ineffective surplusage, and will be known by his tact of omission, by his skilful economy of means, by his selection and self-restraint, and perhaps above all by that conscious artistic structure which is the expression of mind in style. I think I have been wrong in saying that the subject is too abstract. In Mr. Pater's hands it becomes very real to us indeed, and he shows us how, behind the perfection of a man's style, must lie the passion of a man's soul.

As one passes to the rest of the volume, one finds essays on Wordsworth and on Coleridge, on Charles Lamb and on Sir Thomas Browne, on some of Shakespeare's plays and on the English kings that Shakespeare fashioned, on Dante Rossetti, and on William Morris. As that on Wordsworth seems to be Mr. Pater's last work, so that on the singer of "The Defence of Guenevere"[3] is certainly his earliest, or almost his earliest, and it is interesting to mark the change that has taken place in his style. This change is, perhaps, at first sight not very apparent. In 1868 we find Mr. Pater writing with the same exquisite care for words, with the same studied music, with the same temper, and something of the same mode of treatment. But, as he goes on, the architecture of the style becomes richer and more complex, the epithet more precise and intellectual. Occasionally one may be inclined to think that there is, here and there,

3. The title poem of Morris's 1858 collection *The Defence of Guenevere and Other Poems*. Pater's essay on Morris, titled "Aesthetic Poetry"—a revised version of an essay on Morris first published in 1868—appeared only in the 1889 (first) edition of *Appreciations*, not in any subsequent edition.

a sentence which is somewhat long, and possibly, if one may venture to say so, a little heavy and cumbersome in movement. But if this be so, it comes from those side-issues suddenly suggested by the idea in its progress, and really revealing the idea more perfectly; or from those felicitous after-thoughts that give a fuller completeness to the central scheme, and yet convey something of the charm of chance; or from a desire to suggest the secondary shades of meaning with all their accumulating effect, and to avoid, it may be, the violence and harshness of too definite and exclusive an opinion. For in matters of art, at any rate, thought is inevitably coloured by emotion, and so is fluid rather than fixed, and, recognising its dependence upon moods and upon the passion of fine moments, will not accept the rigidity of a scientific formula or a theological dogma. The critical pleasure, too, that we receive from tracing, through what may seem the intricacies of a sentence, the working of the constructive intelligence, must not be overlooked. As soon as we have realised the design, everything appears clear and simple. After a time, these long sentences of Mr. Pater's come to have the charm of an elaborate piece of music, and the unity of such music also. . . .

Finally, one cannot help noticing the delicate instinct that has gone to fashion the brief epilogue that ends this delightful volume. The difference between the classical and romantic spirits in art has often, and with much over-emphasis, been discussed. But with what a light sure touch does Mr. Pater write of it! How subtle and certain are his distinctions! If imaginative prose be really the special art of this century, Mr. Pater must rank amongst our century's most characteristic artists. In certain things he stands almost alone. The age has produced wonderful prose styles, turbid with individualism, and violent with excess of rhetoric. But in Mr. Pater, as in

Cardinal Newman,[4] we find the union of personality with perfection. He has no rival in his own sphere, and he has escaped disciples. And this, not because he has not been imitated, but because in art so fine as his there is something that, in its essence, is inimitable.

4. The theologian and writer John Henry Newman (1801–1890), Victorian Britain's foremost convert to Catholicism, was made a Cardinal in the Catholic Church in 1878 and canonized by Pope Francis in 2019. Wilde was a great admirer of Newman's writings, saying "in what a fine 'temper' Newman always wrote. . . . [How] subtle was his simple mind" (*The Complete Letters of Oscar Wilde,* ed. Merlin Holland and Rupert Hart-Davis [New York: Henry Holt, 2000], 452). Wilde bought many of Newman's books in the summer of 1876, while still a student at Oxford, and nineteen years later Newman's *Apologia Pro Vita Sua* was, along with a number of unspecified works by Walter Pater, among the first books that Wilde was allowed to read in prison. In part one of the "The Critic as Artist," Wilde's avatar Gilbert numbers *Apologia Pro Vita Sua* among history's greatest autobiographies, saying wittily (while disassociating himself from Newman's spiritual beliefs) that "the world will never weary of watching that troubled soul in its progress from darkness to darkness."

ESSAYS AND DIALOGUES

From "The Philosophy of Dress"*

There has been within the last few years, both in America and in England, a marked development of artistic taste. It is impossible to go into the houses of any of our friends without seeing at once

* Published in full under Wilde's name in the *New-York Daily Tribune,* April 19, 1885, 9, subsequently excerpted in *Evening Telegraph* (Dundee, Scotland), May 7, 1885, 4. "The Philosophy of Dress" is based on a lecture that Wilde delivered in England in late 1884 and early 1885 (see Geoff Dibb, *Oscar Wilde, A Vagabond with a Mission,* "Appendix D: Dress and The Philosophy of Dress," [London: The Oscar Wilde Society, 2013], 262). Both the essay and the lecture were part of a broader dress reform *movement* in the early 1880s led by Mary Eliza Haweis, Emily King, and Florence Pomeroy (Viscountess Harberton), authors respectively of *The Art of Dress* (1879), *Rational Dress* (1882), and *Reasons for Reform in Dress* (1884), and in certain respects Wilde's ideas are consistent with those of the Rational Dress Society, which Haweis, King, and Pomeroy cofounded in 1881. For Wilde's debts to Haweis and other British dress reformers of his day, see John Cooper, *Oscar Wilde on Dress* (Philadelphia: CSM Press, 2013), 30–63. For Wilde's essay in full, see Cooper, 81–94; *Fashioning the Victorians: A Critical Sourcebook,* ed. Rebecca N. Mitchell (London: Bloomsbury, 2018), 85–91; also Dibb, *A Vagabond,* 275–282.

When Wilde became editor of the magazine *Woman's World* in 1887, he continued to advance the cause of dress reform, writing in an editorial in the very first number:

Women's dress can easily be modified and adapted to exigencies of [any] kind; but most women refuse to modify or adapt it. They

that a great change has taken place. There is a far greater feeling for color, a far greater feeling for the delicacy of form, as well as a sense that art can touch the commonest things of the household

—————

must follow the fashion, whether it be convenient or the reverse. And, after all, what is a fashion? From the artistic point of view, it is usually a form of ugliness so intolerable that we have to alter it every six months. From the point of view of science, it not unfrequently violates every law of health, every principle of hygiene. While from the point of view of simple ease and comfort it is not too much to say that, with the exception of M. Félix's charming tea gowns, and a few English tailor-made costumes, there is not a single form of really fashionable dress that can be worn without a certain amount of absolute misery to the wearer. . . . [W]ithout freedom there is no such thing as beauty in dress at all. In fact, the beauty of dress depends on the beauty of the human figure, and whatever limits, constrains, and mutilates is essentially ugly, though the eyes of many are so blinded by custom that they do not notice the ugliness till it has become unfashionable.

What women's dress will be in the future it is difficult to say. [A] writer [for] the *Daily News* . . . is of opinion that skirts will always be worn as distinctive of the sex, and it is obvious that men's dress, in its present condition, is not by any means an example of a perfectly rational costume. It is more than probable, however, that the dress of the twentieth century will emphasise distinctions of occupation, not distinctions of sex" ("Literary and Other Notes," *Woman's World*, November 1887, 40)

As well as editorializing on dress, Wilde published in *Woman's World* many illustrated articles on the subject including "The Romance of Dress," "Décolleté Dresses," and "Modern Gloves," by S. William Beck; "Politics and Dress," by Richard Heath; "An Arraignment of Fashion in Dress," by Charlotte Stopes; "Women Wearers of Men's Clothes," by Emily Crawford; "Mourning Dress and Customs," by Viscountess Harberton; and "On Cloaks," by Ella Hepworth-Dixon. He also published—and

into a certain grace and a certain loveliness.[1] But there is also a whole side of the human life which has been left almost entirely untouched. I mean of course the dress of men and of women . . .

I have been sometimes accused of setting too high an importance on dress. To this I answer that dress in itself is a thing to me absolutely unimportant. In fact the more complete a dress looks on the dummy-figure of the milliner's shop, the less suitable it is for being worn.[2] The gorgeous costumes of M. Worth's *atelier* seem to me like those Capo di Monte cups,[3] which are all curves

---

commissioned illustrations for—scholarly articles on historic dress and regular monthly columns on the latest fashions in women's dress. As Loretta Clayton has shown, Wilde used the magazine to "promote unconventional images of female beauty, fashion, and style" and to "mould a specialized female reader, the aesthetic consumer, . . . who spoke a new language of fashion—aesthetic dress reform" ("Oscar Wilde, Aesthetic Dress, and the Modern Woman," in *Wilde Discoveries: Traditions, Histories, Archives,* ed. Joseph Bristow [Toronto: Univ. of Toronto Press, 2013], 143).

1. Wilde alludes here to the Aesthetic Movement of the late 1870s and early 1880s, which he had himself done much to advance, especially through his lectures "The House Beautiful" and "The Decorative Arts," which had been well-attended and widely reported in the press on both sides of the Atlantic. Building on the work of the English designer and craftsman William Morris (1834–1896), Wilde had enjoined British and American audiences to decorate their houses more beautifully, not by spending large sums of money, but "by the procuring of articles which, however cheaply purchased and unpretending, are beautiful and fitted to impart pleasure" (Wilde, "The House Beautiful," in *The Complete Works of Oscar Wilde,* intro. Merlin Holland, 5th ed. [London: Harper-Collins, 2003], 913.

2. A *milliner* is a hatmaker or hatseller. Wilde mistakes a milliner for a dressmaker.

3. The English fashion designer Charles Frederick Worth (1825–1895), widely considered the father of haute couture, founded the House of

Dress, by Charles Frederick Worth, 1880s. "The gorgeous costumes of M. Worth's *atelier* seem to me like . . . Capo di Monte cups," writes Wilde, "all curves and coral handles . . . that is to say, they are curious things to look at, but entirely unfit for use."

and coral handles, and covered over with a Pantheon of gods and goddesses in high excitement and higher relief; that is to say, they are curious things to look at, but entirely unfit for use. The French milliners consider that women are created specially for them by Providence, in order to display their elaborate and expensive wares. I hold that dress is made for the service of Humanity. They think that Beauty is a matter of frills and furbelows. I care nothing at all for frills, and I don't know what furbelows are, but I care a great deal for the wonder and grace of the human Form, and I hold that the very first canon of art is that Beauty is always organic, and comes from within, and not from without, comes from the perfection of its own being and not from any added prettiness.[4] And that consequently the beauty of a dress depends entirely and absolutely on the loveliness it shields, and on the freedom and motion that it does not impede. . . .

It is curious that so many people, while they are quite ready to recognize, in looking at an ordinary drawing-room, that the horizontal line of frieze and dado diminishes the height of the room, and the vertical lines of pillar or panel increase it, yet should not see that the same laws apply to dress also. Indeed in modern costume the horizontal line is used far too often, the vertical line far too rarely, and the oblique line scarcely at all.

Worth, in Paris, in 1858. An *atelier* (Fr.) is a workshop or studio in which an artist or designer works. Often imitated, "Capo di Monte" (sometimes spelt "Capodimonte") is porcelain created or inspired by the Capodimonte porcelain manufactory founded in Naples, Italy, in 1743.

4. A *furbelow* is "a piece of stuff pleated and puckered on a gown or petticoat; a flounce; the pleated border of a petticoat or gown" (OED).

The waist, for instance, is as a rule placed too low down. A long waist implies a short skirt, which is always ungraceful as it conveys an effect of short limbs, whereas a high waist gives an opportunity of a fine series of vertical lines falling in the folds of the dress down to the feet, and giving a sense of tallness and grace. Broad puffed sleeves, again, by intensifying the horizontal line across the shoulders, may be worn by those that are tall and slight, as they diminish any excessive height and give proportion; by those who are small they should be avoided. And the oblique line, which one gets by a cloak falling from the shoulder across the body, or by a gown looped up at the side, is suitable to almost all figures. It is a line which corresponds to the direction of motion, and conveys an impression of dignity as well as of freedom. There are of course many other applications of these lines. I have mentioned merely one or two in order to remind people how identical the laws of architecture and of dress really are, and how much depends on line and proportion. Indeed the test of a good costume is its silhouette, how, in fact, it would look in sculpture.

But besides line there is also color. In decorating a room, unless one wants the room to be either chaos or a museum, one must be quite certain of one's color-scheme. So also in dress. The harmony of color must be clearly settled. If one is small the simplicity of one color has many advantages. If one is taller two colors or three may be used. I do not wish to give a purely arithmetical basis for an aesthetic question, but perhaps three shades of color are the limit. At any rate it should be remembered that in looking at any beautifully dressed person, the eye should be attracted by the loveliness of line and proportion, and the dress should appear a complete harmony from the head to the feet; and that the sudden appearance of any violent contrasting color, in bow or riband, distracts the eye from the dignity of the ensemble, and concentrates it on a mere detail.

Then as regards the kind of colors, I should like to state once for all there is no such thing as a specially artistic color. All good colors are equally beautiful; it is only in the question of their combination that art comes in. And one should have no more preference for one color over another than one has for one note on the piano over its neighbor. Nor are there any sad colors. There are bad colors, such as Albert blue,[5] and magenta, and arsenic green, and the colors of aniline dyes generally, but a good color always gives one pleasure. And the tertiary and secondary colors are for general use the safest, as they do not show wear easily, and besides give one a sense of repose and quiet. A dress should not be like a steam whistle, for all that M. Worth may say.[6]

Then as regards pattern. It should not be too definite. A strong marked check, for instance, has many disadvantages. To begin with, it makes the slightest inequality in the figure, such as between the two shoulders, very apparent; then it is difficult to join the pattern accurately at the seams; and lastly, it distracts the eye away from the proportions of the figure, and gives the mere details an abnormal importance.

Then, again, the pattern should not be too big. I mention this, because I happened lately in London to be looking for some stamped gray plush or velvet, suitable for making a cloak of. Every shop that I went into the man showed me the most enormous patterns, things far too big for an ordinary wall paper, far too big for ordinary curtains, things, in fact, that would require a large public

5. A synthetic substitute for indigo, named for its inventor Ferdinand D'Albert

6. In other words, a dress should not be too shrill or arresting. As John Cooper observes, Wilde had been introduced to the steam-whistle in America in 1882, later telling British lecture audiences that it had often awakened him from sleep.

building to show them off to any advantage. I entreated the shopman to show me a pattern that would be in some rational and relative proportion to the figure of somebody who was not over ten or twelve feet in height. He replied that he was extremely sorry but it was impossible; the smaller patterns were no longer being woven, in fact, the big patterns were in fashion. Now when he said the word *fashion*, he mentioned what is the great enemy of art in this century, as in all centuries. Fashion rests upon folly. Art rests upon law. Fashion is ephemeral. Art is eternal. Indeed what is a fashion really? A fashion is merely a form of ugliness so absolutely unbearable that we have to alter it every six months! It is quite clear that were it beautiful and rational we would not alter anything that combined those two rare qualities. And wherever dress has been so, it has remained unchanged in law and principle for many hundred years. And if any of my practical friends in the States refuse to recognize the value of the permanence of artistic laws, I am quite ready to rest the point entirely on an economic basis.[7] The amount of money that is spent every year in America on dress is something almost fabulous. I have no desire to weary my readers with statistics, but if I were to state the sum that is spent yearly on bonnets alone, I am sure that one-half of the community would be filled with remorse and the other half with despair! I will content myself with saying that it is something quite out of proportion to the splendor of modern dress, and that its reason must be looked for, not in the magnificence of the apparel, but rather in that unhealthy necessity for change which Fashion imposes on its beautiful and misguided votaries.

7. Although based on lectures delivered in Britain, "The Philosophy of Dress" was written and published for an American readership. See headnote p. 93 above.

NEW HATS FROM THE MAISON VIROT.

"The latest Paris Bonnet." During the period of Wilde's editorship (1887–1889), the magazine *Woman's World* featured regular monthly columns on "Paris Fashions" and "The Latest Fashions," with specially commissioned illustrations such as these.

I am told, and I am afraid that I believe it, that if a person has recklessly invested in what is called "the latest Paris bonnet," and worn it to the rage and jealousy of the neighborhood for a fortnight, her dearest friend is quite certain to call upon her, and to mention incidentally that that particular kind of bonnet has gone entirely out of fashion. Consequently a new bonnet has at once to be bought, that Fifth-ave.[8] may be appeased, and more expense entered into. Whereas were the laws of dress founded on art instead of on fashion, there would be no necessity for this constant evolution of horror from horror. What is beautiful looks always new and always delightful, and can no more become old-fashioned than a flower can. Fashion, again, is reckless of the individuality of her worshippers, cares nothing whether they be tall or short, fair or dark, stately or slight, but bids them all be attired exactly in the same way, until she can invent some new wickedness. Whereas Art permits, nay even ordains to each, that perfect liberty which comes from obedience to law, and which is something far better for humanity than the tyranny of tight lacing or the anarchy of aniline dyes. . . .

8. Still the most fashionable street in Manhattan.

The American Invasion*

A terrible danger is hanging over the Americans in London. Their future and their reputation this season depend entirely on the success of Buffalo Bill and Mrs. Brown-Potter.[1] The former is certain

---

* Published unsigned in *The Court and Society Review*, March 23, 1887. In the last decades of the nineteenth century, wealthy American families frequently came to Europe in the summer months, ostensibly to broaden their cultural and social horizons, but also as a way of escaping the stifling East Coast heat. In "The American Man," Wilde observes that rarely were American women accompanied by their menfolk and that "the American invasion has been purely female in character" (p. 113 below).

1. After serving as a scout and dispatch rider for the US Army during the Great Plains Indian Wars of the late 1860s, the buffalo hunter and showman William Frederick Cody (1846–1917), popularly known as "Buffalo Bill," started performing in shows that displayed frontier themes, cowboys, and episodes from the Indian Wars. He founded *Buffalo Bill's Wild West* in 1883, and after several years touring the United States, in 1887 he took his large company on a highly successful and remunerative tour of Great Britain, where over 2.5 million people, including Queen Victoria, watched him perform. Cora Urquhart Brown-Potter (1857–1936), professionally known as "Mrs. Brown Potter" or "Mrs. Brown-Potter," was an American society *belle* and actress. She was warmly received in London society upon her arrival in Britain in the summer of 1886. She made her London stage debut in Wilkie Collins's play *Man and Wife* in March 1887, just days after the publication of "The American Invasion." "[R]esponses to her performances were consistently clouded by her beauty," Catherine

to draw; for English people are far more interested in American barbarism than they are in American civilisation. When they sight Sandy Hook they look to their rifles and ammunition; and, after dining once at Delmonico's, start off for Colorado or California, for Montana or the Yellow Stone Park.[2] Rocky Mountains charm them more than riotous millionaires; they have been known to prefer buffaloes to Boston. Why should they not?[3] The cities of America are inexpressibly tedious. The Bostonians

Hinson writes (*London's West End Actresses and the Origins of Celebrity Charity, 1880–1920* [Iowa City: Univ. of Iowa Press, 2016], 92); in 1892, *Reynold's Newspaper* observed that "Mrs. Brown-Potter has a good stage presence, but she is not an actress" (quoted in Hinson, *London's West End Actresses*, 92). Nonetheless, "throughout the 1880s and 1890s Brown-Potter worked consistently at a range of West End theatres, moving from lead role to lead role" (Hinson, *London's West End Actresses,* 92). In 1898, an impoverished, largely friendless Wilde would enter into a financial agreement with Brown-Potter for a new play that he was never to write.

2. Sandy Hook is a spit of land on the New Jersey shore that marks the southern entrance to New York Bay. It would have been among the first tracts of American land seen by late-Victorian European travelers arriving in New York by steamship. For Delmonico's, see p. 54, n.13 above. Situated on the Yellowstone Caldera in northwest Wyoming and extending into Montana and Idaho, Yellowstone National Park was founded in 1872. It was the first (and, at the time of Wilde's writing, only) national park in the United States, as well as the world's first national park.

3. The remarks about American East Coast cities that follow, as well as the contrasts Wilde draws with the American West, are shaped by Wilde's own experiences lecturing and traveling in America in 1882. In his lecture "Personal Impressions of America," Wilde observes that "the most beautiful part of America is the West" and rhapsodizes about the West's landscape and culture, in comparison with the "great, noisy, modern towns" and "commonplace . . . cities" of the East Coast.

Photoportrait of the American actress Cora Brown-Potter (1859–1936), by B. J. Falk, 1895. Brown-Potter's debut on London's West End stage took place just days after the publication of Wilde's essay "The American Invasion."

take their learning too sadly; culture with them is an accomplishment rather than an atmosphere; their "Hub," as they call it, is the paradise of prigs.[4] Chicago is a sort of monster-shop, full of bustle and bores. Political life at Washington is like political life in a suburban vestry. Baltimore is amusing for a week, but Philadelphia is dreadfully provincial; and though one can dine in New York, one could not dwell there. Better the Far West, with its grizzly bears and its untamed cowboys, its free open-air life and its free open-air manners, its boundless prairie and its boundless mendacity! This is what Buffalo Bill is going to bring to London; and we have no doubt that London will fully appreciate his show.

With regard to Mrs. Brown-Potter, as acting is no longer considered absolutely essential for success on the English stage, there is really no reason why the pretty bright-eyed lady who charmed us all last June by her merry laugh and her nonchalant ways, should not—to borrow an expression from her native language—make a big boom and paint the town red. We sincerely hope she will; for, on the whole, the American invasion has done English society a great deal of good. American women are bright, clever, and wonderfully cosmopolitan. Their patriotic feelings are limited to an admiration for Niagara and a regret for the Elevated Railway; and, unlike the men, they never bore us with Bunker's Hill.[5] They take

4. Boston is still often referred to as "The Hub" or "Hub of the Universe," nicknames derived loosely from Oliver Wendell Holmes, who wrote in *The Autocrat of the Breakfast-Table* (1858): "[The] Boston State-House is the hub of the solar system. You couldn't pry that out of a Boston man, if you had the tire of all creation straightened out for a crowbar."

5. While underground railways were built in many European cities from the 1860s onwards, US cities generally favored noisy elevated railways. *Bunker's Hill* refers to the Battle of Bunker Hill, one of the earliest and most important battles of the Revolutionary War (1775–1783). The

their dresses from Paris, and their manners from Piccadilly, and wear both charmingly. They have a quaint pertness, a delightful conceit, a native self-assertion. They insist on being paid compliments and have almost succeeded in making Englishmen eloquent. For our aristocracy they have an ardent admiration; they adore titles and are a permanent blow to Republican principles. In the art of amusing men they are adepts, both by nature and education, and can actually tell a story without forgetting the point—an accomplishment that is extremely rare among the women of other countries. It is true that they lack repose and that their voices are somewhat harsh and strident when they land first at Liverpool; but after a time one gets to love these pretty whirlwinds in petticoats that sweep so recklessly through society and are so agitating to all duchesses who have daughters.[6] There is something fascinating in their funny, exaggerated gestures and their petulant way of tossing the head. Their eyes have no magic nor mystery in them, but they challenge us for combat; and when we engage we are always worsted. Their lips seem made for laughter, and yet they never

---

battle took place near Boston on June 17, 1775, and it ended in American defeat. But the inexperienced colonial forces inflicted significant casualties on the British and thereby gained an important boost in confidence.

6. One such "pretty whirlwind in petticoats" is Hester Worsley, the American heroine of Wilde's play *A Woman of No Importance,* who possesses many of the characteristics of American young women enumerated here and ends Wilde's play on the point of marrying the young Englishman Gerald Arbuthnot. Worsley has no "ardent admiration" for the British aristocracy, however, observing at one point that "the English aristocracy supply us [Americans] with our curiosities," that "with all your pomp and wealth . . . you [English] don't know how to live," and that "English society seems to me shallow, selfish, foolish."

grimace. As for their voices, they soon get them into tune. Some of them have been known to acquire a fashionable drawl in two seasons; and after they have been presented to Royalty they all roll their R's as vigorously as a young equerry or an old lady-in-waiting. Still, they never really lose their accent, it keeps peeping out here and there, and when they chatter together they are like a bevy of peacocks. Nothing is more amusing than to watch two American girls greeting each other in a drawing-room or in the Row.[7] They are like children, with their shrill staccato cries of wonder, their odd little exclamations. Their conversation sounds like a series of exploding crackers; they are exquisitely incoherent, and use a sort of primitive, emotional language. After five minutes they are left beautifully breathless, and look at each other, half in amusement and half in affection. If a stolid young Englishman is fortunate enough to be introduced to them he is amazed at their extraordinary vivacity, their electric quickness of repartee, their inexhaustible store of curious catchwords. He never really understands them, for their thoughts flutter about with the sweet irresponsibility of butterflies; but he is pleased and amused and feels as if he were in an aviary. On the whole, American girls have a wonderful charm and, perhaps, the chief secret of their charm is that they never talk seriously, except to their dressmaker, and never think seriously, except about amusements.

They have, however, one grave fault—their mothers. Dreary as were those old Pilgrim Fathers, who left our shores more than two centuries ago to found a New England beyond seas, the Pilgrim Mothers, who have returned to us in the nineteenth century, are

7. Rotten Row, in London's Hyde Park. To be seen on horseback or in a carriage in "the Row" was an important Society ritual in Victorian England.

James McNeill Whistler, *Arrangement in Grey and Black No. 1: Portrait of the Artist's Mother.* Lithographic print by Thomas R. Way, 1892, after Whistler's oil painting of 1871. "The American mother is a tedious person," writes Wilde: "The American father is better, for he is never seen in London. . . . The mother, however, is always with us, and, lacking the quick imitative faculty of the younger generation, remains uninteresting and provincial to the last."

drearier still. Here and there, of course, there are exceptions, but as a class they are either dull, dowdy, or dyspeptic.[8] It is only fair

8. *Dyspeptic* literally means "susceptible to or suffering from dyspepsia [indigestion]," but figuratively it means "morbidly despondent or gloomy" (OED). Compare Wilde's remark about American mothers with Mrs. Allonby's reply, in *A Woman of No Importance,* to Lady Caroline's

to the rising generation of America to state that they are not to blame for this. Indeed, they spare no pains at all to bring up their parents properly and to give them a suitable, if somewhat late, education.[9] From its earliest years, every American child spends most of its time in correcting the faults of its father and mother; and no one who has had the opportunity of watching an American family on the deck of an Atlantic steamer, or in the refined seclusion of a New York boarding-house, can fail to have been struck by this characteristic of their civilisation. In America, the young are always ready to give to those who are older than themselves the full benefits of their inexperience. A boy of only eleven or twelve years of age will firmly, but kindly, point out to his father his defects of manner or temper; will never weary of warning him against extravagance, idleness, late hours, unpunctuality, and the other temptations to which the aged are so particularly exposed; and sometimes, should he fancy that he is monopolising too much of the conversation at dinner, will remind him, across the table, of the new child's adage, "Parents should be seen, not

---

comment that Americans "have no ruins, and no curiosities": "What nonsense! They have their mothers"; also Wilde's comment in "The Canterville Ghost" that "many American ladies on leaving their native land adopt an appearance of chronic ill-health, under the impression that it is a form of European refinement."

9. Wilde would elaborate on this joke again in "The Child-Philosopher," his witty review of an article by Mark Twain on "English as She is Taught [in America]," published in *The Court and Society Review,* April 20, 1887. Here Wilde exclaims amusedly "we may all learn wisdom from the lips of babes and sucklings" and says it is "no wonder that the American child educates its father and mother" given how "full of rich suggestion, and pregnant with the very highest philosophy" are the utterances of American children as recorded by Twain.

heard." Nor does any mistaken idea of kindness prevent the little American girl from censuring her mother whenever it is necessary. Often, indeed, feeling that a rebuke conveyed in the presence of others is more truly efficacious than one merely whispered in the quiet of the nursery, she will call the attention of perfect strangers to her mother's general untidiness, her want of intellectual Boston conversation, immoderate love of iced water and green corn, stinginess in the matter of candy, ignorance of the usages of the best Baltimore society, bodily ailments, and the like. In fact, it may be truly said that no American child is ever blind to the deficiencies of its parents, no matter how much it may love them.

Yet, somehow, this educational system has not been so successful as it deserved. In many cases, no doubt, the material with which the children had to deal was crude and incapable of real development; but the fact remains that the American mother is a tedious person. The American father is better, for he is never seen in London. He passes his life entirely in Wall Street, and communicates with his family once a month by means of a telegram in cipher. The mother, however, is always with us, and, lacking the quick imitative faculty of the younger generation, remains uninteresting and provincial to the last. In spite of her, however, the American girl is always welcome. She brightens our dull dinner parties for us and makes life go pleasantly by for a season. In the race for coronets she often carries off the prize; but, once she has gained the victory, she is generous and forgives her English rivals everything, even their beauty.[10] Warned by the example of her

10. In the opening scene of *A Woman of No Importance,* after chastising Hester Worsley that "it is not customary in England . . . for a young

mother that American women do not grow old gracefully, she tries not to grow old at all, and often succeeds. She has exquisite feet and hands, is always *bien chaussée et bien gantée,*[11] and can talk brilliantly upon any subject, provided that she knows nothing about it. Her sense of humour keeps her from the tragedy of a *grande passion,* and, as there is neither romance nor humility in her love, she makes an excellent wife. What her ultimate influence on English life will be, it is difficult to estimate at present; but there can be no doubt that, of all the factors that have contributed to the social revolution of London, there are few more important, and none more delightful, than the American Invasion.

lady to speak with . . . enthusiasm of any person of the opposite sex," Lady Caroline Pontefract observes: "English women conceal their feelings till after they are married," before adding pointedly "they show them then." Later in the same scene, Lady Caroline will declare privately, "These American girls carry off all the good matches. Why can't they stay in their own country? They are always telling us it is the Paradise of women."

11. Beautifully shod and gloved.

The American Man*

One of our prettiest Duchesses enquired the other day of a distinguished traveller whether there was really such a thing as an American man, explaining, as the reason for her question, that, though she knew many fascinating American women, she had never come across any fathers, grandfathers, uncles, brothers, husbands, cousins, or, indeed, male relatives of any kind whatsoever.

The exact answer the Duchess received is not worth recording, as it took the depressing form of useful and accurate information; but there can be no doubt that the subject is an extremely interesting one, pointing, as it does, to the curious fact that, as far as society is concerned, the American invasion has been purely female in character.[1] With the exception of the United States Minister, always a welcome personage wherever he goes, and an occasional

---

* Published unsigned in *Court and Society Review*, April 13, 1887. The essay complements "The American Invasion," which is primarily focused on American women.

1. Wilde implies that by sending their daughters to Europe with a chaperone, wealthy late-Victorian American parents were set on improving their daughters' marriage prospects as well as broadening their horizons. Wilde had anatomized this phenomenon in "The American Invasion."

lion from Boston or the Far West, no American man has any social existence in London.[2] His women-folk, with their wonderful
dresses, and still more wonderful dialogue, shine in our *salons,* and
delight our dinner-parties; our guardsmen are taken captive by
their brilliant complexions, and our beauties made jealous by their
clever wit; but the poor American man remains permanently in
the background, and never rises beyond the level of the tourist.
Now and then he makes an appearance in the Row, looking a
somewhat strange figure in his long frock coat of glossy black cloth,
and his sensible soft-felt hat; but his favourite haunt is the Strand,
and the American Exchange his idea of Heaven.[3] When he is not
lounging in a rocking-chair with a cigar, he is loafing through the
streets with a carpet bag, gravely taking stock of our products, and
trying to understand Europe through the medium of the shop

2. *The United States Minister* is the US ambassador. In Wilde's story
"The Canterville Ghost," Hiram B. Otis is the United States Minister,
although he is so comfortable in British high society that he buys an English stately home. A *lion*—meaning a person of note or celebrity—"is a
man or woman one must have at one's parties," remarked the novelist
W. M. Thackeray.

3. For the Row, see p. 108, n.7 above. The Strand is a major London
thoroughfare connecting London's West End (to the west) with the City
(to the east). Less fashionable than the former and less businesslike than
the latter, the Strand "is a compromise," wrote Charles Dickens Jr.: "there
is somehow an air of greater lightness and gaiety . . . There are more women
among the foot passengers, more looking into shop windows, and an
absence of that hurried walk and preoccupied look which prevail in
the City proper. . . . The Strand is essentially the home of theatres." The
American Exchange was a London base for American travelers, located
in the Strand. For a small monthly fee, the exchange's users could peruse
the largest collection of American newspapers in Europe.

windows. He is M. Renan's *l'homme sensuel moyen*,[4] Mr. Arnold's middle-class Philistine.[5] The telephone is his test of civilisation, and his wildest dreams of Utopia do not rise beyond elevated railways and electric bells.[6] His chief pleasure is to get hold of some unsuspecting stranger, or some sympathetic countryman, and then to indulge in the national game of "matching." With a *naivete* and a nonchalance that are absolutely charming, he will gravely compare St. James' Palace to the grand central depot at Chicago, or Westminster Abbey to the Falls of Niagara. Bulk is his canon of beauty, and size his standard of excellence. To him the greatness of a country consists in the number of square miles that it contains; and he is never tired of telling the waiters at his hotel that the State of Texas is larger than France and Germany put together.[7]

4. Average sensual man. According to both Orthon Guerlac (*Les Citations Françaises* [Paris: Colin, 1931], 236) and Harry Levin (*Refractions: Essays in Comparative Literature* [New York: Oxford Univ. Press, 1966], 197), the phrase—which does not appear anywhere in the writings of the French historian and philologist Ernest Renan (1823–1892)—was invented by Matthew Arnold.

5. "If we look into the thing closely, we shall find that the term *Philistine* . . . gives the notion of something particularly stiff-necked and perverse in the resistance to light and its children, and therein it specially suits our middle-class" (Matthew Arnold, *Culture and Anarchy*, ed. Samuel Lipman [New Haven, CT: Yale Univ. Press, 1994], 68).

6. Following Alexander Graham Bell's invention of the telephone in 1876, the first telephone exchange was founded in New York in 1878. For elevated railways, see p. 106, n.5 above. The electric bell was invented in the United States more or less simultaneously with the telegraph in the 1840s.

7. While Texas is larger than either France or Germany, it is only two-thirds as large as the two put together.

Yet, on the whole, he is happier in London than anywhere else in Europe. Here he can always make a few acquaintances, and, as a rule, can speak the language. Abroad, he is terribly at sea. He knows no one, and understands nothing, and wanders about in a melancholy manner, treating the Old World as if it were a Broadway store, and each city a counter for the sampling of shoddy goods. For him Art has no marvel, and Beauty no meaning, and the Past no message. He thinks that civilisation began with the introduction of steam, and looks with contempt upon all centuries that had no hot-water apparatuses in their houses. The ruin and decay of Time has no pathos in his eyes. He turns away from Ravenna, because the grass grows in her streets, and can see no loveliness in Verona, because there is rust on her balconies. His one desire is to get the whole of Europe into thorough repair. He is severe on the modern Romans for not covering the Colosseum with a glass roof, and utilising the building as a warehouse for dry goods. In a word, he is the Don Quixote of common sense, for he is so utilitarian that he is absolutely unpractical. As a *compagnon de voyage*[8] he is not desirable, for he always looks *deplacé*,[9] and feels depressed. Indeed, he would die of weariness if he were not in constant telegraphic communication with Wall Street; and the only thing that can console him for having wasted a day in a picture-gallery is a copy of the *New York Herald* or the *Boston Times*. Finally, having looked at everything, and seen nothing, he returns to his native land.

There he is delightful. For the strange thing about American civilisation is, that the women are most charming when they are

8. Traveling companion.
9. Out of place.

away from their own country, the men most charming when they are at home.[10]

At home, the American man is the best of companions, as he is the most hospitable of hosts.[11] The young men are especially pleasant, with their bright, handsome eyes, their unwearying energy, their amusing shrewdness. They seem to get a hold on life much earlier than we do. At an age when we are still boys at Eton, or lads at Oxford,[12] they are practising some important profession, making money in some intricate business. Real experience comes to them so much sooner than it does to us, that they are never awkward, never shy, and never say foolish things, except when they ask one how the Hudson River compares with the Rhine, or whether Brooklyn Bridge is not really more impressive than the dome of St. Paul's. Their education is quite different from ours. They know men much better than they know books, and life interests them more than literature. They have no time to study anything but the stock markets, no leisure to read anything but newspapers. Indeed, it is only the women in America who have any leisure at all; and, as a necessary result of this curious state of things, there is no doubt but that, within a century from now, the whole

10. "The home," remarks Gwendolyn in *The Importance of Being Earnest,* "seems to me to be the proper sphere for the man. And certainly once a man begins to neglect his domestic duties, he becomes painfully effeminate."

11. Wilde speaks from experience. See his letters to Charles Eliot Norton, Oliver Wendell Holmes, Joaquin Miller, Henry Ward Beecher, Sam Ward, and Walt Whitman, among others, for an indication of the hospitality Wilde enjoyed from American men during his yearlong lecture tour of America in 1882.

12. Respectively, England's leading private school and leading university for aristocrats and gentlemen.

culture of the New World will be in petticoats. Yet, though these cute young speculators may not have culture, in the sense in which we use it, as the knowledge of the best that has been thought and said in the world,[13] they are by no means dull. There is no such thing as a stupid American. Many Americans are horrid, vulgar, intrusive, and impertinent, just as many English people are also; but stupidity is not one of the national vices. Indeed, in America there is no opening for a fool. They expect brains even from a boot-black, and get them.

As for marriage, it is one of their most popular institutions.[14] From childhood, the husband has been brought up on the most elaborate fetch-and-carry system, and his reverence for the sex has a touch of compulsory chivalry about it; while the wife exercises an absolute despotism, based upon female assertion, and tempered by womanly charm. On the whole, the great success of marriage in the States is due partly to the fact that no American man is ever idle, and partly to the fact that no American wife is considered responsible for the quality of her husband's dinners. In America, the horrors of domesticity are almost entirely unknown. There are no scenes over the soup, nor quarrels over the *entrées,* and as, by a clause inserted in every marriage settlement, the husband solemnly binds himself to use studs and not buttons for his shirts, one of the chief sources of disagreement in ordinary middle-class life is absolutely removed. The habit also of residing in hotels and boarding-houses does away with any necessity for those tedious

13. "[C]ulture [is] a pursuit of our total perfection by means of getting to know . . . the best which has been thought and said in the world, and, through this knowledge, turning a stream of fresh and free thought upon our stock notions and habits" (Arnold, *Culture and Anarchy,* 5).

14. See "A Handbook to Marriage," p. 56, n.2 above.

têtes-à-têtes that are the dream of engaged couples, and the despair of married men.[15] Vulgarising though a *table d'hôte* may be, it is at least better than that eternal duologue about bills and babies to which Benedict and Beatrice so often sink, when the one has lost his wit, and the other her beauty.[16] Even the American freedom of divorce, questionable though it undoubtedly is on many grounds, has at least the merit of bringing into marriage a new element of romantic uncertainty. When people are tied together for life they too often regard manners as a mere superfluity, and courtesy as a thing of no moment; but where the bond can be easily broken, its very fragility makes its strength, and reminds the husband that he should always try to please, and the wife that she should never cease to be charming.

As a consequence of this liberty of action, or, it may be, in spite of it, scandals are extremely rare in America, and should one occur, so paramount in society is female influence, that it is the man who is never forgiven. America is the only country in the world where Don Juan is not appreciated, and where there is sympathy for Georges Dandin.[17]

15. Wilde himself frequently resided in London hotels for long periods in the early 1890s as a way of escaping from his marriage and satisfying his need for homosexual relationships.

16. The lovers Benedick (not Benedict) and Beatrice marry at the end of Shakespeare's *Much Ado About Nothing* after a courtship involving a great deal of verbal duelling. But Wilde means "Benedict and Beatrice" in the proverbial sense of "any newly married couple."

17. In Spanish legend, Don Juan, the subject of Mozart's *Don Giovanni* and Byron's *Don Juan,* was a notorious womanizer and libertine. Georges Dandin is the foolish, cuckolded protagonist of Moliere's play *Georges Dandin, or Le Mari Confondu* (Georges Dandin, or The Confounded Husband).

On the whole, then, the American man at home is a very worthy person. There is just one point in which he is disappointing. American humour is a mere travellers' tale. It has no real existence. Indeed, so far from being humorous, the male American is the most abnormally serious creature who ever existed. He talks of Europe as being old; but it is he himself who has never been young. He knows nothing of the irresponsible light-heartedness of boyhood, of the graceful *insouciance* of animal spirits. He has always been prudent, always practical, and pays a heavy penalty for having committed no mistakes. It is only fair to admit that he can exaggerate; but even his exaggeration has a rational basis. It is not founded on wit or fancy; it does not spring from any poetic imagination; it is simply an earnest attempt on the part of language to keep pace with the enormous size of the country. It is evident that where it takes one twenty-four hours to go across a single parish, and seven days' steady railway travelling to keep a dinner engagement in another State, the ordinary resources of human speech are quite inadequate to the strain put on them, and new linguistic forms have to be invented, new methods of description resorted to. But this is nothing more than the fatal influence of geography upon adjectives; for naturally humorous the American man certainly is not. It is true that when we meet him in Europe his conversation keeps us in fits of laughter; but this is merely because his ideas are so absolutely incongruous with European surroundings. Place him in his own environment, in the midst of the civilisation that he has made for himself, and the life that is the work of his own hands, and the very same observations will fail even to excite a smile. They have sunk to the level of the commonplace truism, or the sensible remark; and what seemed a paradox when we listened to it in London, becomes a platitude when we hear it in Milwaukee.

America has never quite forgiven Europe for having been discovered somewhat earlier in history than itself. Yet how immense are its obligations to us! How enormous its debt! To gain a reputation for humour, its men have to come to London; to be famous for their *toilettes,*[18] its women have to shop in Paris.

Yet, though the American man may not be humorous, he is certainly humane. He is keenly conscious of the fact that there is a great deal of human nature in man, and tries to be pleasant to every stranger who lands on his shores. He has a healthy freedom from all antiquated prejudices, regards introductions as a foolish relic of mediaeval etiquette, and makes every chance visitor feel that he is the favoured guest of a great nation. If the English girl ever met him, she would marry him; and if she married him, she would be happy. For, though he may be rough in manner, and deficient in the picturesque insincerity of romance, yet he is invariably kind and thoughtful, and has succeeded in making his own country the Paradise of Women.

This, however, is perhaps the reason why, like Eve, the women are always so anxious to get out of it.

18. Ways of dressing, get-ups.

From "London Models"*

Professional models are a purely modern invention.[1] To the Greeks, for instance, they were quite unknown. Mr. Mahaffy, it is true, tells us that Pericles used to present peacocks to the great ladies of Athenian society in order to induce them to sit to his

* Published over Wilde's signature in *English Illustrated Magazine* 6, no.64 (January 1889), illustrated with fifteen drawings by R. G. Harper Pennington, who had previously painted a full-length oil portrait of Wilde as a wedding gift in 1884. On December 24, 1888, the *Pall Mall Gazette* observed "the *English Illustrated* for January has a really good article on 'London Models' written by Mr. Oscar Wilde. . . . Mr. Wilde's letterpress is very entertaining, and lends an air of unaccustomed sprightliness to the magazine." Wilde's essay was widely extracted and positively noticed in the English press around this time.

1. Wilde means *professional artist's models,* or what the novelist Nathaniel Hawthorne once termed "living models . . . whom artists convert into saints or assassins, according as their pictorial purposes demand" (Hawthorne, *The Marble Faun,* ed. Susan Manning [Oxford: Oxford Univ. Press, 2002], 17). The late nineteenth century was "the golden age of the artist's model," says Frances Borzello: artists frequently relied on human models, both paid and unpaid, to provide a realistic foundation—and in many cases, imaginative inspiration—for their art (*The Artist's Model* [London: Junction Books, 1982], 35). Modeling in the flesh, no longer restricted to the confines of state-approved academies, had become a source of livelihood and professional pride for many models, especially women, who had until very recently been largely excluded from live modeling. See also n.4 below. Two of Wilde's fictions center on the

friend Pheidias,[2] and we know that Polygnotus introduced into his picture of the Trojan women the face of Elpinice, the celebrated sister of the great Conservative leader of the day,[3] but these *grandes dames* clearly do not come under our category. As for the old masters, they undoubtedly made constant studies from their

---

highly charged model-artist relationship. In Wilde's story "The Model Millionaire," on seeing the painter Alan Trevor "putting the finishing touches to a wonderful life-size picture of a beggar-man" and noticing "the beggar himself . . . standing on a raised dais in the corner of the studio," Hughie Erskine declares, "what an amazing model"; and in *The Picture of Dorian Gray,* before painting Dorian Gray's portrait, the painter Basil Hallward depicts Gray "stood as Paris in dainty armour, and as Adonis in huntsman's cloak and polished boar-spear," later acknowledging that "I paint from him, draw from him, model from him."

2. For Mahaffy, see headnote p. 67 above. In *Social Life in Greece,* Mahaffy observes: "Whoever thinks for a moment of the pure and noble types of female beauty in Greek art, can hardly conceive the models to have been anything but the very highest and best of society. I imagine Pericles and Phidias to have been under great difficulties in procuring the best models, owing to the seclusion of women at Athens, and I conjecture that they were induced with difficulty to come to the sculptor's studio, where Pericles no doubt often met them, and that they were rewarded upon some few occasions with the present of a peacock, as money payments would have been unseemly" (Mahaffy, *Social Life in Greece from Homer to Menander,* 5th ed. [London: Macmillan, 1883], 215–216). Pericles (c. 495–429 BCE) was a Greek politician and general during Athens's golden age. For Phidias, see p. 335, n. 7 below.

3. "Plutarch tells us that the celebrated sister of Cimon, Elpinice, who appears from various anecdotes to have gone about Athens with some liberty, is said to have transgressed with the painter Polygnotus, and that accordingly when painting the Trojan women (in his famous portico called *pœcile*) he made his figure of Laodice a portrait of Elpinice" (Mahaffy, *Social Life in Greece,* 216).

pupils and apprentices, and even their religious pictures are full of the portraits of their friends and relations, but they do not seem to have had the inestimable advantage of the existence of a class of people whose sole profession is to pose. In fact the model, in our sense of the word, is the direct creation of Academic Schools.[4]

Every country now has its own models, except America. In New York, and even in Boston, a good model is so great a rarity that most of the artists are reduced to painting Niagara and million-aires.[5] In Europe, however, it is different. Here we have plenty of models, and of every nationality. The Italian models are the best.[6]

4. The earliest professional models were men because the academic system of art training considered drawing from the male body to be the intellectual foundation of high art. See n.20 and n.25 below. In the second half of the nineteenth century, art academies began to admit female models, but even still "the paucity of female models [in academies] from the 1860s to the 1880s was compensated by their ubiquitous presence in the studio, which in turn fuelled the cult of the female model in the last decades of the nineteenth century" (Martin Postle, "The Professional Life Model in British Art," in *Model and Supermodel: The Model in British Art and Culture,* ed. Jane Desmarais et al. [Manchester: Manchester Univ. Press, 2006], 15).

5. "The moral climate of the United States during the eighteenth and nineteenth centuries made it difficult or impossible for most artists to work from nude life models" (Sarah R. Phillips, *Modeling Life: Art Models Speak about Nudity, Sexuality, and the Creative Process* [Albany: SUNY Press, 2006], 7).

6. As Wilde implies, the late-Victorian ideal of personal beauty was not formulated in terms of gender alone: the model's ethnicity, race, and class began to invade representations too, and "by mid-century, due to an influx of Italian immigrants, . . . the Italian became a distinct ethnic type. . . . The *Italienne* was prized as an ideal beauty and a talented poser . . . with an instinctive feeling for the ways of the *atelier*" (Marie Lathers, "Changing Tastes: Ethnicity and the Artist's Model," in *Dictio-nary of Artists' Models,* ed. Jill Berk Jimenez [London: Fitzroy Dearborn,

The natural grace of their attitudes, as well as the wonderful pic-turesqueness of their colouring, makes them facile—often too facile—subjects for the painter's brush. The French models, though not so beautiful as the Italian, possess a quickness of intellectual sympathy, a capacity, in fact, of understanding the artist, which is quite remarkable. They have also a great command over the varie-ties of facial expression, are peculiarly dramatic, and can chatter the *argot* of the *atelier*[7] as cleverly as the critic of the *Gil Blas*.[8] The English models form a class entirely by themselves. They are not so picturesque as the Italian, nor so clever as the French, and they have absolutely no tradition, so to speak, of their order.[9] Now and then some old veteran knocks at the studio door, and proposes to sit as Ajax defying the lightning, or as King Lear upon the blasted heath. One of them some time ago called on a popular painter who, happening at the moment to require his services, engaged him, and told him to begin by kneeling down in the attitude of prayer. "Shall I be Biblical or Shakespearean, sir?" asked the veteran.

2001], 14–18). In Henry James's short story "The Real Thing," the penniless, working-class Italian model Oronte has an instinctive and uncultivated "*sentiment de la pose*" (real feel for posing).

7. For the *argot* of the *atelier,* see p. 48, n.14 above. Jane Desmarais writes that the young French female model "was regarded as a modern woman, assured, coquettish, aware of herself in a way that her Italian counterpart was not" ("The Model in Fiction from Balzac to du Maurier," in *Model and Supermodel,* 52).

8. An avant-garde French periodical founded in 1879, named after the picaresque novel of the same name by Alain-René Lesage. Wilde is prob-ably thinking of critics such as Paul Bourget and Camille Lemonnier, who wrote for *Gil Blas.*

9. Jane Desmarais contrasts the popularity of French and Italian models with "the absence of a popular 'English' model on the studio circuits in London and Paris" ("The Model in Fiction," 54).

"Well—Shakespearean," answered the artist, wondering by what subtle nuance of expression the model would convey the difference. "All right, sir," said the professor of posing, and he solemnly knelt down and began to wink with his left eye! This class, however, is dying out. As a rule the model, nowadays, is a pretty girl, from about twelve to twenty-five years of age, who knows nothing about art, cares less, and is merely anxious to earn seven or eight shillings a day without much trouble. English models rarely look at a picture, and never venture on any aesthetic theories. In fact, they realise very completely Mr. Whistler's idea of the function of an art critic, for they pass no criticisms at all.[10] They accept all schools of art with the grand catholicity of the auctioneer, and sit to a fantastic young impressionist as readily as to a learned and laborious academician. They are neither for the Whistlerites nor against them;[11] the quarrel between the school of facts and the school of effects touches them not; idealistic and naturalistic are words that convey no meaning to their ears; they merely desire that the studio shall be warm, and the lunch hot, for all charming artists give their models lunch.

As to what they are asked to do they are equally indifferent. On Monday they will don the rags of a beggar-girl for Mr. Pumper,

10. In his pamphlet *Whistler v. Ruskin: Art and Art Critics,* Whistler wrote, "the art critic alone would I extinguish. . . . Let work . . . be received in silence, as it was in the days to which the penmen still point as an era when art was at its apogee." See, too, "Mr. Whistler's Ten O'Clock."

11. In their hostility to the narrative and pictorializing impulse in Victorian painting, as well as their embrace of abstraction and tone-painting, Whistler's paintings, etchings, and lithographs were in the artistic avant-garde. Whistler formalized his artistic principles on numerous occasions, notably in his "Ten O'Clock Lecture."

whose pathetic pictures of modern life draw such tears from the public, and on Tuesday they will pose in a peplum for Mr. Phoebus, who thinks that all really artistic subjects are necessarily B.C.[12] They career gaily through all centuries and through all costumes, and, like actors, are interesting only when they are not themselves. They are extremely good-natured, and very accommodating. "What do you sit for?" said a young artist to a model who had sent him in her card (all models, by the way, have cards and a small black bag). "Oh, for anything you like, sir," said the girl, "landscape if necessary!"

Intellectually, it must be acknowledged, they are Philistines, but physically they are perfect—at least some are.[13] Though none of them can talk Greek, many can look Greek, which to a nineteenth-century painter is naturally of great importance.[14] If

12. Mr. Pumper is a sentimental liberal, who uses his art to highlight the injustices of modern life, while Mr. Phoebus—named ironically after Phoebus Apollo, the Greco-Roman god of the arts—is a Classicist, who pursues accurate historicism at the expense of any other consideration. Neither figure, in Wilde's view, is a good artist. As Stokes and Turner observe, to *pump* was Victorian slang for *to weep*. A *peplum* is "the part of a woman's jacket or tunic which hangs below the waist; a jacket or tunic having such a design" (OED). The word derives from *peplos,* a body-length garment worn by Greek women before 500 BCE.

13. For Philistines, see p. 43, n.2 and p. 117, n.5 above.

14. Ancient Greece was of vital interest to Victorian artists and thinkers, and *Hellenism*—designating ideals associated with Ancient Greek culture and thought—was promoted by a number of prominent Victorian thinkers as an antidote to the uniformity and authoritarianism of industrial modernity. For John Stuart Mill and George Grote, the Hellenism of fifth-century Athens represented "generous tolerance towards social dissent, and spontaneity of individual taste" while for Matthew Arnold, Hellenism meant a "play of thought" and "spontaneity of consciousness,"

they are allowed, they chatter a great deal, but they never say anything. Their observations are the only *banalités* heard in Bohemia.[15] However, though they cannot appreciate the artist as artist, they are quite ready to appreciate the artist as a man. They are very sensitive

---

contrasting sharply with the "Hebraic" authoritarianism of mid-Victorian England (Grote, quoted in Linda Dowling, *Hellenism and Homosexuality in Victorian Oxford* [Ithaca: Cornell Univ. Press, 1994], 61; Arnold, *Culture and Anarchy* ed. Samuel Lipman [New Haven: Yale Univ. Press, 1994], 147). According to Walter Pater, the Greek or "Hellenic" ideal is that "in which man is at unity with himself, with his physical nature, [and] with the outward world" (Pater, *The Renaissance: Studies in Art and Poetry*, ed. Donald L. Hill [Berkeley: Univ. of California Press, 1980], 177). To "look Greek" was, for many of Wilde's original readers, to embody this Hellenic ideal and thereby to seem invested with what Arnold called "a kind of aerial ease, clearness, and radiancy" (Arnold, *Culture and Anarchy*, 151). However, there is a subversive and erotic inflection to Wilde's invocation of the Greek ideal here, on which many readers of Walter Pater and John Addington Symonds would have picked up. As Linda Dowling has shown, Wilde, like Pater and Symonds before him, frequently invokes Hellenism as a "counterdiscourse" in order to celebrate male same-sex love and the male body in ideal or transcendental terms, particularly terms associated with the "spiritual procreancy" of Plato's *Symposium* or with Ancient Greece more generally (Dowling, *Hellenism and Homosexuality*, xiii). Wilde does not here specify the gender of the "physically . . . perfect" model who "looks Greek," but he nevertheless eroticizes the traditional ideal by describing this model as "ready to appreciate the artist as a man."

15. Bohemia is literally a region of what is now the Czech Republic, but Wilde means *Bohemia* in its figurative sense of "the realm in which non-traditional artists, writers, musicians and thinkers dwell." The term *Bohemian* came into English in the mid-nineteenth century, via France, as a way of equating the cultural avant-garde with the perceived free spirit of Romany gypsies, who had reached Western Europe via Bohemia. "Banalités" means *banalities*.

to kindness, respect and generosity. A beautiful model who had sat for two years to one of our most distinguished English painters, got engaged to a street vendor of penny ices. On her marriage the painter sent her a pretty wedding present, and received in return a nice letter of thanks with the following remarkable postscript: "Never eat the green ices!"

When they are tired a wise artist gives them a rest. Then they sit in a chair and read penny dreadfuls,[16] till they are roused from the tragedy of literature to take their place again in the tragedy of art. A few of them smoke cigarettes. This, however, is regarded by the other models as showing a want of seriousness, and is not generally approved of. They are engaged by the day and by the half-day. The tariff is a shilling an hour, to which great artists usually add an omnibus fare.[17] The two best things about them are their extraordinary prettiness, and their extreme respectability. As a class they are very well behaved, particularly those who sit for the figure, a fact which is curious or natural according to the view one takes of human nature. They usually marry well, and sometimes they marry the artist. For an artist to marry his model is as fatal as for a *gourmet* to marry his cook: the one gets no sittings, and the other gets no dinners.

On the whole the English female models are very naive, very natural, and very good-humoured. The virtues which the artist values most in them are prettiness and punctuality. Every sensible

16. Victorian term for "cheaply published crime stor[ies] written in a sensational or morbidly exciting style" (OED).

17. In Wilde's day, models earned more than London dockers, and modeling was often "not their only source of income, especially since many of them modelled principally during the evening and took on other forms of employment by day" (Postle, "The Professional Life Model in British Art," 11).

"Do you want a model?" engraved illustration, by R. G. Harper Pennington, accompanying "London Models" on its publication in *The English Illustrated Magazine* in 1889. "As a rule," says Wilde, "the model, nowadays, is a pretty girl, from about twelve to twenty-five years of age, who knows nothing about art, cares less, and is merely anxious to earn seven or eight shillings a day without much trouble." Five years earlier, Pennington had painted a full-length oil portrait of Wilde as a wedding gift. It is likely that he illustrated "London Models" at Wilde's request.

model consequently keeps a diary of her engagements, and dresses neatly. The bad season is, of course, the summer, when the artists are out of town. However, of late years some artists have engaged their models to follow them, and the wife of one of our most charming painters has often had three or four models under her charge in the country, so that the work of her husband and his friends should not be interrupted. In France the models migrate *en masse* to the little seaport villages or forest hamlets where the painters congregate. The English models, however, wait patiently in London, as a rule, till the artists come back. Nearly all of them live with their parents, and help to support the house. They have every qualification for being immortalised in art except that of beautiful hands. The hands of the English model are nearly always coarse and red.[18]

As for the male models, there is the veteran whom we have mentioned above. He has all the traditions of the grand style, and is rapidly disappearing with the school he represents. An old man who talks about Fuseli[19] is, of course, unendurable, and, besides,

18. The Victorians considered the hand "the talisman by which we are to penetrate the arcana of character" and also "the index of the human soul" (Anon. and Alexandre Dumas, quoted in Aviva Briefel, *The Racial Hand in the Victorian Imagination* [Cambridge: Cambridge Univ. Press, 2015], 2). Wilde was sensitive to the expressiveness of the human hand, and he had more than a passing interest in the pseudoscience of *cheiromancy* (palm reading), which was taken seriously by the late-Victorian elite. In *The Picture of Dorian Gray,* Wilde quotes from the second of two "Etudes de Mains [Studies of Hands]" by Théophile Gautier, as his protagonist reflects on the expressive quality of his own fingers; and his short story "Lord Arthur Savile's Crime: A Study of Cheiromancy" turns on an act of palm reading.

19. Henry Fuseli (1741–1825), British painter of Swiss origin and, from 1804, keeper of the Royal Academy, influential during the Romantic era.

patriarchs have ceased to be fashionable subjects. Then there is the true Academy model.[20] He is usually a man of thirty, rarely good-looking, but a perfect miracle of muscles. In fact he is the apotheosis of anatomy, and is so conscious of his own splendour that he tells you of his tibia and his thorax, as if no one else had anything of the kind. Then come the Oriental models. The supply of these is limited, but there are always about a dozen in London. They are very much sought after as they can remain immobile for hours, and generally possess lovely costumes. However, they have a very poor opinion of English art, which they regard as something between a vulgar personality and a commonplace photograph. Next we have the Italian youth who has come over specially to be a model, or takes to it when his organ is out of repair.[21] He is often quite charming with his large melancholy eyes, his crisp hair, and his slim brown figure. It is true he eats garlic, but then he can stand like a faun and couch like a leopard, so he is forgiven. He is always full of pretty compliments, and has been known to have kind words of encouragement for even our greatest artists. As for the English lad of the same age, he never sits at all. Apparently he does not regard the career of a model as a serious profession. In any case he is rarely, if ever, to be got hold of. English boys, too, are difficult

20. The academic ideal or "true Academy model" was "a nude male standing with legs spread wide and arms raised in a pose designed to display clearly his broad shoulders and well-developed musculature" (Susan S. Waller, *The Invention of the Model: Artists and Models in Paris, 1830–1870* [Aldershot, England: Ashgate, 2006], 1). See also n.4 above.

21. "Italian male models earned a reputation for reliability and resourcefulness, readily supplementing their earnings as models by selling chestnuts, ice cream and working as organ grinders" (Martin Postle, "The Professional Life Model in British Art," 19). Street organs, popular during the Victorian period, were often played by Italian immigrants.

to find. Sometimes an ex-model who has a son will curl his hair, and wash his face, and bring him the round of the studios, all soap and shininess. The young school don't like him, but the older school do, and when he appears on the walls of the Royal Academy he is called *The Infant Samuel.*[22] Occasionally also an artist catches a couple of *gamins*[23] in the gutter and asks them to come to his studio. The first time they always appear, but after that they don't keep their appointments. They dislike sitting still, and have a strong and perhaps natural objection to looking pathetic. Besides, they are always under the impression that the artist is laughing at them. . . .

Besides the professional posers of the studio there are posers of the Row, the posers at afternoon teas, the posers in politics and the circus posers.[24] All four classes are delightful, but only the last class is ever really decorative. Acrobats and gymnasts can give the young painter infinite suggestions, for they bring into their art an element of swiftness of motion and of constant change that the studio model necessarily lacks.[25] What is interesting in these "slaves of the ring" is that with them Beauty is an unconscious result not

22. Wilde is referring to over-sentimental paintings in the mode of Sir Joshua Reynolds's "The Infant Samuel" (1776), such as the "Infant Samuel" (c. 1853) of James Sant R. A. (1820–1916), the official portraitist of Queen Victoria. But his remark is implicitly a critique of adult constructions of childhood too, especially of the idealism and innocence often projected onto children by an "older school."

23. *Gamin,* originally a French word, means a boy left to run wild in the streets.

24. For the Row, see p. 108, n.7.

25. Male acrobats and gymnasts often numbered among the professional male models who sat for life-drawing from the nude in the state-run academies of art.

a conscious aim, the result in fact of the mathematical calculation of curves and distances, of absolute precision of eye, of the scientific knowledge of the equilibrium of forces, and of perfect physical training. A good acrobat is always graceful, though grace is never his object; he is graceful because he does what he has to do in the best way in which it can be done—graceful because he is natural. If an ancient Greek were to come to life now, which considering the probable severity of his criticisms would be rather trying to our conceit, he would be found far oftener at the circus than at the theatre. A good circus is an oasis of Hellenism[26] in a world that reads too much to be wise, and thinks too much to be beautiful. If it were not for the running-ground at Eton, the towing-path at Oxford, the Thames swimming-baths, and the yearly circuses, humanity would forget the plastic perfection of its own form, and degenerate into a race of short-sighted professors and spectacled *précieuses*.[27] Not that the circus proprietors are, as a rule, conscious of their high mission. Do they not bore us with the *haute école*,[28] and weary us with Shakespearean clowns? Still, at least, they give us acrobats, and the acrobat is an artist. The mere fact that he never speaks to the audience shows how well he appreciates the great truth that the aim of art is not to reveal personality but to please. The clown may be blatant, but the acrobat is always beautiful. He is an interesting combination of the spirit of Greek sculpture with the spangles of the modern costumier. . . .

26. See n.14 above.

27. People "aspiring to or affecting a refined delicacy of language and taste; . . . over-refined or absurdly fastidious" (OED).

28. A French term, literally meaning "high school," for the most difficult feats of horsemanship.

From "The Soul of Man Under Socialism"*

The chief advantage that would result from the establishment of Socialism is, undoubtedly, the fact that Socialism would relieve us from that sordid necessity of living for others which, in the

* "The Soul of Man Under Socialism" was first published over Wilde's signature in the February 1891 number of *Fortnightly Review*. An anonymous reviewer at the time described it as one "of the most paradoxical articles we have recently seen even in magazines. Mr. Oscar Wilde . . . has apparently set himself to galvanise his readers, and does it in a series of . . . literary bullets [that] are shot out in defence of the thesis that men should be themselves, in contempt . . . of all law which restricts their individualism. The article, if serious, would be thoroughly unhealthy, but it leaves on us the impression of being written merely to startle and excite talk" (Anon., "The Magazines," *Spectator* 66, no. 3267 [February 7, 1891]: 213). The essay was republished with very slight changes as a small book titled simply *The Soul of Man* in May 1895, shortly after Wilde's criminal conviction. This was a private publication, consisting of just fifty copies in light brown paper wrappers, overseen by Arthur Humphries, the manager of Hatchard's bookstore and a personal friend of Wilde and his wife. According to Josephine Guy, Wilde "did not . . . even attempt to rework the periodical text" for Humphries's publication and "had little active involvement in it" (Wilde, *Criticism: Historical Criticism, Intentions, The Soul of Man*, ed. Josephine Guy, vol. 4 of *The Complete Works of Oscar Wilde* [Oxford: Oxford Univ. Press, 2007], lxxviii–lxxix). The *Fortnightly* text is given here.

present condition of things, presses so hardly upon almost everybody. In fact, scarcely anyone at all escapes.

Now and then, in the course of the century, a great man of science, like Darwin; a great poet, like Keats; a fine critical spirit,

---

Socialism was both new and fashionable among British intellectuals in the early 1890s, in part because of the activities and writings of the acclaimed poet and designer William Morris, who founded the Socialist League in 1885 and spent the latter half of the 1880s writing, lecturing, and organizing for the revolutionary socialist cause. In the period leading up to his composition of "The Soul of Man Under Socialism," Wilde attended lectures in the coach house attached to Morris's home, where Socialist League meetings took place, and also subscribed to the League's official organ *The Commonweal* (edited by Morris), in which Morris serialized his important Utopian novel *News From Nowhere* in 1890. Morris was a key influence earlier in Wilde's career too, and a month or two after the publication of "The Soul of Man Under Socialism," Wilde told Morris, "I have loved your work since boyhood." As one might expect of an accomplished poet and designer, Morris, like Wilde, was especially interested in socialism's implications for art and the individual (and vice versa), and Wilde was familiar with Morris's 1882 essay collection *Hopes and Fears for Art* as well as with Morris's 1884 tract "Art and Socialism." Shortly after its British publication, "The Soul of Man Under Socialism" was published in an American pamphlet together with Morris's recent essay "The Socialist Ideal: Art."

Wilde's essay also reflects his interests in two other strands of contemporary political thought besides socialism: the scientific and evolutionary anarchism of Count Peter Kropotkin, whose 1889 lectures on "Social Evolution" Wilde helped to promote; and the political philosophy of *individualism* as espoused in the 1880s and 1890s by T. H. Green, Herbert Spencer, and the Libertarian Auberon Herbert. Kropotkin and Herbert were both frequent contributors to the *Nineteenth Century,* the monthly magazine in which three of the four prose pieces in Wilde's *Intentions* (see p. 183 below) originally appeared, and Wilde would have known both men's writings well. For Kropotkin's influence, see Masolino D'Amico,

Peter Alexeyevich Kropotkin (1842–1921), photographer and date unknown. Trained as an evolutionary biologist and geographer, Kropotkin was the father of modern anarchist thought. Exiled from his native Russia in 1876, he was well known among London intellectuals and exerted a great influence on Wilde's "Soul of Man Under Socialism." Years later, in *De Profundis,* Wilde was to call Kropotkin "a man with the soul of that beautiful white Christ that seems coming out of Russia."

"Oscar Wilde between 'Socialism' and Aestheticism," *English Miscellany* 18 (1967): 111–139; Deaglán Ó Donghail, *Oscar Wilde and The Radical Politics of the Fin de Siècle* (Edinburgh: Edinburgh Univ. Press, 2020), 110–123; also n.32 below. For the influence of Morris and other socialist thinkers, see Kristian Williams, "The Roots of Wilde's Socialist *Soul:* Ibsen and Shaw, or Morris and Crane," *Oscholars* (Spring 2010); also Williams, "The Basis

like M. Renan;[1] a supreme artist, like Flaubert, has been able to isolate himself, to keep himself out of reach of the clamorous claims of others, to stand "under the shelter of the wall," as Plato puts it,[2] and so to realise the perfection of what was in him, to his own incomparable gain, and to the incomparable and lasting gain of the whole world. These, however, are exceptions. The majority of people spoil their lives by an unhealthy and exaggerated altruism—are forced, indeed, so to spoil them. They find themselves surrounded by hideous poverty, by hideous ugliness, by hideous starvation. It is inevitable that they should be strongly moved by all this. The emotions of man are stirred more quickly than man's intelligence; and, as I pointed out some time ago in an article on the function of criticism, it is much more easy to have sympathy with suffering than it is to have sympathy with thought.[3] Accordingly, with admirable, though misdirected intentions, they very

---

for a New Civilization: Art and Labor, Artists and Workers, Aestheticism and Socialism," chapter 2 of his *Resist Everything Except Temptation: The Anarchist Philosophy of Oscar Wilde* (Chico, CA: AK Press, 2020), 61–97. For the influence of Herbert and of political Individualism, see Josephine Guy, "'The Soul of Man Under Socialism,' A (Con) Textual History," in *Wilde Writings: Contextual Conditions,* ed. Joseph Bristow (Toronto: Univ. of Toronto Press, 2003), esp. 69–77.

1. See p. 115, n.4 above.

2. A reference to Plato's description of the embattled philosopher at odds with the madness and savagery of his own age, who "remains quiet, minds his own affair, and, as it were, standing under the shelter of a wall in a storm, . . . is content if in any way he can keep himself free from iniquity and unholy deeds" (Plato, *Republic*, bk. 6, 496d-e).

3. In part two of "The Critic as Artist," published in serial form in *Nineteenth Century* in Sept. 1890, Wilde had written "The intellectual ideal is difficult of attainment [and] . . . will be for years to come unpopular with the crowd. It is so easy for people to have sympathy with suffering.

seriously and very sentimentally set themselves to the task of remedying the evils that they see. But their remedies do not cure the disease: they merely prolong it. Indeed, their remedies are part of the disease.

They try to solve the problem of poverty, for instance, by keeping the poor alive; or, in the case of a very advanced school, by amusing the poor.

But this is not a solution: it is an aggravation of the difficulty. *The proper aim is to try and reconstruct society on such a basis that poverty will be impossible.* And the altruistic virtues have really prevented the carrying out of this aim. Just as the worst slave-owners were those who were kind to their slaves, and so prevented the horror of the system being realised by those who suffered from it, and understood by those who contemplated it, so, in the present state of things in England, the people who do most harm are the people who try to do most good; and at last we have had the spectacle of men who have really studied the problem and know the life—educated men who live in the East End[4]—coming forward and imploring the community to restrain its altruistic impulses of

---

It is so difficult for them to have sympathy with thought" (Wilde, *Criticism*, 183).

4. An allusion to the Settlement Movement, a reformist social movement begun in the early 1880s, whose goal was for the rich and poor to live more closely together in an interdependent community. It aimed to realize this goal through the establishment of "settlement houses" in poor urban areas such as London's East End, in which highly educated, volunteer "settlement workers" would provide food, shelter, and education to local residents. By "educated men," Wilde is thinking of such original settlement workers as Canon Samuel Barnett (1844–1913), dean of the parish of St. Jude's, Whitechapel, who, together with his wife Henrietta Barnett, founded one of the East End's first settlement houses, Toynbee Hall, in 1884.

charity, benevolence, and the like.[5] They do so on the ground that such charity degrades and demoralizes.[6] They are perfectly right. Charity creates a multitude of sins.[7]

There is also this to be said. It is immoral to use private property in order to alleviate the horrible evils that result from the institution of private property. It is both immoral and unfair.

Under Socialism all this will, of course, be altered. There will be no people living in fetid dens and fetid rags, and bringing up unhealthy, hunger-pinched children in the midst of impossible and absolutely repulsive surroundings. The security of society will not depend, as it does now, on the state of the weather. If a frost comes we shall not have a hundred thousand men out of work, tramping about the streets in a state of disgusting misery, or whining to their neighbours for alms, or crowding round the doors of loathsome shelters to try and secure a hunch of bread and a night's unclean lodging. Each member of the society will share in the general pros-

5. In "Relief Funds and The Poor" (1886), Samuel Barnett, reflecting on the recent failure of the Mansion House Relief Fund, writes that "the rich would not be so cruel if they would think. . . . Never were needs so delicate left to mercies so clumsy; needs intertwined with the sorrows and sufferings with which no stranger could intermeddle have been met with the brutal generosity of gifts given often with little thought or cost. The result has been an increase of the causes which make poverty and a decrease of good-will among men" (Samuel Barnett and Henrietta Barnett, *Practicable Socialism: Essays on Social Reform* [London: Longmans, Green, 1888], 30–31).

6. Wilde means *deprives or vacuates [the recipient] of moral responsibility.*

7. An inversion of the Biblical notion that "charity covers a multitude of sins," as well as a reformulation of Wilde's idea, first expressed in part one of "The Critic as Artist" on its serial publication the previous year, that "charity . . . creates a multitude of evils." See p. 301 below.

perity and happiness of the society, and if a frost comes no one will practically be anything the worse.

Upon the other hand, *Socialism itself will be of value simply because it will lead to Individualism.*

Socialism, Communism, or whatever one chooses to call it, by converting private property into public wealth, and substituting co-operation for competition, will restore society to its proper condition of a thoroughly healthy organism, and insure the material well-being of each member of the community. It will, in fact, give Life its proper basis and its proper environment. But for the full development of Life to its highest mode of perfection, something more is needed. What is needed is Individualism. If the Socialism is Authoritarian; if there are Governments armed with economic power as they are now with political power; if, in a word, we are to have Industrial Tyrannies, then the last state of man will be worse than the first. At present, in consequence of the existence of private property, a great many people are enabled to develop a certain very limited amount of Individualism. They are either under no necessity to work for their living, or are enabled to choose the sphere of activity that is really congenial to them, and gives them pleasure. These are the poets, the philosophers, the men of science, the men of culture—in a word, the real men, the men who have realised themselves, and in whom all Humanity gains a partial realisation. Upon the other hand, there are a great many people who, having no private property of their own, and being always on the brink of sheer starvation, are compelled to do the work of beasts of burden, to do work that is quite uncongenial to them, and to which they are forced by the peremptory, unreasonable, degrading Tyranny of want. These are the poor, and amongst them there is no grace of manner, or charm of speech, or civilization, or culture, or refinement in pleasures, or joy of life. From their collective force Humanity gains much in material prosperity. But it is only the material result that it gains, and the man who is poor is in himself absolutely of no importance. He is merely the infinitesimal atom of a force that, so far from regarding him, crushes him: indeed, prefers him crushed, as in that case he is far more obedient.

Of course, it might be said that the Individualism generated under conditions of private property is not always, or even as a rule, of a fine or wonderful type, and that the poor, if they have not culture and charm, have still many virtues. Both these statements would be quite true. The possession of private property is very often extremely demoralising, and that is, of course, one of the reasons why Socialism wants to get rid of the institution. In fact, property is really a nuisance. Some years ago people went about the country saying that property has duties. They said it so often and so tediously that, at last, the Church has begun to say it.[8] One hears

8. As Josephine Guy has shown, this sentence, along with the six following it and the two preceding it (from "In fact, property is really a nuisance" to "we must get rid of it") was a late addition to the text. These sentences were probably written in response to a series of articles on "Irresponsible Wealth," penned by two leading British churchmen and a leading rabbi, that appeared in the *Nineteenth Century* in December 1890. These articles were in turn prompted by "The Gospel of Wealth," the foundational document of modern philanthropy, by the American industrialist and philanthropist Andrew Carnegie, which had been enthusiastically appraised by none other than the onetime (and future) Prime Minister W. E. Gladstone in the *Nineteenth Century* the previous month. In May 1891, three months after the publication of "The Soul of Man Under Socialism," Pope Leo XIII issued his *Rerum Novarum* on "the Rights and Duties of Capital and Labor," in which he proclaimed that, while "Private ownership . . . is the natural right of man," it is "more blessed to give than to receive" and so "Whoever has received from the

it now from every pulpit. It is perfectly true. Property not merely has duties, but has so many duties that its possession to any large extent is a bore. It involves endless claims upon one, endless attention to business, endless bother. If property had simply pleasures, we could stand it; but its duties make it unbearable. In the interest of the rich we must get rid of it. The virtues of the poor may be readily admitted, and are much to be regretted. We are often told that the poor are grateful for charity. Some of them are, no doubt, *but the best amongst the poor are never grateful.* They are ungrateful, discontented, disobedient, and rebellious. They are quite right to be so. Charity they feel to be a ridiculously inadequate mode of partial restitution, or a sentimental dole, usually accompanied by some impertinent attempt on the part of the sentimentalist to tyrannize over their private lives. Why should they be grateful for the crumbs that fall from the rich man's table? They should be seated at the board, and are beginning to know it. As for being discontented, a man who would not be discontented with such surroundings and such a low mode of life would be a perfect brute. Disobedience, in the eyes of anyone who has read history, is man's original virtue. It is through disobedience that progress has been made, through disobedience and through rebellion. Sometimes the poor are praised for being thrifty. But to recommend thrift to the poor is both grotesque and insulting. It is like advising a man who is starving to eat less. For a town or country labourer to practise thrift would be absolutely immoral. Man should not be ready to show that he can live like a badly-fed animal. He should

---

divine bounty a large share of temporal blessings . . . has received them . . . that he may employ them, as the steward of God's providence, for the benefit of others."

decline to live like that, and should either steal or go on the rates,[9] which is considered by many to be a form of stealing. As for begging, it is safer to beg than to take, but it is finer to take than to beg. No: a poor man who is ungrateful, unthrifty, discontented, and rebellious, is probably a real personality, and has much in him. He is at any rate a healthy protest. As for the virtuous poor, one can pity them, of course, but one cannot possibly admire them. They have made private terms with the enemy, and sold their birthright for very bad pottage. They must also be extraordinarily stupid. I can quite understand a man accepting laws that protect private property, and admit of its accumulation, as long as he himself is able under those conditions to realise some form of beautiful and intellectual life. But it is almost incredible to me how a man whose life is marred and made hideous by such laws can possibly acquiesce in their continuance.

However, the explanation is not really difficult to find. It is simply this. Misery and poverty are so absolutely degrading, and exercise such a paralysing effect over the nature of men, that no class is ever really conscious of its own suffering. They have to be told of it by other people, and they often entirely disbelieve them. What is said by great employers of labour against agitators is unquestionably true. Agitators are a set of interfering, meddling people, who come down to some perfectly contented class of the community, and sow the seeds of discontent amongst them. That is the reason why agitators are so absolutely necessary. Without them, in our incomplete state, there would be no advance towards civilization. Slavery was put down in America, not in consequence of any action on the part of the slaves, or even any express desire on their part that they should be free. It was put down entirely

9. For *go on the rates,* see p. 83, n.25 above.

through the grossly illegal conduct of certain agitators in Boston and elsewhere, who were not slaves themselves, nor owners of slaves, nor had anything to do with the question really.[10] It was, undoubtedly, the Abolitionists who set the torch alight, who began the whole thing. And it is curious to note that from the slaves themselves they received, not merely very little assistance, but hardly any sympathy even; and when at the close of the war the slaves found themselves free, found themselves indeed so absolutely free that they were free to starve, many of them bitterly regretted the new state of things.[11] To the thinker, the most tragic fact in

10. The life, writings, and speeches of the black American abolitionist, statesman, and escaped slave Frederick Douglass stand in contradiction to this claim. To be sure, in "What Are The Colored People Doing For Themselves?" (1848), Douglass wrote that "while the oppressed of the old world are making efforts, by holding public meetings, putting forth addresses, passing resolutions, and in various other ways making their wishes known to the world, . . . it is a shame that we, who are enduring wrongs far more grievous than any other portion of the great family of man, are comparatively idle and indifferent about our welfare." Nonetheless Douglass felt that "our elevation as a race is almost wholly dependent upon our own exertions" and "the oppressed nation has always taken a prominent part in the conflict." For useful surveys of black abolitionism, slave rebellions, and the agitations of ex-slaves, see Gerald Sorin, *Abolitionism: A New Perspective* (New York: Praeger, 1972), 99–119; Benjamin Quarles, *Black Abolitionists* (New York: Da Capo, 1991); and Richard S. Newman, "The Rise of Black Abolitionism and Global Antislavery Struggles," in his *Abolitionism: A Very Short Introduction* (Oxford: Oxford Univ. Press, 2018), 29–46.

11. The notion that, after the conclusion of the American Civil War, Reconstruction foundered through the indifference or incompetence of black Americans was famously challenged by W. E. B. Du Bois among others. See especially "The Propaganda of History," the final chapter of Du Bois's essential *Black Reconstruction in America* (1935).

the whole of the French Revolution is not that Marie Antoinette was killed for being a queen, but that the starved peasant of the Vendee voluntarily went out to die for the hideous cause of feudalism.[12]

It is clear, then, that no Authoritarian Socialism will do. For while under the present system a very large number of people can lead lives of a certain amount of freedom and expression and happiness, under an industrial-barrack system, or a system of economic tyranny, nobody would be able to have any such freedom at all. It is to be regretted that a portion of our community should be practically in slavery, but to propose to solve the problem by enslaving the entire community is childish. Every man must be left quite free to choose his own work. No form of compulsion must be exercised over him. If there is, his work will not be good for him, will not be good in itself, and will not be good for others. And by work I simply mean activity of any kind.

I hardly think that any Socialist, nowadays, would seriously propose that an inspector should call every morning at each house to see that each citizen rose up and did manual labour for eight hours. Humanity has got beyond that stage, and reserves such a form of life for the people whom, in a very arbitrary manner, it chooses to

12. An allusion to the unsuccessful Royalist rebellion and counterrevolution that took place in the Vendée region of western France from 1793–1776, in the wake of the execution of Louis XVI, when the rest of France was under firm revolutionary control. As Wilde indicates, the rebellion—initially, a popular reaction to the revolutionary government's restrictions on Catholic worship—was conducted by peasants of the region, where priests were poor and devoted, and the nobility, scarcely richer than the clergy, were equally attached to the people.

call criminals.[13] But I confess that many of the socialistic views that I have come across seem to me to be tainted with ideas of authority, if not of actual compulsion. Of course, authority and compulsion are out of the question. All association must be quite voluntary. *It is only in voluntary associations that man is fine.*

But it may be asked how Individualism, which is now more or less dependent on the existence of private property for its development, will benefit by the abolition of such private property. The answer is very simple. It is true that, under existing conditions, a few men who have had private means of their own, such as Byron, Shelley, Browning, Victor Hugo, Baudelaire, and others, have been able to realise their personality more or less completely. Not one of these men ever did a single day's work for hire. They were relieved from poverty. They had an immense advantage. The question is whether it would be for the good of Individualism that such an advantage should be taken away. Let us suppose that it is taken away. What happens then to Individualism? How will it benefit?

It will benefit in this way. Under the new conditions Individualism will be far freer, far finer, and far more intensified than it is now. I am not talking of the great imaginatively-realised Individualism of such poets as I have mentioned, but of the great actual

13. Penal servitude, or imprisonment with hard labor, was widely prescribed as punishment by British courts in the nineteenth century, both for severe and petty crimes. As late as 1885, 75 percent of all prison inmates were involved in some sort of penal servitude or forced labor, and it was not till 1948 that penal servitude was abolished in law. Wilde was himself subject to a severe and debilitating regimen of hard labor upon his imprisonment for gross indecency in 1895 (see Nicholas Frankel, *Oscar Wilde: The Unrepentant Years* [Cambridge, MA: Harvard Univ. Press, 2017], 39–41; also *The Annotated Prison Writings of Oscar Wilde,* ed. Frankel [Cambridge, MA: Harvard Univ. Press, 2018], 338, n.35).

Individualism latent and potential in mankind generally. For the recognition of private property has really harmed Individualism, and obscured it, by confusing a man with what he possesses. It has led Individualism entirely astray. It has made gain not growth its aim. So that man thought that the important thing was to have, and did not know that the important thing is to be. *The true perfection of man lies, not in what man has, but in what man is.*

Private property has crushed true Individualism, and set up an Individualism that is false. It has debarred one part of the community from being individual by starving them. It has debarred the other part of the community from being individual by putting them on the wrong road, and encumbering them. Indeed, so completely has man's personality been absorbed by his possessions that the English law has always treated offences against a man's property with far more severity than offences against his person, and property is still the test of complete citizenship.[14] The industry necessary for the making money is also very demoralising. In a community like ours, where property confers immense distinction, social position, honour, respect, titles, and other pleasant things of the kind, man, being naturally ambitious, makes it his aim to accumulate this property, and goes on wearily and tediously accumulating it long after he has got far more than he wants, or can use, or enjoy, or perhaps even know of. Man will kill himself by

14. Prior to 1832, the right to vote in England had been restricted to a small landowning portion of the male populace. The Reform Bills of 1832, 1867, and 1884 widened the franchise, so that by Wilde's day about 60 percent of adult males had the vote. But voting rights were still restricted to men paying an annual rental of £10 or holding land valued at £10. It was not till 1918 that all men were granted the right to vote in England, regardless of property qualifications, and not till 1928 that all women were granted this right.

overwork in order to secure property, and really, considering the enormous advantages that property brings, one is hardly surprised. One's regret is that society should be constructed on such a basis that man has been forced into a groove in which he cannot freely develop what is wonderful, and fascinating, and delightful in him—in which, in fact, he misses the true pleasure and joy of living. He is also, under existing conditions, very insecure. An enormously wealthy merchant may be—often is—at every moment of his life at the mercy of things that are not under his control. If the wind blows an extra point or so, or the weather suddenly changes, or some trivial thing happens, his ship may go down, his speculations may go wrong, and he finds himself a poor man, with his social position quite gone. Now, nothing should be able to harm a man except himself. Nothing should be able to rob a man at all. What a man really has, is what is in him. What is outside of him should be a matter of no importance.

With the abolition of private property, then, we shall have true, beautiful, healthy Individualism. Nobody will waste his life in accumulating things, and the symbols for things. One will live. To live is the rarest thing in the world. Most people exist, that is all.

It is a question whether we have ever seen the full expression of a personality, except on the imaginative plane of art. In action, we never have. Caesar, says Mommsen, was the complete and perfect man.[15] But how tragically insecure was Caesar! Wherever there is a

---

15. In his massive *History of Rome*, the German historian Theodor Mommsen had praised Julius Caesar as "filled with republican ideas and at the same time born to be a king. . . . The entire and perfect man" (4: 457). Wilde admired Mommsen's history greatly, drawing upon it for his undergraduate thesis, and copying passages into his commonplace book. For Wilde's inclusion of *The History of Rome* in a short list of "books to read," see "To Read, or Not to Read," below.

man who exercises authority, there is a man who resists authority. Caesar was very perfect, but his perfection travelled by too dangerous a road. Marcus Aurelius was the perfect man, says Renan.[16] Yes; the great emperor was a perfect man. But how intolerable were the endless claims upon him! He staggered under the burden of the empire. He was conscious how inadequate one man was to bear the weight of that Titan and too vast orb.[17] What I mean by a perfect man is one who develops under perfect conditions; one who is not wounded, or worried or maimed, or in danger. *Most personalities have been obliged to be rebels. Half their strength has been wasted in friction.* Byron's personality, for instance, was terribly wasted in its battle with the stupidity, and hypocrisy, and Philistinism of the English.[18] Such battles do not always intensify strength:

16. In *Marc-Aurèle et le fin de la monde antique* (Marcus Aurelius and the End of The Antique World), the seventh volume of his monumental *Histoire des Origines du Christianisme* (History of the Origins of Christianity), the French historian Ernest Renan (see p. 115, n.4 above) refers to Marcus Aurelius (r. 161–180 CE), the most benign of Roman emperors, as "le plus pieux des homes, non parce qu'il était païen, mais parce qu'il était un home accompli" (the most pious of men, not because he was pagan, but because he was a perfect man).

17. Titan, named for the legendary race of powerful deities who governed ancient Greece, is the largest moon orbiting Saturn. Wilde is likening Julius Caesar to Atlas, a Titan deity for whom another of Saturn's moons is named, who bore the spheres of the heavens on his back.

18. *Philistinism* means the embrace of unenlightened or uneducated values. See also p. 43, n.2 above. Lord Byron (1788–1824) left England permanently following his scandalous separation from his wife in 1816, and it is certainly the case that Byron's hostility to English prudery and conservatism—vividly on display in *English Bards and Scotch Reviewers* (1809)—colors much of his writing. Nevertheless, it remains debatable

they often exaggerate weakness. Byron was never able to give us what he might have given us. Shelley escaped better. Like Byron, he got out of England as soon as possible. But he was not so well known. If the English had had any idea of what a great poet he really was, they would have fallen on him with tooth and nail, and made his life as unbearable to him as they possibly could. But he was not a remarkable figure in society, and consequently he escaped, to a certain degree. Still, even in Shelley the note of rebellion is sometimes too strong. The note of the perfect personality is not rebellion, but peace.

It will be a marvellous thing—the true personality of man—when we see it. It will grow naturally and simply, flowerlike, or as a tree grows. It will not be at discord. It will never argue or dispute. It will not prove things. It will know everything. And yet it will not busy itself about knowledge. It will have wisdom. Its value will not be measured by material things. It will have nothing. And yet it will have everything, and whatever one takes from it, it will still have, so rich will it be. It will not be always meddling with others, or asking them to be like itself. It will love them because they will be different. And yet while it will not meddle with others, it will help all, as a beautiful thing helps us, by being what it is. The personality of man will be very wonderful. It will be as wonderful as the personality of a child.

In its development it will be assisted by Christianity, if men desire that; but if men do not desire that, it will develop none the

---

whether Byron's personality was "wasted by" or realized through his hostility to England. The works he wrote and published during his self-imposed exile from England—not least, *Don Juan, Manfred, Cain, A Vision of Judgment,* and the final two cantos of *Childe Harold's Pilgrimage*—are among his finest.

less surely. For it will not worry itself about the past, nor care whether things happened or did not happen. Nor will it admit any laws but its own laws; nor any authority but its own authority. Yet it will love those who sought to intensify it, and speak often of them. And of these Christ was one.

"Know thyself" was written over the portal of the antique world.[19] Over the portal of the new world, "Be thyself" shall be written. And the message of Christ to man was simply "Be thyself." That is the secret of Christ.

When Jesus talks about the poor he simply means personalities, just as when he talks about the rich he simply means people who have not developed their personalities. Jesus moved in a community that allowed the accumulation of private property just as ours does, and the gospel that he preached was not that in such a community it is an advantage for a man to live on scanty, unwholesome food, to wear ragged, unwholesome clothes, to sleep in horrid, unwholesome dwellings, and a disadvantage for a man to live under healthy, pleasant, and decent conditions. Such a view would have been wrong there and then, and would, of course, be still more wrong now and in England; for as man moves northwards the material necessities of life become of more vital importance, and our society is infinitely more complex, and displays far greater extremes of luxury and pauperism than any society of the antique world. What Jesus meant, was this. He said to man, "You have a wonderful personality. Develop it. Be yourself. Don't imagine that your perfection lies in accumulating or possessing external things. Your affection is inside of you. If only you could realise that, you

19. "Know thyself" was written over the entrance to the temple of Apollo at Delphi, on the slopes of Mount Parnassus, where the Delphic oracle, the most important of ancient Greek oracles, resided.

would not want to be rich. Ordinary riches can be stolen from a man. Real riches cannot. In the treasury-house of your soul, there are infinitely precious things, that may not be taken from you. And so, try to so shape your life that external things will not harm you. And try also to get rid of personal property. It involves sordid pre-occupation, endless industry, continual wrong. Personal property hinders Individualism at every step." It is to be noted that Jesus never says that impoverished people are necessarily good, or wealthy people necessarily bad. That would not have been true. Wealthy people are, as a class, better than impoverished people, more moral, more intellectual, more well-behaved. *There is only one class in the community that thinks more about money than the rich, and that is the poor.* The poor can think of nothing else. That is the misery of being poor. What Jesus does say is that man reaches his perfection, not through what he has, not even through what he does, but entirely through what he is. And so the wealthy young man who comes to Jesus is represented as a thoroughly good citizen, who has broken none of the laws of his state, none of the command-ments of his religion.[20] He is quite respectable, in the ordinary sense of that extraordinary word. Jesus says to him, "You should give up private property. It hinders you from realising your per-fection. It is a drag upon you. It is a burden. Your personality does not need it. It is within you, and not outside of you, that you will find what you really are, and what you really want." To his own

20. In Matthew 19:16–23, a wealthy young man of unassailable moral character comes to Jesus asking, "what good thing must I do to get eternal life?" Jesus replies "If you want to be perfect, go, sell your possessions and give to the poor, and you will have treasure in heaven." Upon seeing the young man's reluctance to relinquish his earthly wealth, Jesus re-marks to his disciples "it is easier for a camel to go through the eye of a needle than for a rich man to enter the kingdom of God."

friends he says the same thing.[21] He tells them to be themselves, and not to be always worrying about other things. What do other things matter? Man is complete in himself. When they go into the world, the world will disagree with them. That is inevitable. The world hates Individualism. But that is not to trouble them. They are to be calm and self-centred. If a man takes their cloak, they are to give him their coat, just to show that material things are of no importance.[22] If people abuse them, they are not to answer back. What does it signify? The things people say of a man do not alter a man. He is what he is. Public opinion is of no value whatsoever.[23] Even if people employ actual violence, they are not to be violent

21. As Guy has observed, Wilde is probably thinking of Christ's Sermon on the Mount: "Do not store up for yourselves treasures on earth . . . do not worry about your life, what you will eat or drink; or about your body, what you will wear. Is not life more important than food, and the body more important than clothes? Look at the birds of the air; they do not sow or reap or store away in barns . . . Who of you by worrying can add a single hour to his life? And why do you worry about clothes? See how the lilies of the field grow. They do not labor or spin" (Matthew 6:19–28).

22. "If any man will sue thee at the law, and take away thy coat, let him have thy cloke also" (Matthew 5:40).

23. Here and elsewhere, Wilde's essay shows the influence of Ralph Waldo Emerson, who had argued in "Self-Reliance" as follows: "Whoso would be a man must be a nonconformist. He who would gather immortal palms must not be hindered by the name of goodness, but must explore if it be goodness. Nothing is at last sacred but the integrity of your own mind. Absolve you to yourself, and you shall have the suffrage of the world. . . . No law can be sacred to me but that of my nature. Good and bad are but names very readily transferable to that or this; the only right is what is after my constitution, the only wrong what is against it. A man is to carry himself in the presence of all opposition, as if every thing were titular and ephemeral but he."

in turn. That would be to fall to the same low level. After all, even in prison, a man can be quite free. His soul can be free. His personality can be untroubled. He can be at peace. And, above all things, they are not to interfere with other people or judge them in any way. Personality is a very mysterious thing. A man cannot always be estimated by what he does. He may keep the law, and yet be worthless. He may break the law, and yet be fine. He may be bad, without ever doing anything bad. He may commit a sin against society, and yet realise through that sin his true perfection.

There was a woman who was taken in adultery.[24] We are not told the history of her love, but that love must have been very great; for Jesus said that her sins were forgiven her, not because she

24. Wilde is conflating different biblical stories. In John 8:3–7, the Pharisees and Sadducees bring to Jesus a woman caught in the act of adultery, looking for Jesus's agreement to stone her, as prescribed by Old Testament law. Jesus replies "Let him who is without sin among you be the first to throw a stone at her." In Luke 7:36–47, when dining at the house of a Pharisee named Simon the Leper, Jesus's feet are washed with tears, kissed, and anointed with costly ointment by a woman who has lived a sinful life. When Simon recoils at this act, Jesus tells him "Do you see this woman? I came into your house. You did not give me any water for my feet, but she wet my feet with her tears and wiped them with her hair. . . . You did not put oil on my head, but she has poured perfume on my feet. Therefore, I tell you, her many sins have been forgiven—for she loved much." In Mark and Matthew, it is Christ's head, not his feet, that are anointed in this way, and in Matthew 26:8–9, it is his disciples who object, not Simon the Leper, on the grounds of waste and expense, not the character of the woman. The remark with which Wilde concludes this paragraph, that "the world worships the woman, even now, as a saint," indicates that he conflates the sinful women in these different stories with Mary Magdalene, the most important of his female disciples, whom Christ healed of "evil spirits" (Luke 8:2) and who is now venerated as saint.

repented, but because her love was so intense and wonderful. Later on, a short time before his death, as he sat at a feast, the woman came in and poured costly perfumes on his hair. His friends tried to interfere with her, and said that it was an extravagance, and that the money that the perfume cost should have been expended on charitable relief of people in want, or something of that kind. Jesus did not accept that view. He pointed out that the material needs of Man were great and very permanent, but that the spiritual needs of Man were greater still, and that in one divine moment, and by selecting its own mode of expression, a personality might make itself perfect. The world worships the woman, even now, as a saint.

Yes; there are suggestive things in Individualism. Socialism annihilates family life, for instance. With the abolition of private property, marriage in its present form must disappear. This is part of the programme. Individualism accepts this and makes it fine. It converts the abolition of legal restraint into a form of freedom that will help the full development of personality, and make the love of man and woman more wonderful, more beautiful, and more ennobling. Jesus knew this. He rejected the claims of family life, although they existed in his day and community in a very marked form. "Who is my mother? Who are my brothers?" he said, when he was told that they wished to speak to him.[25] When one of his followers asked leave to go and bury his father, "Let the dead bury the dead," was his terrible answer.[26] He would allow no claim whatsoever to be made on personality.

And so he who would lead a Christ-like life is he who is perfectly and absolutely himself. He may be a great poet, or a great man of science; or a young student at a University, or one who

25. Mark 3:31–35 and Matthew 12:46–50.
26. Matthew 8:21–22 and Luke 9:59–60

watches sheep upon a moor; or a maker of dramas, like Shake-speare, or a thinker about God, like Spinoza;[27] or a child who plays in a garden, or a fisherman who throws his net into the sea.[28] It does not matter what he is, as long as he realises the perfection of the soul that is within him. All imitation in morals and in life is wrong. Through the streets of Jerusalem at the present day crawls one who is mad and carries a wooden cross on his shoulders. He is a symbol of the lives that are marred by imitation. Father Damien was Christ-like when he went out to live with the lepers, because in such service he realised fully what was best in him.[29] But he was not more Christ-like than Wagner, when he realised his soul in music; or than Shelley, when he realised his soul in song.[30] There is no one type for man. There are as many perfections as there are imperfect men. And while to the claims of charity a man may yield and yet be free, to the claims of conformity no man may yield and remain free at all.

27. The Dutch-Jewish rationalist theologian and philosopher Baruch de Spinoza (1632–1677).

28. Wilde here invokes characters who feature prominently in his stories "The Selfish Giant" and "The Fisherman and His Soul."

29. Canonized by Pope Benedict XVI in 2009, Father Damien (1840–1889), born Jozef De Veuster, was a Belgian Roman Catholic priest who ministered for sixteen years to the leper colony at Kalaupapa, on the island of Moloka'i in the Kingdom of Hawai'i, before dying of the leprosy he had contracted at the colony. Called "the Apostle of the Lepers" by the *Catholic Encyclopedia*, Damien is widely considered a "martyr of charity," the spiritual patron of lepers and outcasts, and the patron saint of Hawai'i.

30. Wilhelm Richard Wagner (1813–1883), German composer and librettist; Percy Bysshe Shelley (1792–1822), one of the preeminent poets of the Romantic Era.

Individualism, then, is what through Socialism we are to attain to. As a natural result the State must give up all idea of government. It must give it up because, as a wise man once said many centuries before Christ, there is such a thing as leaving mankind alone; there is no such thing as governing mankind.[31] *All modes of government are failures.*[32] Despotism is unjust to everybody, including the despot, who was probably made for better things. Oligarchies are unjust to the many, and ochlocracies are unjust to the few.[33] High hopes were once formed of democracy; but democracy means simply the bludgeoning of the people by the people

31. Wilde is quoting Chuang Tzŭ. See p. 79, n.11 above.

32. In his rejection of governmental authority, Wilde reflects the influence of the anarchist philosopher Peter Kropotkin, whose 1889 lectures on "Social Evolution" he helped to promote, and whom Wilde was later to call "a man with the soul of that beautiful white Christ that seems coming out of Russia." In "The Scientific Bases of Anarchy"—one of fourteen articles that Kropotkin published in *The Nineteenth Century* in the mid-1880s—Kropotkin argued that "the ideal of the political organisation of society is a condition of things where the functions of government are reduced to a minimum, and the individual recovers his full liberty of initiative and action for satisfying, by means of free groups and federations—freely constituted—all the infinitely varied needs of the human being." Similarly, in "The Coming Anarchy" Kropotkin argued: "if we carefully watch the present development of civilised nations, we cannot fail to discover in it a marked and ever-growing movement towards limiting more and more the sphere of action of government, so as to leave more and more liberty to the initiative of the individual. After having tried all kinds of government, . . . humanity is trying now to free itself from the bonds of any government whatever."

33. An oligarchy is a "form of government in which the exercise of power is restricted to a few people or families (in later use, frequently a wealthy elite)" (OED). Ochlocracy is "government by the populace; mob rule; a state, etc., ruled or dominated by the populace" (OED).

for the people.[34] It has been found out. I must say that it was high time, for all authority is quite degrading. It degrades those who exercise it, and degrades those over whom it is exercised. When it is violently, grossly, and cruelly used, it produces a good effect, by creating, or at any rate bringing out, the spirit of revolt and individualism that is to kill it. When it is used with a certain amount of kindness, and accompanied by prizes and rewards, it is dreadfully demoralising. People, in that case, are less conscious of the horrible pressure that is being put on them, and so go through their lives in a sort of coarse comfort, like petted animals, without ever realising that they are probably thinking other people's thoughts, living by other people's standards, wearing practically what one may call other people's second-hand clothes, and never being themselves for a single moment. "He who would be free," says a fine thinker, "must not conform."[35] And authority, by bribing people to conform, produces a very gross kind of over-fed barbarism amongst us.

With authority, punishment will pass away. This will be a great gain—a gain, in fact, of incalculable value. As one reads history, not in the expurgated editions written for school-boys and passmen,[36] but in the original authorities of each time, one is absolutely

34. A parody of Lincoln's famous phrase, from the Gettysburg Address, "government of the people, by the people, and for the people." Wilde's "bludgeoning" comment was timely given the events of Bloody Sunday (November 13, 1887), when a peaceful demonstration in London's Trafalgar Square was violently suppressed by the combined forces of the police and the army. See William Morris, "London in a State of Siege," *The Commonweal* (November 19, 1887).

35. Wilde is paraphrasing Emerson. See n.23 above.

36. At the all-male Oxford and Cambridge universities, a *passman* was a student who graduated with a minimum "pass," without taking an honours degree.

sickened, not by the crimes that the wicked have committed, but by the punishments that the good have inflicted; *and a community is infinitely more brutalised by the habitual employment of punishment, than it is by the occurrence of crime.*[37] It obviously follows that the more punishment is inflicted the more crime is produced, and most modern legislation has clearly recognised this, and has made it its task to diminish punishment as far as it thinks it can. Wherever it has really diminished it, the results have always been extremely good. The less punishment, the less crime. When there is no punishment at all, crime will either cease to exist, or, if it occurs, will be treated by physicians as a very distressing form of dementia, to be cured by care and kindness.[38] For what are called criminals nowadays are not criminals at all. Starvation, and not sin, is the parent of modern crime. That indeed is the reason why our criminals are, as a class, so absolutely uninteresting from any psychological point of view. They are not marvellous Macbeths and

37. A prophetic sentence: Wilde's late prison writings eloquently testify to the brutalism of the punitive prison regime of "hard labor, hard board, and hard fare" under which he would himself suffer in the years 1895–1897. As a result of his imprisonment, Wilde would reach a very different conclusion about the extent to which modern legislation "has made it its task to diminish punishment." See Wilde, *Annotated Prison Writings*, especially *The Ballad of Reading Gaol* and "Letter to the *Daily Chronicle*, 23 March 1898" (317–383).

38. For Wilde's argument that the criminal offense ("gross indecency") for which he was himself imprisoned in May 1895 was a form of sexual madness and a "disease to be cured by a physician, rather than [a crime] to be punished by a judge," see his "Clemency Petition to the Home Secretary, 2 July 1896" in Wilde, *Annotated Prison Writings*, 41.

terrible Vautrins.[39] They are merely what ordinary, respectable, commonplace people would be if they had not got enough to eat. When private property is abolished there will be no necessity for crime, no demand for it; it will cease to exist. Of course, all crimes are not crimes against property, though such are the crimes that the English law, valuing what a man has more than what a man is, punishes with the harshest and most horrible severity, if we except the crime of murder, and regard death as worse than penal servitude, a point on which our criminals, I believe, disagree. But though a crime may not be against property, it may spring from the misery and rage and depression produced by our wrong system of property-holding, and so, when that system is abolished, will disappear.[40] When each member of the community has sufficient for his wants, and is not interfered with by his neighbour, it will not be an object of any interest to him to interfere with anyone else. Jealousy, which is an extraordinary source of crime in modern life, is an emotion closely bound up with our conceptions of property, and under Socialism and Individualism will die out. It is remarkable that in communistic tribes jealousy is entirely unknown.

39. Vautrin is the master-criminal who dominates Balzac's *La Comédie Humaine* (The Human Comedy), the epic series of novels in which he dramatized the corruptions and mannerisms of Parisian life during the Second Empire.

40. An idea indebted to William Morris's Utopian novel *News From Nowhere,* which Wilde would have read upon its serialization in *The Commonweal* in 1890. In Morris's Utopian future society, "private property being abolished, all the laws and all the legal 'crimes' which it had manufactured of course came to an end" (*News From Nowhere and Other Writings*, ed. Clive Wilmer [Harmondsworth: Penguin Books, 1993], 112).

Now as the State is not to govern, it may be asked what the State is to do. The State is to be a voluntary association that will organize labour, and be the manufacturer and distributor of necessary commodities. *The State is to make what is useful. The individual is to make what is beautiful.*[41] And as I have mentioned the word labour, I cannot help saying that a great deal of nonsense is being written and talked nowadays about the dignity of manual labour. There is nothing necessarily dignified about manual labour at all, and most of it is absolutely degrading. It is mentally and morally injurious to man to do anything in which he does not find pleasure, and many forms of labour are quite pleasureless activities, and should be regarded as such. To sweep a slushy crossing for eight hours on a day when the east wind is blowing is a disgusting occupation.[42] To sweep it with mental, moral, or physical dignity seems to me to be impossible. To sweep it with joy would be appalling. Man is made for something better than disturbing dirt. All work of that kind should be done by a machine.

And I have no doubt that it will be so. Up to the present, man has been to a certain extent, the slave of machinery, and there is something tragic in the fact that as soon as man had invented a machine to do his work he began to starve. This, however, is, of

41. In 1882, when lecturing on "The House Beautiful," Wilde had enjoined Americans to "Have nothing in your house that is not useful or beautiful"—a verbatim echo of William Morris's mantra "Have nothing in your houses that you do not know to be useful or . . . beautiful." By 1890, however, Wilde had diverged considerably from Morris where it came to the need to reconcile utility with beauty. See p. 357, n.11 below.

42. Because of the ubiquity of horse-drawn transport, the streets of nineteenth-century cities were covered in horse manure. Crossing sweepers were informally employed at street crossings to sweep the street so that pedestrians could cross without becoming soiled.

course, the result of our property system and our system of competition. One man owns a machine which does the work of five hundred men. Five hundred men are, in consequence, thrown out of employment, and, having no work to do, become hungry and take to thieving. The one man secures the produce of the machine and keeps it, and has five hundred times as much as he should have, and probably, which is of much more importance, a great deal more than he really wants. Were that machine the property of all, every one would benefit by it. It would be an immense advantage to the community. All unintellectual labour, all monotonous, dull labour, all labour that deals with dreadful things, and involves unpleasant conditions, must be done by machinery. Machinery must work for us in coal mines, and do all sanitary services, and be the stoker of steamers, and clean the streets, and run messages on wet days, and do anything that is tedious or distressing.[43] *At present*

43. Wilde's discussion of machinery as a substitute for "tedious or depressing" manual labor was topical. In his bestselling Utopian novel *Looking Backward, 2000–1887* (1888), the American author and socialist Edward Bellamy suggested that the labor problem could be solved if society "recognized and co-operated" with "industrial evolution." But in a forceful critique of Bellamy's novel, William Morris objected to Bellamy's optimism about "making labour tolerable . . . by means of fresh and ever fresh developments in machinery" (Morris, review of *Looking Backward*, in *News From Nowhere and Other Writings*, 357). While recognizing that Bellamy's optimism would be shared by "many Socialists with whom I might otherwise agree," Morris argued that "the multiplication of machinery will just—multiply machinery," while in his own Utopian novel *News From Nowhere* Morris remarks that labor-saving machines are "made to 'save labour' . . . on one piece of work in order that it might be expended . . . on another" and that "all . . . devices for cheapening labour simply result in increasing the burden of labour" (*News From Nowhere and Other Writings*, 139). Rather than looking for a "reduction of labour to a

machinery competes against man. Under proper conditions machinery will serve man. There is no doubt at all that this is the future of machinery, and just as trees grow while the country gentleman is asleep, so while Humanity will be amusing itself, or enjoying cultivated leisure—which, and not labour, is the aim of man—or making beautiful things, or reading beautiful things, or simply contemplating the world with admiration and delight, machinery will be doing all the necessary and unpleasant work. The fact is, that civilisation requires slaves. The Greeks were quite right there. Unless there are slaves to do the ugly, horrible, uninteresting work, culture and contemplation become almost impossible. Human slavery is wrong, insecure, and demoralising. On mechanical slavery, on the slavery of the machine, the future of the world depends. And when scientific men are no longer called upon to go down to a depressing East End and distribute bad cocoa and worse blankets to starving people, they will have delightful leisure in which to devise wonderful and marvellous things for their own joy and the joy of everyone else. There will be great storages of force for every city, and for every house if required, and this force man will convert into heat, light, or motion, according to his needs. Is this Utopian? A map of the world that does not include Utopia is not worth even glancing at, for it leaves out the one country at which Humanity is always landing. And when Humanity lands there, it looks out, and, seeing a better country, sets sail. Progress is the realisation of Utopias.

Now, I have said that the community by means of organization of machinery will supply the useful things, and that the beautiful things will be made by the individual. This is not merely necessary, but it is the only possible way by which we can get either the

---

minimum," Morris wrote in response to Bellamy, the ideal should be "the reduction of *pain in labour* to a minimum" (357).

one or the other. An individual who has to make things for the use of others, and with reference to their wants and their wishes, does not work with interest, and consequently cannot put into his work what is best in him. Upon the other hand, whenever a community or a powerful section of a community, or a government of any kind, attempts to dictate to the artist what he is to do, Art either entirely vanishes, or becomes stereotyped, or degenerates into a low and ignoble form of craft. *A work of art is the unique result of a unique temperament. Its beauty comes from the fact that the author is what he is. It has nothing to do with the fact that other people want what they want.* Indeed, the moment that an artist takes notice of what other people want, and tries to supply the demand, he ceases to be an artist, and becomes a dull or an amusing craftsman, an honest or a dishonest tradesman. He has no further claim to be considered as an artist.[44] *Art is the most intense mode of Individualism*

44. Wilde's comments about the artist's need to resist accommodating their art to "what other people want" were born out of experience. In the spring of 1890, his novel *The Picture of Dorian Gray* had been censored by its editor without Wilde's knowledge, although this did not prevent a critical firestorm from erupting when the novel was finally published in *Lippincott's Monthly Magazine* in June 1890. To the editor of the *St. James's Gazette,* for instance, Wilde remarked: "that the editor of a paper like yours should appear to countenance the monstrous theory that the Government of a country should exercise a censorship over imaginative literature . . . is a theory against which I, and all men of letters of my acquaintance, protest most strongly" (*The Complete Letters of Oscar Wilde,* ed. Merlin Holland and Rupert Hart-Davis [New York: Henry Holt, 2000], 431). As Wilde prepared the novel for book publication the following year, he came under pressure to mute further the novel's representations of male same-sex desire. See textual introduction to *The Picture of Dorian Gray: An Annotated, Uncensored Edition,* ed. Nicholas Frankel (Cambridge, MA: The Belknap Press of Harvard Univ. Press, 2011).

that the world has known. I am inclined to say that it is the only real mode of Individualism that the world has known. Crime, which, under certain conditions, may seem to have created Individualism, must take cognisance of other people and interfere with them. It belongs to the sphere of action. But alone, without any reference to his neighbours, without any interference, the artist can fashion a beautiful thing; and if he does not do it solely for his own pleasure, he is not an artist at all.[45]

And it is to be noted that it is the fact that Art is this intense form of Individualism that makes the public try to exercise over it in an authority that is as immoral as it is ridiculous, and as corrupting as it is contemptible. It is not quite their fault. The public has always, and in every age, been badly brought up. They are continually asking Art to be popular, to please their want of taste, to flatter their absurd vanity, to tell them what they have been told before, to show them what they ought to be tired of seeing, to amuse them when they feel heavy after eating too much, and to distract their thoughts when they are wearied of their own stupidity. *Now Art should never try to be popular. The public should try to make itself artistic.* There is a very wide difference. If a man of science were told that the results of his experiments, and the conclusions that he arrived at, should be of such a character that they would not upset the received popular notions on the subject, or disturb popular prejudice, or hurt the sensibilities of people who knew nothing about science; if a philosopher were told that he had a perfect right to speculate in the highest spheres of thought, provided that he arrived at the same conclusions as were held by those who had never thought in any sphere at all— well, nowadays the man of science and the philosopher would be

45. An anticipation of the first and final aphorisms in the Preface to *The Picture of Dorian Gray.* See p. 353 and p. 357 below.

considerably amused. Yet it is really a very few years since both philosophy and science were subjected to brutal popular control, to authority in fact—the authority of either the general ignorance of the community, or the terror and greed for power of an ecclesiastical or governmental class. Of course, we have to a very great extent got rid of any attempt on the part of the community, or the Church, or the Government, to interfere with the individualism of speculative thought, but the attempt to interfere with the individualism of imaginative art still lingers. In fact, it does more than linger; it is aggressive, offensive, and brutalizing.

In England, *the arts that have escaped best are the arts in which the public take no interest.* Poetry is an instance of what I mean. We have been able to have fine poetry in England because the public do not read it, and consequently do not influence it. The public like to insult poets because they are individual, but once they have insulted them, they leave them alone. In the case of the novel and the drama, arts in which the public do take an interest, the result of the exercise of popular authority has been absolutely ridiculous.[46] No country produces such badly-written fiction, such tedious, common work in the novel form, such silly, vulgar plays as England. It must necessarily be so. The popular standard is of such a character that no artist can get to it. It is at once too easy and too difficult to be a popular novelist. It is too easy, because the

---

46. One such "ridiculous ... result of the exercise of popular authority" was the outcry over Wilde's own *The Picture of Dorian Gray*, in which Wilde faced public calls for prosecution. Other recent examples included the successful criminal prosecution and imprisonment for obscenity of Henry Vizetelly, the English publisher of Emile Zola, in 1889; and the censorship of Thomas Hardy's novel *Tess of the D'Urbervilles* by magazine editors, against which Hardy loudly protested in his important article "Candour in English Fiction" (1890).

requirements of the public as far as plot, style, psychology, treatment of life, and treatment of literature are concerned are within the reach of the very meanest capacity and the most uncultivated mind. It is too difficult, because to meet such requirements the artist would have to do violence to his temperament, would have to write not for the artistic joy of writing, but for the amusement of half-educated people, and so would have to suppress his individualism, forget his culture, annihilate his style, and surrender everything that is valuable in him. In the case of the drama, things are a little better: the theatre-going public like the obvious, it is true, but they do not like the tedious; and burlesque and farcical comedy, the two most popular forms, are distinct forms of art. Delightful work may be produced under burlesque and farcical conditions, and in work of this kind the artist in England is allowed very great freedom.[47] It is when one comes to the higher forms of the drama that the result of popular control is seen.[48] The one thing that the public dislike is novelty. Any attempt to extend the subject-matter of art is extremely distasteful to the public; and yet the vitality and progress of art depend in a large measure on the continual extension of subject-matter. The public dislike novelty because they are afraid of it. It represents to them a mode of Individualism, an assertion on the part of the artist that he selects his own subject, and treats it as he chooses. The public are quite right in their attitude. Art is

47. An insight that does much to explain the genius of Wilde's own *The Importance of Being Earnest,* first performed in 1895 under the subtitle "A Trivial Comedy for Serious People."

48. Another prophetic sentence: in 1892 Wilde's symbolist drama *Salomé* would be banned by the censor on the grounds that it contravened an obscure statute prohibiting the staged representation of biblical subjects, leading Wilde to protest once again that he could not tolerate "a country that shows such narrowness in its artistic judgment."

Individualism, and Individualism is a disturbing and disintegrating force. Therein lies its immense value. For what it seeks to disturb is monotony of type, slavery of custom, tyranny of habit, and the reduction of man to the level of a machine. In Art, the public accept what has been, because they cannot alter it, not because they appreciate it. They swallow their classics whole, and never taste them. They endure them as the inevitable, and as they cannot mar them, they mouth about them. Strangely enough, or not strangely, according to one's own views, this acceptance of the classics does a great deal of harm. The uncritical admiration of the Bible and Shakespeare in England is an instance of what I mean. With regard to the Bible, considerations of ecclesiastical authority enter into the matter, so that I need not dwell upon the point.

But in the case of Shakespeare it is quite obvious that the public really see neither the beauties nor the defects of his plays. If they saw the beauties, they would not object to the development of the drama; and if they saw the defects, they would not object to the development of the drama either. *The fact is, the public make use of the classics of a country as a means of checking the progress of Art.* They degrade the classics into authorities. They use them as bludgeons for preventing the free expression of Beauty in new forms. They are always asking a writer why he does not write like somebody else, or a painter why he does not paint like somebody else, quite oblivious of the fact that if either of them did anything of the kind he would cease to be an artist. A fresh mode of Beauty is absolutely distasteful to them, and whenever it appears they get so angry and bewildered that they always use two stupid expressions—one is that the work of art is grossly unintelligible; the other, that the work of art is grossly immoral. What they mean by these words seems to me to be this. When they say a work is grossly unintelligible, they mean that the artist has said or made a beautiful thing that is new;

when they describe a work as grossly immoral, they mean that the artist has said or made a beautiful thing that is true. The former expression has reference to style; the latter to subject matter. But they probably use the words very vaguely, as an ordinary mob will use ready-made paving-stones. *There is not a single real poet or prose-writer of this century, for instance, on whom the British public have not solemnly conferred diplomas of immorality,* and these diplomas practically take the place, with us, of what in France, is the formal recognition of an Academy of Letters, and fortunately make the establishment of such an institution quite unnecessary in England. Of course, the public are very reckless in their use of the word. That they should have called Wordsworth an immoral poet, was only to be expected. Wordsworth was a poet. But that they should have called Charles Kingsley an immoral novelist is extraordinary.[49] Kingsley's prose was not of a very fine quality. Still, there is the word, and they use it as best they can. An artist is, of course, not disturbed by it. The true artist is a man who believes absolutely in himself, because he is absolutely himself.[50] But I can fancy that if an artist produced a work of art in England that immediately on its appearance was recognised by the public, through their medium, which is the public press, as a work that was quite intelligible and highly moral, he would begin to seriously question whether in its creation he had really been himself at all, and consequently whether the work was not quite unworthy of him, and either of a thoroughly second-rate order, or of no artistic value whatsoever.

49. In 1863, Edward Pusey, Regius Professor of Hebrew at Oxford, objected to the novelist Charles Kingsley being awarded an honorary degree on the grounds that his 1853 novel *Hypatia* was an "immoral book."'

50. See, too, Wilde's aphorism "When critics disagree the artist is in accord with himself," p. 356 below

Perhaps, however, I have wronged the public in limiting them to such words as "immoral," "unintelligible," "exotic," and "unhealthy."[51] There is one other word that they use. That word is "morbid."[52] They do not use it often. The meaning of the word is so simple that they are afraid of using it. Still, they use it sometimes,

51. In an undated letter probably written in January 1891 to an unidentified recipient at the *Fortnightly Review*, Wilde complained that "there is an error of setting in my article, which pray correct at once, if possible. The passage (p. 307) on morbidity, beginning 'Perhaps however' and ending with 'King Lear,' must be transferred to p. 308 and put after 'healthy work of art'.... [I]t is out of place at present" (*Complete Letters*, 462). The correction was not carried out in either edition published in Wilde's lifetime, and the paragraph order has similarly been left uncorrected here. For the corrected ordering of paragraphs, see Wilde, *Criticism*, lxxii–lxxv. The later passage to which Wilde refers, containing the phrase "healthy work of art," has not been included in the present excerpt.

52. The phenomenon Wilde describes here reached its apogee in Max Nordau's hysterical (though influential) screed *Degeneration* (orig. publ. in German in 1892; translated into English in 1895), in which Nordau used the term *morbid* over forty times to denigrate the latest trends in Western art and culture, including Henrik Ibsen's plays, Wagner's operas, the fiction of Zola, Maupassant and Tolstoy, the paintings of the Pre-Raphaelites, the poetry of Baudelaire and Whitman, and of course the writings of Oscar Wilde. For Nordau, "the originators of all the *fin-de-siècle* movements in art and literature" were subject to a "morbid mobility of ... mind" and an "excessive excitability of ... imagination [that] conveys to ... consciousness all sorts of queer and senseless ideas" (*Degeneration*, translator unknown [New York; Appleton, 1895], 17–25). Sadly, in one of several unsuccessful appeals for clemency while incarcerated for "gross indecency" from 1895–1897, Wilde would cite Nordau approvingly and confess that he was indeed "the sure prey of morbid passions, and obscene fancies, and thoughts that defile," while arguing that the offences for which he was imprisoned were "diseases to be cured

and, now and then, one comes across it in popular newspapers. It is, of course, a ridiculous word to apply to a work of art. For what is morbidity but a mood of emotion or a mode of thought that one cannot express? The public are all morbid, because the public can never find expression for anything. *The artist is never morbid. He expresses everything.* He stands outside his subject, and through its medium produces incomparable and artistic effects. To call an artist morbid because he deals with morbidity as his subject matter is as silly as if one called Shakespeare mad because he wrote "King Lear."

On the whole, an artist in England gains something by being attacked. His individuality is intensified. He becomes more completely himself. Of course, the attacks are very gross, very impertinent, and very contemptible. But then no artist expects grace from the vulgar mind, or style from the suburban intellect. Vulgarity and stupidity are two very vivid facts in modern life. One regrets them, naturally. But there they are. They are subjects for study, like everything else. And it is only fair to state, with regard to modern journalists, that they always apologise to one in private for what they have written against one in public.

. . . . People sometimes inquire what form of government is most suitable for an artist to live under. To this question there is only one answer. *The form of government that is most suitable to the artist is no government at all.* Authority over him and his art is ridiculous. It has been stated that under despotisms artists have produced lovely work. This is not quite so. Artists have visited despots, not as subjects to be tyrannized over, but as wandering wonder-makers, as fascinating vagrant personalities, to be entertained and charmed

by a physician, rather than crimes to be punished by a judge" ("Clemency Petition," in Wilde, *Annotated Prison Writings,* 41–47).

and suffered to be at peace, and allowed to create. There is this to be said in favour of the despot, that he, being an individual, may have culture, while the mob, being a monster, has none. One who is an Emperor and King may stoop down to pick up a brush for a painter,[53] but when the democracy stoops down it is merely to throw mud. And yet the democracy have not so far to stoop as the emperor. In fact, when they want to throw mud they have not to stoop at all. But there is no necessity to separate the monarch from the mob; all authority is equally bad.

There are three kinds of despots. There is the despot who tyrannizes over the body. There is the despot who tyrannizes over the soul. There is the despot who tyrannizes over the soul and body alike. The first is called the Prince. The second is called the Pope. The third is called the People. The Prince may be cultivated. Many Princes have been. Yet in the Prince there is danger. One thinks of Dante at the bitter feast in Verona,[54] of Tasso in Ferrara's madman's cell.[55] It is better for the artist not to live with Princes. The Pope

53. According to Carlo Ridolfi's *Life of Titian*, when Titian was painting his third portrait of the Emperor Charles V, he dropped a brush, where-upon the emperor picked it up saying, "Titian deserves to be served by Caesar." The event was memorialized by the French historical painter Pierre-Nolasque Bergeret in his 1808 painting *L'Empéreur Charles-Quint remassant le panceau de Titien* (The Emperor Charles V Picking Up the Brush of Titian).

54. The mistreatment of the poet Dante Alighieri (1265–1321) at the hands of his patron Can Grande della Scala (1291–1329), ruler of Verona, is the subject of Dante Gabriel Rossetti's poem "Dante At Verona" (published 1870) as well as of Wilde's own 1881 poem "At Verona." In the latter, Dante remarks "O how salt and bitter is the bread / Which falls from this Hound's table."

55. From 1579 to 1586, the Italian poet Torquato Tasso (1544–1595) was imprisoned in the madhouse of St. Anna, on the orders of his patron

may be cultivated. Many Popes have been; the bad Popes have been. The bad Popes loved Beauty, almost as passionately, nay, with as much passion as the good Popes hated Thought. To the wickedness of the Papacy humanity owes much. The goodness of the Papacy owes a terrible debt to humanity. Yet, though the Vatican has kept the rhetoric of its thunders, and lost the rod of its lightning, it is better for the artist not to live with Popes. It was a Pope who said of Cellini to a conclave of Cardinals that common laws and common authority were not made for men such as he; but it was a Pope who thrust Cellini into prison, and kept him there till he sickened with rage, and created unreal visions for himself, and saw the gilded sun enter his room, and grew so enamoured of it that he sought to escape, and crept out from tower to tower, and falling through dizzy air at dawn, maimed himself, and was by a vine-dresser covered with vine leaves, and carried in a cart to one who, loving beautiful things, had care of him.[56] There is danger in Popes. And as for the People, what of them and their authority? Perhaps of them and their authority one has spoken enough. Their

Alfonso II (1533–1597), Duke of Ferrara. Alfonso's "danger" (he is widely reputed to have ordered the murder of his first wife, Lucrezia di Cosimo de Medici) is mythologized in Robert Browning's poem "My Last Duchess."

56. In 1534, the Italian Renaissance sculptor and goldsmith Benvenuto Cellini (1500–1571) committed a murder, only to be pardoned by the newly-elected Pope Pius III with the words "Know . . . that men like Benvenuto, unique in their profession, stand above the law" (*The Autobiography of Benvenuto Cellini* [1558–63], tr. John Addington Symonds [New York: P. F. Collier, 1910], bk. 1, ch. 74, p. 152). Four years later, Pius imprisoned Cellini on an apparently false charge of having embezzled gems belonging to the Pope. Wilde here adapts events described in *The Autobiography of Benvenuto Cellini*, bk 1, chs. 102–128, pp. 212–262. For Wilde's inclusion of Cellini's *Autobiography* among "books to read," see "To Read, or Not to Read," below.

authority is a thing blind, deaf, hideous, grotesque, tragic, amusing, serious, and obscene. It is impossible for the artist to live with the People. All despots bribe. The people bribe and brutalize. Who told them to exercise authority? They were made to live, to listen, and to love. Someone has done them a great wrong. They have marred themselves by imitation of their inferiors. They have taken the sceptre of the Prince. How should they use it? They have taken the triple tiar of the Pope.[57] How should they carry its burden? They are as a clown whose heart is broken. They are as a priest whose soul is not yet born. Let all who love Beauty pity them. Though they themselves love not Beauty, yet let them pity themselves. Who taught them the trick of tyranny?

There are many other things that one might point out. One might point out how the Renaissance was great, because it sought to solve no social problem, and busied itself not about such things, but suffered the individual to develop freely, beautifully, and naturally, and so had great and individual artists, and great and individual men. One might point out how Louis XIV, by creating the modern state, destroyed the individualism of the artist, and made things monstrous in their monotony of repetition, and contemptible in their conformity to rule, and destroyed throughout all France all those fine freedoms of expression that had made tradition new in beauty, and new modes one with antique form. But the past is of no importance. The present is of no importance. It is with the future that we have to deal. For the past is what man should

57. The papal *tiar* or *tiara* was an ornate, jewel-encrusted crown worn by each new pope at his coronation, from the eighth to the mid-twentieth centuries, while the *triple tiar* or "triple crown" refers to the three-tiered version adopted from the fourteenth century onwards. Although no longer worn as part of the pope's regalia, the papal tiara still appears on the coats of arms of the Holy See.

not have been. The present is what man ought not to be. The future is what artists are.

It will, of course, be said that such a scheme as is set forth here is quite unpractical, and goes against human nature. This is perfectly true. It is unpractical, and it goes against human nature. This is why it is worth carrying out, and that is why one proposes it. For what is a practical scheme? *A practical scheme is either a scheme that is already in existence, or a scheme that could be carried out under existing conditions.* But it is exactly the existing conditions that one objects to; and any scheme that could accept these conditions is wrong and foolish. The conditions will be done away with, and human nature will change. The only thing that one really knows about human nature is that it changes. Change is the one quality we can predicate of it. The systems that fail are those that rely on the permanency of human nature, and not on its growth and development. The error of Louis XIV was that he thought human nature would always be the same. The result of his error was the French Revolution. It was an admirable result. All the results of the mistakes of governments are quite admirable.

It is to be noted also that Individualism does not come to man with any sickly cant about duty, which merely means doing what other people want because they want it; or any hideous cant about self-sacrifice, which is merely a survival of savage mutilation. *In fact, it does not come to man with any claims upon him at all. It comes naturally and inevitably out of man.* It is the point to which all development tends. It is the differentiation to which all organisms grow. It is the perfection that is inherent in every mode of life, and towards which every mode of life quickens. And so Individualism exercises no compulsion over man. On the contrary, it says to man that he should suffer no compulsion to be exercised over him. It does not try to force people to be good. It knows that people are good when they are let alone. Man will develop Individualism out of himself. Man is now so developing Individualism. To ask whether Individualism is practical is like asking whether Evolution is practical. *Evolution is the law of life, and there is no evolution except towards Individualism.* Where this tendency is not expressed, it is a case of artificially-arrested growth, or of disease, or of death.

Individualism will also be unselfish and unaffected. It has been pointed out that one of the results of the extraordinary tyranny of authority is that words are absolutely distorted from their proper and simple meaning, and are used to express the obverse of their right signification. What is true about Art is true about Life. A man is called affected, nowadays, if he dresses as he likes to dress. But in doing that he is acting in a perfectly natural manner. Affectation, in such matters, consists in dressing according to the views of one's neighbour, whose views, as they are the views of the majority, will probably be extremely stupid. Or a man is called selfish if he lives in the manner that seems to him most suitable for the full realisation of his own personality; if, in fact, the primary aim of his life is self-development. But this is the way in which everyone should live. *Selfishness is not living as one wishes to live,* it is asking others to live as one wishes to live. And unselfishness is letting other people's lives alone, not interfering with them. Selfishness always aims at creating around it an absolute uniformity of type. Unselfishness recognises infinite variety of type as a delightful thing, accepts it, acquiesces in it, enjoys it. It is not selfish to think for oneself. A man who does not think for himself does not think at all. It is grossly selfish to require of one's neighbour that he should think in the same way, and hold the same opinions. Why should he? If he can think, he will probably think differently. If he cannot think, it is monstrous to require thought of any kind from him. A red rose is not selfish because it wants to be a red rose. It would be horribly selfish if it wanted all the other flowers in the garden to be both red and roses. Under Individualism people will be quite natural and absolutely unselfish, and will know the meanings of the words, and realise them in their free, beautiful lives. Nor will men be egotistic as they are now. For the egotist is he who makes claims upon others, and the Individualist will not desire to do that. It will not give him pleasure. When man has realised Individualism, he will also realise sympathy and exercise it freely and spontaneously. Up to the present man has hardly cultivated sympathy at all. He has merely sympathy with pain, and sympathy with pain is not the highest form of sympathy. *All sympathy is fine, but sympathy with suffering is the least fine mode.* It is tainted with egotism. It is apt to become morbid. There is in it a certain element of terror for our own safety. We become afraid that we ourselves might be as the leper or as the blind, and that no man would have care of us. It is curiously limiting, too. One should sympathise with the entirety of life, not with life's sores and maladies merely, but with life's joy and beauty and energy and health and freedom. The wider sympathy is, of course, the more difficult. It requires more unselfishness. Anybody can sympathise with the sufferings of a friend, but it requires a very fine nature—it requires, in fact, the nature of a true Individualist—to sympathise with a friend's success. In the modern stress of competition and struggle for place, such sympathy is naturally rare, and is also very much stifled by the immoral ideal of uniformity of type and conformity to rule which is so prevalent everywhere, and is perhaps most obnoxious in England.

Sympathy with pain there will, of course, always be. It is one of the first instincts of man. The animals which are individual, the higher animals, that is to say, share it with us. But it must be remembered that while sympathy with joy intensifies the sum of joy in the world, sympathy with pain does not really diminish the amount of pain. It may make man better able to endure evil, but the evil remains. Sympathy with consumption does not cure consumption; that is what Science does. And when Socialism has solved the problem of poverty, and Science solved the problem of disease, the area of the sentimentalists will be lessened, and the sympathy of man will be large, healthy, and spontaneous. Man will have joy in the contemplation of the joyous life of others.

For it is through joy that the Individualism of the future will develop itself. *Christ made no attempt to reconstruct society, and consequently the Individualism that he preached to man could be realised only through pain or in solitude.* The ideals that we owe to Christ are the ideals of the man who abandons society entirely, or of the man who resists society absolutely. But man is naturally social. Even the Thebaid became peopled at last.[58] And though the cenobite realises his personality, it is often an impoverished personality that he so realises. Upon the other hand, the terrible truth that pain is a mode through which man may realise himself exercises a wonderful fascination over the world. Shallow speakers and shallow thinkers in pulpits and on platforms often talk about the world's worship of pleasure, and whine against it. But it is rarely in the world's

58. The Thebaid, which takes its name from its proximity to the ancient Egyptian capital of Thebes, was a desert region in ancient Egypt extending from Abydos, in the north, to Aswan in the south. In the fourth and fifth centuries, it became a place of retreat for early Christian eremitic monks, who each lived alone in huts, caves, and cells. Eventually, however, *cenobitic* communities developed under the direction of St. Pachomius (c. 292–348), who organized most of the Thebaid's monks into monasteries, each comprising one large building or complex, where they lived together and held possessions in common, under the leadership of an abbot or abbess. "Cenobites," derived from the Greek for "common life," means "members of a religious monastic order."

history that its ideal has been one of joy and beauty. The worship of pain has far more often dominated the world. Mediaevalism, with its saints and martyrs, its love of self-torture, its wild passion for wounding itself, its gashing with knives, and its whipping with rods—Mediaevalism is real Christianity, and the mediaeval Christ is the real Christ. When the Renaissance dawned upon the world, and brought with it the new ideals of the beauty of life and the joy of living, men could not understand Christ. Even Art shows us that. The painters of the Renaissance drew Christ as a little boy playing with another boy in a palace or a garden, or lying back in his mother's arms, smiling at her, or at a flower, or at a bright bird; or as a noble, stately figure moving nobly through the world; or as a wonderful figure rising in a sort of ecstasy from death to life. Even when they drew him crucified they drew him as a beautiful God on whom evil men had inflicted suffering. But he did not preoccupy them much. What delighted them was to paint the men and women whom they admired, and to show the loveliness of this lovely earth. They painted many religious pictures— in fact, they painted far too many, and the monotony of type and motive is wearisome, and was bad for art. It was the result of the authority of the public in art-matters, and is to be deplored. But their soul was not in the subject. Raphael was a great artist when he painted his portrait of the Pope. When he painted his Madonnas and infant Christs, he was not a great artist at all. Christ had no message for the Renaissance, which was wonderful because it brought an ideal at variance with his, and to find the presentation of the real Christ we must go to mediaeval art. There he is one maimed and marred; one who is not comely to look on, because Beauty is a joy; one who is not in fair raiment, because that may be a joy also: he is a beggar who has a marvellous soul;

he is a leper whose soul is divine; he needs neither property nor health; he is a God realising his perfection through pain.

The evolution of man is slow. The injustice of men is great. It was necessary that pain should be put forward as a mode of self-realisation. Even now, in some places in the world, the message of Christ is necessary. No one who lived in modern Russia could possibly realise his perfection except by pain.[59] A few Russian artists have realised themselves in Art; in a fiction that is mediaeval in character, because its dominant note is the realisation of men through suffering. But for those who are not artists, and to whom there is no mode of life but the actual life of fact, pain is the only door to perfection. A Russian who lives happily under the present system of government in Russia must either believe that man has no soul, or that, if he has, it is not worth developing. A Nihilist who rejects all authority, because he knows authority to be evil, and welcomes all pain, because through that he realises his personality, is a real Christian. To him the Christian ideal is a true thing.

And yet, Christ did not revolt against authority. He accepted the imperial authority of the Roman Empire and paid tribute. He endured the ecclesiastical authority of the Jewish Church, and would not repel its violence by any violence of his own. He had,

59. An allusion to the autocratic regime of Tsar Alexander III, who ruled Russia with an iron fist after the assassination of his father, Alexander II, in 1881 until his own death in 1894. Alexander III tolerated no dissent, whether political, linguistic, or religious: he authorized the violent pogroms that led to the decimation of Russia's Jewish population, and suppressed any vestiges of German, Polish, and Swedish institutions that remained in Russia's outlying regions. Wilde's antipathy to the Tsarist regime, as well as his support for the revolutionary anarchists who sought its overthrow, is apparent in his early drama *Vera, or The Nihilist*.

as I said before, no scheme for the reconstruction of society. But the modern world has schemes. It proposes to do away with poverty and the suffering that it entails. It desires to get rid of pain, and the suffering that pain entails. It trusts to Socialism and to Science as its methods. What it aims at is an Individualism expressing itself through joy. This Individualism will be larger, fuller, lovelier than any Individualism has ever been. Pain is not the ultimate mode of perfection. It is merely provisional and a protest. It has reference to wrong, unhealthy, unjust surroundings. When the wrong, and the disease, and the injustice are removed, it will have no further place. It will have done its work. It was a great work, but it is almost over. Its sphere lessens every day.

Nor will man miss it. *For what man has sought for is, indeed, neither pain nor pleasure, but simply Life.* Man has sought to live intensely, fully, perfectly. When he can do so without exercising restraint on others, or suffering it ever, and his activities are all pleasurable to him, he will be saner, healthier, more civilized, more himself. Pleasure is Nature's test, her sign of approval. When man is happy, he is in harmony with himself and his environment. The new Individualism, for whose service Socialism, whether it wills it or not, is working, will be perfect harmony. It will be what the Greeks sought for, but could not, except in Thought, realise completely, because they had slaves, and fed them; it will be what the Renaissance sought for, but could not realise completely except in Art, because they had slaves, and starved them. It will be complete, and through it each man will attain to his perfection. The new Individualism is the new Hellenism.[60]

60. For *Hellenism*, see pp. 127–128, n.14 above.

From *Intentions**

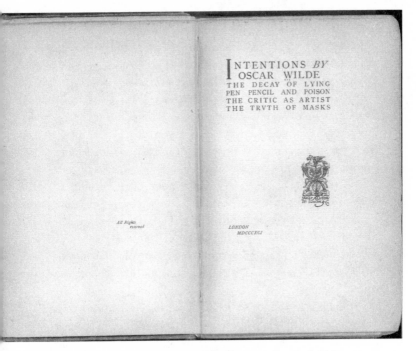

Oscar Wilde, *Intentions* (London: Osgood McIlvaine & Co., 1891). Title page.

* As its title indicates, *Intentions* begs to be understood as Wilde's artistic manifesto. It appeared in May 1891, the first of three books by Wilde that were copublished in 1891 by Osgood McIlvaine and Co. (in England) and Dodd, Mead, and Co. (in America). Like the other two volumes (*Lord Arthur Savile's Crime and Other Stories* and *A House of Pomegranates*), *Intentions* was a gathering of pieces that Wilde had previously published in periodicals, although Wilde revised the four constituent pieces of *Intentions* carefully, even retitling two of them. He had been contemplating a volume of "essays and studies" since 1889, to include both "The Decay of Lying" and "Pen Pencil and Poison," and at one point he considered

From "The Decay of Lying: An Observation"†

including "The Portrait of Mr. W. H." as well. Some months after *Intentions* appeared in English, Wilde gave permission for a French translation, saying "je ne veux pas qu'il traduise le dernier essai, 'La Vérité des Masques"; je ne l'aime plus. Au lieu de cela, on pourra mettre l'essai paru dans le *Fortnightly Review* de février dernier sur 'L'Ame de l'Homme,' qui contient une partie de mon esthétique" (*The Complete Letters of Oscar Wilde,* ed. Merlin Holland and Rupert Hart-Davis [New York: Henry Holt, 2000], 487; "I don't want the final essay, 'The Truth of Masks,' to be translated; I don't like it anymore. Instead you could include the essay that appeared in the *Fortnightly Review* last February on 'The Soul of Man,' which contains part of my aesthetic").

† "The Decay of Lying" is Wilde's wittiest, most paradoxical reflection on the nature of art, as well as a fine embodiment of Wilde's ideas about the art of conversation. First published, signed, in *Nineteenth Century*, January 1889, as "The Decay of Lying: A Dialogue," it was heavily revised for republication in *Intentions,* where it first appeared with its present subtitle. The present extract is derived from the *Intentions* version.

With his original subtitle "a dialogue" (relegated to the opening stage direction in 1891), Wilde highlighted his formal debts to an ancient tradition for the imaginative discussion of ideas that includes the dialogues of Plato, Lucian's *Dialogues of the Dead,* Hume's *Dialogues Concerning Natural Religion,* Landor's *Imaginary Conversations,* and, in Wilde's own day, "A Dialogue on Poetic Morality" by Wilde's onetime friend "Vernon Lee" (Violet Paget). Wilde was to utilize the dialogue form again in "The Critic as Artist," where Gilbert self-reflexively describes it as a "wonderful literary form" in which the thinker "can both reveal and conceal himself, and give form to every fancy, and reality to every mood. By its means he can exhibit the object from each point of view, and show it to us in the round, as a sculptor shows us things, gaining in this manner all the richness and reality of effect that comes from those side issues that are suddenly suggested by the central idea in its progress" (Wilde, *Criticism: Historical Criticism, Intentions, The Soul of Man,* ed. Josephine Guy, vol. 4

A Dialogue.
Persons: Cyril and Vivian.[1]
Scene: The Library of a Country House in Nottinghamshire.[2]

Cyril (coming in through the open window from the terrace). My
dear Vivian, don't coop yourself up all day in the library. It is
a perfectly lovely afternoon. The air is exquisite. There is a

---

of *The Complete Works of Oscar Wilde* [Oxford: Oxford Univ. Press,
2007], 186–187). Wilde was especially fond of Plato's *Symposium,* which
he called "of all the Platonic dialogues perhaps the most perfect, as it is
the most poetical" and praised for its "subtle suggestions of sex in soul,"
for "the curious analogies it draws between intellectual enthusiasm and
the physical passion of love," and for "its dream of the incarnation of the
Idea in a beautiful and living form" ("Appendix: Extracts from the Extended Version of 'The Portrait of Mr. W. H.,'" in *The Short Stories of
Oscar Wilde: An Annotated Selection*, ed. Nicholas Frankel [Cambridge,
MA.: Harvard Univ. Press, 2020], 288–289).

1. Cyril and Vivian (sometimes spelt "Vyvyan") were the names of Wilde's two children—aged three and two respectively when "The Decay of
Lying" was first published. Cyril is also the name of one of two interlocutors in Vernon Lee's "Dialogue on Poetic Morality" (1881), from which
Wilde borrows several important aesthetic principles while stripping them
of the ethical import and high moral tone with which Lee invests them.

2. In the periodical version of 1889, "a dialogue" was the subtitle, not
part of the opening stage direction, and the setting was "the library of a
country house in England." Josephine Guy (Wilde, *Criticism*, 360) says
of the altered setting that Wilde may have had a specific country house
in Nottinghamshire in mind. Horst Schroeder agrees, although whereas
Guy suggests Bingham Rectory (where Wilde stayed in 1876) as a possibility, Schroeder convincingly suggests Clumber House, near Worksop,
the seat of the Duke of Newcastle, where Wilde stayed twice in the late
1880s (Schroeder, "The OET *Complete Works* Vol IV: IV: 'The Decay of
Lying,'" *The Wildean* 37 [July 2010], 22).

mist upon the woods, like the purple bloom upon a plum.[3] Let us go and lie on the grass, and smoke cigarettes, and enjoy Nature.[4]

Vivian. Enjoy Nature! I am glad to say that I have entirely lost that faculty. People tell us that Art makes us love Nature more than we loved her before; that it reveals her secrets to us; and that after a careful study of Corot and Constable we see things in her that had escaped our observation.[5] My own experience is that the more we study Art, the less we care for Nature. What Art really reveals to us is Nature's lack of design, her curious crudities, her extraordinary monotony, her absolutely unfinished condition.[6] Nature has good intentions of course, but, as Aristotle once said, she cannot carry them out.[7] When I look at a landscape I cannot help seeing all its defects. It is fortunate for us, however, that Nature is

3. This sentence and the previous one, from "There is . . ." to "a plum," added 1891.

4. In the periodical version of 1889, the terms *Art* and *Nature* began without a capital letter.

5. Jean Baptiste Corot (1796–1875) and John Constable (1776–1837), both admired in Wilde's day for their depictions of nature.

6. Wilde breaks decisively here with his onetime mentor John Ruskin, whose writings about art had been founded on the principles of "Truth to Nature" and "Vital Beauty." See introduction, p. 7 above. Wilde's ideas about art's supremacy to nature are indebted to Whistler and to the cult of anti-nature in the works of Baudelaire and Huysmans.

7. This sentence was added in 1891. According to Josephine Guy, Wilde alludes here to Aristotle's *Poetics,* in which Aristotle "suggests that the function of the poet is to say not what has happened, but [rather] the kind of thing that *would* happen" (Wilde, *Criticism,* 362.)

so imperfect, as otherwise we should have had no art at all. Art is our spirited protest, our gallant attempt to teach Nature her proper place.[8] As for the infinite variety of Nature, that is a pure myth.[9] It is not to be found in Nature herself. It resides in the imagination, or fancy, or cultivated blindness of the man who looks at her.

Cyril. Well, you need not look at the landscape. You can lie on the grass and smoke and talk.

Vivian. But Nature is so uncomfortable. Grass is hard and lumpy and damp, and full of dreadful black insects. Why, even Morris' poorest workman could make you a more comfortable seat than the whole of Nature can.[10] Nature pales before the furniture of "the street from which Oxford has borrowed its name," as the poet you love so much once vilely

8. As Horst Schroeder has observed, this sentence contains an echo of Charles Baudelaire's proclamation that "la première affaire d'un artiste est de substituer l'homme à la nature, et de protester contre elle [*An artist's first duty is to substitute man for nature and to protest against her*]" (Baudelaire, *Salon de 1846* [Paris: Michel Levy, 1846], 91)

9. A direct challenge to John Addington Symonds, as Schroeder observes. Symonds had written in 1887 that "Art will never match the infinite variety and subtlety of nature" ("The Model," *Fortnightly Review*, n.s., 42 [Jul.–Dec. 1887], 859). The phrase "infinite variety" is an echo of Shakespeare's "Age cannot with her, nor custom stale / Her infinite variety" (*Antony and Cleopatra*, act 2, scene 2).

10. William Morris, whose decorating company, Morris and Co., founded in 1861, made exquisite handmade furniture and home furnishings for a wealthy artistic clientele. Morris and the company he founded are now widely regarded as the fountainhead of the Arts and Crafts movement.

William Morris and Company, London. "Sussex" armchair, c. 1865. Ebonized birch and matted rush. "Nature is so uncomfortable," remarks Vivian in "The Decay of Lying": "even Morris' poorest workman could make you a more comfortable seat than the whole of Nature can."

phrased it.[11] I don't complain. If Nature had been comfortable, mankind would never have invented architecture, and I prefer houses to the open air. In a house we all feel of the proper proportions. Everything is subordinated to us, fashioned for our use and our pleasure. Egotism itself, which is so necessary to a proper sense of human dignity, is entirely the result of indoor life. Out of doors one becomes abstract and impersonal. One's individuality absolutely leaves one. And then Nature is so indifferent, so unappreciative. Whenever I am walking in the park here, I always feel that I am no more to her than the cattle that browse on the slope, or the burdock that blooms in the ditch. Nothing is clearer than that Nature hates Mind. Thinking is the most unhealthy thing in the world, and people die of it just as they die of any other disease. Fortunately, in England at any rate, thought is not catching. Our splendid physique as a people is entirely due to our national stupidity. I only hope that we shall be able to keep this great historic bulwark of our happiness for many years to come; but I am afraid that we are beginning to be over-educated;[12] at least everybody who is incapable of learning

11. Vivian, who is clearly not fond of the nature-loving poet, is misquoting William Wordsworth, who in "The Power of Music" had called London's Oxford Street "the street that from Oxford hath borrowed its name." From 1877 onward, Oxford Street was home to the shop and showroom of Morris and Co. (see previous annotation). In the 1889 version of "The Decay of Lying," Wilde referred here not to Oxford Street, but rather to London's Tottenham Court Road, home of the luxury furniture store Maple & Co. Similarly, in the previous sentence, he referred not to Morris, but to Maple.

12. An idea that occurs repeatedly in Wilde's writings. In *The Importance of Being Earnest*, for instance, Lady Bracknell responds to Jack's

has taken to teaching—that is really what our enthusiasm for education has come to. In the meantime, you had better go back to your wearisome uncomfortable Nature, and leave me to correct my proofs.

Cyril. Writing an article! That is not very consistent after what you have just said.

Vivian. Who wants to be consistent?[13] The dullard and the doctrinaire, the tedious people who carry out their principles to the bitter end of action, to the *reductio ad absurdum* of practice.[14] Not I. Like Emerson, I write over the door of my library the word "Whim."[15] Besides, my article is really a most salutary and valuable warning. If it is attended to, there may be a new Renaissance of Art.[16]

---

confession that he "knows nothing" with "I am pleased to hear it . . . The whole theory of modern education is radically unsound. Fortunately in England, at any rate, education produces no effect whatsoever." Like many of his generation, Wilde was skeptical about wide-reaching educational reforms that followed in the wake of the 1870 and 1880 Elementary Education Acts.

13. For "the pleasure of being inconsistent," see p. 333 below. And for Wilde's aphorism "The well-bred contradict other people. The wise contradict themselves," see p. 364 below.

14. For a more substantial critique of action, see "From 'The Critic as Artist,'" pp. 298–299 below.

15. "I shun father and mother and wife and brother, when my genius calls me. I would write on the lintels of the door-post 'Whim.'" (Ralph Waldo Emerson, "Self-Reliance")

16. Inspired by Walter Pater's *Studies in the History of the Renaissance* (see p. 30, n.9 above), Wilde had first called for a new English "renaissance" of art in 1882: "I call it our English Renaissance because it is indeed a sort of new birth of the spirit of man, like the great Italian Re-

Cyril. What is the subject?

Vivian. I intend to call it "The Decay of Lying: A Protest."

Cyril. Lying! I should have thought our politicians kept up that habit.

Vivian. I assure you that they do not. They never rise beyond the level of misrepresentation, and actually condescend to prove, to discuss, to argue. How different from the temper of the true liar, with his frank, fearless statements, his superb irresponsibility, his healthy, natural disdain of proof of any kind! After all, what is a fine lie? Simply that which is its own evidence. If a man is sufficiently unimaginative to produce evidence in support of a lie, he might just as well speak the truth at once. No, the politicians won't do. Something may, perhaps, be urged on behalf of the Bar.[17] The mantle of the

---

naissance of the fifteenth century, in its desire for a more gracious and comely way of life, its passion for physical beauty, its exclusive attention to form, its seeking for new subjects for poetry, new forms of art, new intellectual and imaginative enjoyments" ("The English Renaissance of Art," in *Miscellanies,* vol. 14 of *The Complete Works of Oscar Wilde,* ed. Robert Ross [London: Methuen, 1908], 243).

17. This sentence and the next ten, from "Something may, perhaps" to "either the lawyer or the journalist," were added for the 1891 version of "The Decay of Lying." In London's Inns of Court, where English trial lawyers or "barristers" train to this day, the *bar* originally referred to "a barrier or partition separating the seats of the benchers or readers from the rest of the hall, to which students, after they had attained a certain standing, were 'called' from the body of the hall, for the purpose of taking a principal part in the mootings or exercises of the house" (OED). However, "the Bar" has for centuries been a metonym for the profession of the barrister: to be "called to the Bar" is to attain full accreditation as an advocate or trial lawyer.

Sophist has fallen on its members. Their feigned ardours and unreal rhetoric are delightful. They can make the worse appear the better cause, as though they were fresh from Leontine schools, and have been known to wrest from reluctant juries triumphant verdicts of acquittal for their clients, even when those clients, as often happens, were clearly and unmistakeably innocent. But they are briefed by the prosaic, and are not ashamed to appeal to precedent. In spite of their endeavours, the truth will out. Newspapers, even, have degenerated. They may now be absolutely relied upon. One feels it as one wades through their columns. It is always the unreadable that occurs. I am afraid that there is not much to be said in favour of either the lawyer or the journalist. Besides, what I am pleading for is Lying in art.[18] Shall I read you what I have written? It might do you a great deal of good.

Cyril. Certainly, if you give me a cigarette. Thanks. By the way, what magazine do you intend it for?

Vivian. For the *Retrospective Review.* I think I told you that the elect had revived it.[19]

Cyril. Whom do you mean by "the elect"?

Vivian. Oh, The Tired Hedonists of course. It is a club to which I belong. We are supposed to wear faded roses in our button-holes when we meet, and to have a sort of cult for

18. Here and below, "Lying" began with a lowercase *l* in 1889.

19. *The Retrospective Review*, an antiquarian magazine, published in England from 1820–1828. For Wilde's notion that "They are the elect to whom beautiful things mean only Beauty," see p. 354 below.

Domitian.[20] I am afraid you are not eligible. You are too fond of simple pleasures.

Cyril. I should be black-balled[21] on the ground of animal spirits, I suppose?

Vivian. Probably. Besides, you are a little too old. We don't admit anybody who is of the usual age.[22]

Cyril. Well, I should fancy you are all a good deal bored with each other.

Vivian. We are. That is one of the objects of the club. Now, if you promise not to interrupt too often, I will read you my article.

Cyril. You will find me all attention.

Vivian (reading in a very clear, musical voice). "THE DECAY OF LYING: A PROTEST.—One of the chief causes of the curiously commonplace character of most of the literature of our age is undoubtedly the decay of Lying as an art, a science, and a social pleasure. The ancient historians gave us delightful fiction in the form of fact; the modern novelist presents us with dull facts under the guise of fiction. The Blue-Book[23] is

20. Domitian (51–96 CE) was among the most decadent of Roman emperors. In *The Picture of Dorian Gray*, Wilde compares Dorian to Domitian, "sick with that *ennui,* that terrible *taedium vitae,* that comes to those to whom life denies nothing."
21. Excluded by an adverse vote of the club's members.
22. cf. "The old believe everything. The middle-aged suspect everything. The young know everything" (p. 367 below).
23. Government publications or official reports, named for their blue covers.

rapidly becoming his ideal both for method and manner. He has his tedious '*document humain*,'[24] his miserable little '*coin de la création*,'[25] into which he peers with his microscope. He is to be found at the Librairie Nationale,[26] or at the British Museum, shamelessly reading up his subject. He has not even the courage of other people's ideas,[27] but insists on going directly to life for everything, and ultimately, between encyclopaedias and personal experience, he comes to the ground, having drawn his types from the family circle or from the weekly washerwoman,[28] and having acquired an amount of useful information from which never, even in his most meditative moments, can he thoroughly free himself.

"The loss that results to literature in general from this false ideal of our time can hardly be overestimated. People have a careless way of talking about a 'born liar,' just as they talk about a 'born poet.' But in both cases they are wrong. Lying and poetry are arts—arts, as Plato saw,[29] not unconnected

24. *Human document.* The phrase appears as a chapter title in Emile Zola's *Le Roman Experimentale* (1880; *The Experimental Novel*).

25. *Corner of creation.* Another direct quotation from Zola, this time from *Mes Haines* (1866, *My Hatreds*).

26. A slip for the Bibliothèque Nationale, the national library of France.

27. A deliberate echo—and transvaluation—of James McNeill Whistler's charge that "Oscar . . . has the courage of the opinions . . . of others" (letter published in *The World,* November 17, 1886, rpt. [although misdated] in Whistler, *The Gentle Art of Making Enemies* [London: Heinemann, 1890], 164).

28. An allusion to Zola's novel *L'Assommoir* (*The Drinking Den*), whose heroine works in a laundry.

29. In *The Republic,* Book X, Plato had argued, through his mouthpiece Socrates, that the "imitative poet" is a "manufacturer of images and is very far removed from the truth."

with each other—and they require the most careful study, the most disinterested devotion. Indeed, they have their technique, just as the more material arts of painting and sculpture have, their subtle secrets of form and colour, their craft-mysteries, their deliberate artistic methods. As one knows the poet by his fine music, so one can recognize the liar by his rich rhythmic utterance, and in neither case will the casual inspiration of the moment suffice.[30] Here, as elsewhere, practice must precede perfection. But in modern days while the fashion of writing poetry has become far too common, and should, if possible, be discouraged, the fashion of lying has almost fallen into disrepute. Many a young man starts in life with a natural gift for exaggeration which, if nurtured in congenial and sympathetic surroundings, or by the imitation of the best models, might grow into something really great and wonderful. But, as a rule, he comes to nothing. He either falls into careless habits of accuracy—"

Cyril. My dear fellow!

Vivian. Please don't interrupt in the middle of a sentence. "He either falls into careless habits of accuracy, or takes to frequenting the society of the aged and the well-informed.[31] Both things are equally fatal to his imagination, as indeed they would be fatal to the imagination of anybody, and in a short time he develops a morbid and unhealthy faculty of truth-telling, begins to verify all statements made in his presence, has no hesitation in contradicting people who are much

30. See, too, p. 215 below; and for Wilde's notion that the liar "is a far more civilized being than the blockhead," see p. 68 above.
31. "Those whom the Gods love grow young" (p. 361 below).

younger than himself, and often ends by writing novels which are so like life that no one can possibly believe in their probability. This is no isolated instance that we are giving. It is simply one example out of many; and if something cannot be done to check, or at least to modify, our monstrous worship of facts, Art will become sterile, and Beauty will pass away from the land.

"Even Mr. Robert Louis Stevenson, that delightful master of delicate and fanciful prose, is tainted with this modern vice, for we know positively no other name for it. There is such a thing as robbing a story of its reality by trying to make it too true, and *The Black Arrow* is so inartistic as not to contain a single anachronism to boast of, while the transformation of Dr. Jekyll reads dangerously like an experiment out of the *Lancet*.[32] As for Mr. Rider Haggard, who really has, or had once, the makings of a perfectly magnificent liar, he is now so afraid of being suspected of genius that when he does tell us anything marvellous, he feels bound to invent a personal reminiscence, and to put it into a footnote as a kind of cowardly corroboration.[33] Nor are our other novelists much better. Mr. Henry James writes fiction as if it were a painful

32. *The Lancet* is still Britain's leading medical journal. Like his short story "The Body Snatcher," Stevenson's novella *The Strange Case of Dr. Jekyll and Mr. Hyde* (1886) is deeply preoccupied with the experiments, behaviors, and characters of licensed medical professionals. *The Black Arrow* is a historical romance set during the Wars of the Roses.

33. Wilde is thinking of Haggard's novels *Allan Quatermain* (1887) and *Maiwa's Revenge* (1888), into which Haggard had inserted numerous mock-serious pseudo-footnotes purporting to corroborate the fictional details. Many of these notes were based on Haggard's own experiences in Africa, where these novels are set.

duty, and wastes upon mean motives and imperceptible 'points of view'[34] his neat literary style, his felicitous phrases, his swift and caustic satire. . . . Mrs. Oliphant prattles pleasantly about curates, lawn-tennis parties, domesticity, and other wearisome things.[35] Mr. Marion Crawford has immolated himself upon the altar of local colour.[36] He is like the lady in the French comedy who is always talking about 'le beau ciel d'Italie.'[37] Besides, he has fallen into a bad habit of uttering moral platitudes. At times he is almost edifying. *Robert Elsmere* is of course a masterpiece—a masterpiece of the 'genre ennuyeux,'[38] the one form of literature that the English people seem to thoroughly enjoy. A thoughtful young friend of ours once told us that it reminded him of the sort of conversation that goes on at a meat tea in the house of a serious Nonconformist family, and we can quite believe it.[39]

34. "I see dramas within dramas . . . and innumerable points of view" (Henry James, "The Art of Fiction").

35. Margaret Oliphant (1828–1897) was best known for her *Chronicles of Carlingford* (1863–1866).

36. Francis Marion Crawford (1854–1909), prolific American author, many of whose novels were set in India, Italy, or Asia.

37. *The beautiful sky of Italy.* The lady and the French comedy to which Wilde attributes this phrase are unknown.

38. *Robert Elsmere* (1888), by Mrs. Humphrey Ward, was a bestselling three-volume novel describing a young Anglican clergyman's crisis of faith. Shortly after the publication of "The Decay of Lying," Wilde wrote to Mrs. George Lewis, "I have blown my trumpet against the gate of dullness, and I hope some shaft has hit *Robert Elsmere* between the joints of his nineteenth edition." The phrase "genre ennuyeux" (boring genre) derives from Voltaire's *L'Enfant Prodigue* (1736): "*Tous les genres sont bons hors le genre ennuyeux*" ("All genres are good except for the boring kind").

39. This sentence added 1891.

Indeed it is only in England that such a book could be produced. England is the home of lost ideas.[40] As for that great and daily increasing school of novelists for whom the sun always rises in the East-End, the only thing that can be said about them is that they find life crude, and leave it raw.[41]

"In France, though nothing so deliberately tedious as *Robert Elsmere* has been produced, things are not much better. M. Guy de Maupassant, with his keen mordant irony and his hard vivid style, strips life of the few poor rags that still cover her, and shows us foul sore and festering wound. He writes lurid little tragedies in which everybody is ridiculous; bitter comedies at which one cannot laugh for very tears. . . . [I]f a novelist is base enough to go to life for his personages he should at least pretend that they are creations, and not boast of them as copies. The justification of a character in a novel is not that other persons are what they are, but that the author is what he is.[42] Otherwise the novel is not a work of art. As for M. Paul Bourget, the master of the *roman psychologique*,[43] he commits the error of imagining that the men and women

40. This sentence added 1891.

41. Wilde refers here to the early novels of George Gissing and Walter Besant, many of which take place in the slums of London's impoverished and multi-ethnic East End. In later years, Wilde owned novels by Israel Zangwill and Arthur Morrison, the 1890s masters of East End fiction, though whether these novels changed his views about "novelists for whom the sun always rises in the East-End" cannot be determined.

42. This sentence and the next, from "The justification" to "work of art," added 1891.

43. Psychological novel. Paul Bourget (1852–1935) was one of France's leading intellectuals. His early novels, such as *Cruelle Énigme* (1885), *Un Crime d'amour* (1886), and *André Cornélis* (1887), were careful psychological studies.

of modern life are capable of being infinitely analyzed for an innumerable series of chapters. In point of fact what is interesting about people in good society—and M. Bourget rarely moves out of the Faubourg St. Germain, except to come to London[44]—is the mask that each one of them wears, not the reality that lies behind the mask. It is a humiliating confession, but we are all of us made out of the same stuff. In Falstaff there is something of Hamlet, in Hamlet there is not a little of Falstaff.[45] The fat knight has his moods of melancholy, and the young prince his moments of coarse humor. Where we differ from each other is purely in accidentals: in dress, manner, tone of voice, religious opinions,[46] personal appearance, tricks of habit, and the like. The more one analyses people, the more all reasons for analysis disappear. Sooner or later one comes to that dreadful universal thing called human nature. Indeed, as any one who has ever worked among the poor knows only too well, the brotherhood of man is no mere poet's dream, it is a most depressing and humiliating reality; and if a writer insists upon analysing the upper classes, he might just as well write of match-girls and costermongers at once." However, my dear Cyril, I will not detain you any

44. In the 1889 version of "The Decay of Lying," Bourget "never" moved out of the Faubourg St. Germain, the Parisian neighbourhood most associated with the French aristocracy, roughly comparable to London's Mayfair. In 1891, Wilde altered "never" to "rarely" and added "except to come to London."

45. The corpulent Sir John Falstaff ("the fat knight") is the bawdy and irreverent foil to Prince Hal ("the young prince") in Shakespeare's *Henry IV, Part One*. Hamlet is now a byword for youthful angst, self-doubt, and noble purity of purpose.

46. "religious opinions" added 1891.

further just here. I quite admit that modern novels have many good points. All I insist on is that, as a class, they are quite unreadable.

Cyril. That is certainly a very grave qualification, but I must say that I think you are rather unfair in some of your strictures. I like . . . *Mr. Isaacs,* and as for *Robert Elsmere* I am quite devoted to it.[47] Not that I can look upon it as a serious work. As a statement of the problems that confront the earnest Christian it is ridiculous and antiquated. It is simply Arnold's *Literature and Dogma* with the literature left out.[48] It is as much behind the age as Paley's *Evidences,*[49] or Colenso's method of Biblical exegesis.[50] Nor could anything be less impressive than the unfortunate hero gravely heralding a dawn that rose long ago, and so completely missing its true

47. F. Marion Crawford, *Mr. Isaacs: A Tale of Modern India* (1882). For *Robert Elsmere,* see n.38 above.

48. In *Literature and Dogma* (1873), Matthew Arnold had challenged orthodox Christian belief and sought to establish a more vital, humanistic Christianity through the study of literature and the development of human culture.

49. *A View of the Evidences of Christianity* (1794), by William Paley (1743–1805). Paley's effort to unite natural science and Christian theology was rendered obsolete by the work of Charles Darwin in the mid-nineteenth century. For Wilde's inclusion of Paley's *Evidences* among "books not to read at all," see "To Read, or Not to Read" below.

50. In a series of treatises (1862–1879) on the Pentateuch and the book of Joshua, the biblical scholar John William Colenso (1814–1883) courted immense controversy by questioning the literal and historical truthfulness of the first five books of the Old Testament. Though Wilde disparages Colenso's methods, Colenso's work is now recognized as contributing significantly to biblical scholarship.

significance that he proposes to carry on the business of the old firm under the new name.[51] On the other hand, it contains several clever caricatures, and a heap of delightful quotations, and Green's philosophy very pleasantly sugars the somewhat bitter pill of the author's fiction.[52] I also cannot help expressing my surprise that you have said nothing about the two novelists whom you are always reading, Balzac and George Meredith. Surely they are realists, both of them?[53]

Vivian. Ah! Meredith! Who can define him? His style is chaos illumined by flashes of lightning. As a writer he has mastered everything except language; as a novelist he can do everything, except tell a story: as an artist he is everything, except articulate. Somebody in Shakespeare—Touchstone, I think—talks about a man who is always breaking his shins over his own wit,[54] and it seems to me that this might serve as the basis of a criticism of Meredith's style. But whatever he is, he is not a realist. Or rather I would say that he is a child of realism who is not on speaking terms with his father. By deliberate choice he has made himself a romanticist. He has refused to bow the

51. After resigning his position as Anglican rector, Elsmere establishes a religious brotherhood in the slums of London's East End.

52. The ideas of T. H. Green (1836–1882), England's leading moral philosopher, saturate *Robert Elsmere*. Green appears within the novel as Henry Grey, an Oxford don who balances Christian faith with social idealism and rational skepticism.

53. Honoré de Balzac (1799–1850) and George Meredith (1828–1909) were among Wilde's favorite novelists. The latter was (and still is) infamous for the allusiveness and obscurity of his style.

54. In Shakespeare's *As You Like It,* Touchstone, the wise fool, remarks, "I shall ne'er be ware of my own wit till I break my shins against it."

knee to Baal,[55] and after all, even if the man's fine spirit did not revolt against the noisy assertions of realism, his style would be quite sufficient of itself to keep life at a respectful distance. By its means he has planted round his garden a hedge full of thorns, and red with wonderful roses. As for Balzac, he was a most remarkable combination of the artistic temperament with the scientific spirit. The latter he bequeathed to his disciples: the former was entirely his own. The difference between such a book as M. Zola's *L'Assommoir* and Balzac's *Illusions Perdues* is the difference between unimaginative realism and imaginative reality.[56] "All Balzac's characters," said Baudelaire, "are gifted with the same ardour of life that animated himself. All his fictions are as deeply coloured as dreams. Each mind is a weapon loaded to the muzzle with will. The very scullions have genius."[57] A steady course of Balzac reduces our living friends to shadows, and our acquaintances to the shadows of shades. His characters have a kind of fervent fiery-coloured existence. They dominate us, and defy scepticism. One of the greatest tragedies of

55. In the Old Testament, Baal is a false idol condemned by the Hebrew prophets. To "bow the knee to Baal" is a proverbial expression, as Schroeder points out, deriving from 1 Kings 19:18: "I have left me seven thousand in Israel, all the knees which have not bowed to Baal."

56. "unimaginative realism and imaginative reality" is an unacknowledged plagiarism of Algernon Swinburne's *A Study of Shakespeare* (1879), where Swinburne had, like Wilde, contrasted Balzac and Zola to the latter's detriment.

57. The quotation derives from Baudelaire's 1859 essay "Théodore Gautier," but as Patricia Clements has observed, Wilde is quoting Swinburne's translation in *A Study of Shakespeare.*

my life is the death of Lucien de Rubempré.[58] It is a grief from which I have never been able to completely rid myself. It haunts me in my moments of pleasure.[59] I remember it when I laugh. But Balzac is no more a realist than Holbein[60] was. He created life, he did not copy it. I admit, however, that

58. Lucien de Rubempré, a talented, ambitious, but impoverished young writer from the provinces, is a principal character in Balzac's *Illusions Perdues (Lost Illusions)* and *Splendeurs et Misères des Courtesans (A Harlot High and Low)*. Towards the end of *Illusions Perdues*, Lucien is seduced in a carriage by the roguish Vautrin. He dies by suicide in a prison cell towards the end of *Splendeurs et Misères des Courtesans*. Richard Ellmann writes that "Lucien de Rubempré became in fact the nineteenth-century type of the homosexual beloved" (Ellmann, "A Late Victorian Love-Affair," *New York Rev. of Books* [August 4, 1977]: 6). Vivian's reaction to Lucien's death is thus "part of Wilde's subtle effort to bring to light and so gain countenance for sexual feelings like his own, an effort that involved small yet continual affronts to conventional moral expectations. Under cover of aestheticism, Wilde was claiming that there could be a homosexual as well as a heterosexual gallery of lovers" (Ellmann, "A Late Victorian Love-Affair," 6). Proust once remarked that there is "something particularly dramatic about Oscar Wilde in his most brilliant days having been drawn to Lucien de Rubempré, and moved by his death. . . . But one can't help thinking how a few years later he was himself to be Lucien de Rubempré; and Lucien de Rubempré in the prison . . . brought down by the proof that he had been living in close friendship with a convict, was but a foreshadowing . . . of just what was going to happen to Wilde" (*By Way of Sainte-Beuve,* tr. Sylvia Townsend-Warner [London: Chatto & Windus, 1958], 134).

59. This sentence and the next, from "It haunts" to "I laugh," added 1891.

60. Hans Holbein the Younger (c. 1497–1543), German portrait-painter and printmaker.

he set far too high a value on modernity of form, and that, consequently, there is no book of his that, as an artistic masterpiece, can rank with *Salammbô* or *Esmond,* or *The Cloister and the Hearth,* or the *Vicomte de Bragelonne.*[61]

Cyril. Do you object to modernity of form, then?

Vivian. Yes. It is a huge price to pay for a very poor result. Pure modernity of form is always somewhat vulgarizing. It cannot help being so. The public imagine that, because they are interested in their immediate surroundings, Art should be interested in them also, and should take them as her subject-matter. But the mere fact that they are interested in these things makes them unsuitable subjects for Art. The only beautiful things, as somebody once said, are the things that do not concern us.[62] As long as a thing is useful or necessary to us, or affects us in any way, either for pain or for pleasure, or appeals strongly to our sympathies, or is a vital part of the environment in which we live, it is outside the proper sphere of art.[63] To art's subject-matter we should be more or less in-

61. Gustave Flaubert, *Salammbô* (1862); William Makepeace Thackeray, *The History of Henry Esmond* (1852); Charles Reade, *The Cloister and The Hearth* (1861); Alexandre Dumas, *Le Vicomte de Bragelonne* (1848–1850).

62. Wilde is paraphrasing Théophile Gautier, who had argued in his preface to *Mademoiselle de Maupin* (ed. and tr. Helen Constantine [London: Penguin, 2005], 23) that "The only things that are really beautiful are those which have no use."

63. Wilde's rejection of utility as a criterion for art is a challenge to the principal tenet of the Arts and Crafts movement, whose founder William Morris insisted repeatedly in the 1870s and 1880s that "nothing can be a work of art that is not useful" ("The Lesser Arts").

different. We should, at any rate, have no preferences, no prejudices, no partisan feeling of any kind. It is exactly because Hecuba is nothing to us that her sorrows are such an admirable motive for a tragedy.[64] I do not know anything in the whole history of literature sadder than the artistic career of Charles Reade. He wrote one beautiful book, *The Cloister and the Hearth,* a book as much above *Romola* as *Romola* is above *Daniel Deronda,*[65] and wasted the rest of his life in a foolish attempt to be modern, to draw public attention to the state of our convict prisons, and the management of private lunatic asylums.[66] Charles Dickens was depressing enough in all conscience when he tried to arouse our sympathy for the victims of the poor-law administration;[67] but Charles Reade, an artist, a scholar, a man with a true sense of beauty, raging and

64. According to Greek myth, Hecuba, Queen of Troy, was inconsolable at the death of her children and the loss of her homeland. Her tragedy was the subject of Euripides's plays *Hecuba* and *The Trojan Women.* Wilde is here alluding to—and endorsing—Hamlet's remark, about the power of the tragic actor: "For Hecuba! / What's Hecuba to him, or he to Hecuba, / That he should weep for her?"

65. George Eliot, *Romola* (1862–1863) and *Daniel Deronda* (1876). In a passage of "The Decay of Lying" omitted from the present excerpt, Wilde quoted approvingly John Ruskin's description of Eliot's characters as "being like the sweepings of a Pentonville omnibus" (Wilde, *Criticism,* 79).

66. After writing the much-praised historical novel *The Cloister and The Hearth* (1861), set in the fifteenth century, Charles Reade (1814–1884) tackled contemporary topics in his novels and plays. *Hard Cash* (1863) describes the abuses common in private lunatic asylums; and *It Is Never Too Late to Mend* (1865) shocked audiences with its depictions of torture and inhumanity in English prisons.

67. See Charles Dickens, *Oliver Twist.*

THE CRITICAL WRITINGS OF OSCAR WILDE

roaring over the abuses of contemporary life like a common pamphleteer or a sensational journalist, is really a sight for the angels to weep over.[68] Believe me, my dear Cyril, modernity of form and modernity of subject-matter are entirely and absolutely wrong. We have mistaken the common livery of the age for the vesture of the Muses, and spend our days in the sordid streets and hideous suburbs of our vile cities when we should be out on the hill-side with Apollo.[69] Certainly we are a degraded race, and have sold our birthright for a mess of facts.[70]

Cyril. There is something in what you say, and there is no doubt that whatever amusement we may find in reading a purely modern novel, we have rarely any artistic pleasure in re-reading it. And this is perhaps the best rough test of what is literature and what is not. If one cannot enjoy reading a book over and over again, there is no use reading it at all. But what do you say about the return to Life and Nature? This is the panacea that is always being recommended to us.

68. Vivian's disparagement of the later career of Charles Reade is ironic given that Wilde himself later adopted the manner of the pamphleteer in order to rage against the state of Victorian prisons and the cruelty of the Victorian justice system. See Wilde, *The Annotated Prison Writings of Oscar Wilde,* ed. Nicholas Frankel (Cambridge, MA: Harvard Univ. Press, 2018), 293–383.

69. Apollo, the Greek god of music, poetry, and the arts, resided on Mount Olympus.

70. In Genesis 25:29–34, Esau sells his birthright for a meal of lentil stew. Esau's poor bargain was described by English biblical commentators of the Renaissance as "selling his birthright for a mess of pottage" and the phrase thereafter became proverbial for any action that produces a result of little or no value.

Vivian. I will read you what I say on that subject. The passage comes later on in the article, but I may as well give it to you now:

"The popular cry of our time is 'Let us return to Life and Nature; they will recreate Art for us, and send the red blood coursing through her veins; they will give her feet swiftness and make her hand strong.' But, alas! we are mistaken in our amiable and well-meaning efforts. Nature is always behind the age. And as for Life, she is the solvent that breaks up Art, the enemy that lays waste her house."

Cyril. What do you mean by saying that Nature is always behind the age?

Vivian. Well, perhaps that is rather cryptic. What I mean is this. If we take Nature to mean natural simple instinct as opposed to self-conscious culture, the work produced under this influence is always old-fashioned, antiquated, and out of date. One touch of Nature may make the whole world kin, but two touches of Nature will destroy any work of Art.[71] If, on the other hand, we regard Nature as the collection of phenomena external to man, people only discover in her what they bring to her. She has no suggestions of her own. Wordsworth went to the lakes, but he was never a lake poet.[72] He found in stones the sermons he had already hidden there. He went moralizing about the district, but his good work

71. This sentence added 1891.

72. William Wordsworth (1770–1850) was born in the English Lake District and resided there for all but thirteen years of his life. This district was the inspiration for much of Wordsworth's finest poetry; in Wilde's day Wordsworth was still widely regarded as *the* poet of "the Lakes."

was produced when he returned, not to Nature but to poetry. Poetry gave him "Laodamia," and the fine sonnets, and the great Ode, such as it is.[73] Nature gave him "Martha Ray" and "Peter Bell" and the address to Mr. Wilkinson's spade.[74]

Cyril. I think that view might be questioned. I am rather inclined to believe in the "impulse from a vernal wood,"[75] though of course the artistic value of such an impulse depends entirely on the kind of temperament that receives it, so that the return to Nature would come to mean simply the advance to a great personality.[76] You would agree with that, I fancy. However, proceed with your article.

Vivian (reading). "Art begins with abstract decoration, with purely imaginative and pleasurable work dealing with what is unreal and non-existent. This is the first stage. Then Life becomes fascinated with this new wonder, and asks to be admitted into the charmed circle. Art takes life as part of her rough material, recreates it, and refashions it in fresh forms,

73. By "fine sonnets" Wilde likely means "The World Is Too Much With Us," "Composed Upon Westminster Bridge, September 3, 1802," and other sonnets first published in Wordsworth's *Poems, In Two Volumes* (1807). By "great Ode," he means Wordsworth's "Ode: Intimations of Immortality," first published in 1807.

74. Martha Ray is a character in Wordsworth's poem "The Thorn" (1798). By "address to Mr. Wilkinson's spade," Wilde means Wordsworth's poem "To the Spade of a Friend (An Agriculturalist)" (1804).

75. "one impulse from a vernal wood / May teach you more of man; / Of moral evil and of good, / Than all the sages can" (Wordsworth, "The Tables Turned" [1798]). As Guy observes, in the late 1870s Wilde copied these lines into his Commonplace Book.

76. The last phrase of this sentence, from "so that" to "great personality," added 1891.

is absolutely indifferent to fact, invents, imagines, dreams, and keeps between herself and reality the impenetrable barrier of beautiful style, of decorative or ideal treatment. The third stage is when Life gets the upper hand, and drives Art out into the wilderness. This is the true decadence, and it is from this that we are now suffering.[77]

"Take the case of the English drama. At first in the hands of the monks Dramatic Art was abstract, decorative, and mythological. Then she enlisted Life in her service, and using some of life's external forms, she created an entirely new race of beings, whose sorrows were more terrible than any sorrow man has ever felt, whose joys were keener than lover's joys, who had the rage of the Titans and the calm of the gods, who had monstrous and marvellous sins, monstrous and marvellous virtues. To them she gave a language different from that of actual use, a language full of resonant music and sweet

77. In the last decades of the nineteenth century, conservative cultural critics throughout Europe were preoccupied with the thought that their age represented a decline from the values that had made their nations great powers—a decline roughly comparable to the decay or "decadence" of imperial Rome or fifteenth-century Venice. See Max Nordau, "The Dusk of The Nations" in his *Degeneration,* translator unknown (New York: Appleton, 1895), 1–6; also Jerome H. Buckley, "The Idea of Decadence," in his *The Triumph of Time* (Cambridge, MA: The Belknap Press of Harvard Univ. Press, 1966), 66–93. For Nordau, *fin de siècle* art and literature exemplified and were even partly responsible for this decline, representing a "decadent movement" at large in Europe's capitals. See p. 171, n.52 above. By insisting that present-day efforts to suppress or censor art represented "the true decadence . . . from [which] we are now suffering" (Wilde added the word "true" in 1891), Wilde transvalued the notion of *decadence* and turned the tables on art's conservative detractors.

rhythm, made stately by solemn cadence, or made delicate by fanciful rhyme, jewelled with wonderful words, and enriched with lofty diction. She clothed her children in strange raiment and gave them masks, and at her bidding the antique world rose from its marble tomb. A new Caesar stalked through the streets of risen Rome, and with purple sail and flute-led oars another Cleopatra passed up the river to Antioch.[78] Old myth and legend and dream took shape and substance. History was entirely rewritten, and there was hardly one of the dramatists who did not recognize that the object of Art is not simple truth but complex beauty. In this they were perfectly right. Art itself is really a form of exaggeration; and selection, which is the very spirit of art, is nothing more than an intensified mode of over-emphasis.

"But Life soon shattered the perfection of the form. Even in Shakespeare we can see the beginning of the end. It shows itself by the gradual breaking up of the blank-verse in the later plays, by the predominance given to prose, and by the over-importance assigned to characterization. The passages in Shakespeare—and they are many—where the language is uncouth, vulgar, exaggerated, fantastic, obscene even, are entirely due to Life calling for an echo of her own voice, and rejecting the intervention of beautiful style, through which alone should Life be allowed to find expression. Shakespeare is not by any means a flawless artist. He is too fond of going directly to life, and borrowing life's natural utterance. He forgets that when Art surrenders her imaginative medium she surrenders everything. Goethe says somewhere 'In der Bes-

<hr>

78. Wilde is alluding to Shakespeare's plays *Julius Caesar* and *Antony and Cleopatra*.

chränkung zeigt sich erst der Meister' ('It is in working within limits that the master reveals himself'),[79] and the limitation, the very condition, of any art is style. However, we will not linger any longer over Shakespeare's realism. The *Tempest* is the most perfect of palinodes.[80] All that we desired to point out was, that the magnificent work of the Elizabethan and Jacobean artists contained within itself the seeds of its own dissolution, and that, if it drew some of its strength from using life as rough material, it drew all its weakness from using life as an artistic method. As the inevitable result of this substitution of an imitative for a creative medium, this surrender of an imaginative form, we have the modern English melodrama. The characters in these plays talk on the stage exactly as they would talk off it; they have neither aspirations nor aspirates;[81] they are taken directly from life and reproduce its vulgarity down to the smallest detail; they present the gait, manner, costume, arid accent of real people; they would pass unnoticed in a third-class railway carriage. And yet how wearisome the plays are! They do not succeed in producing even that impression of reality at which they aim, and which is their only reason for existing. As a method, realism is a complete failure.

79. Johann Wolfgang von Goethe, "Natur und Kunst" (Nature and Art) (1802). Goethe's line was often quoted in Britain in the 1880s—in an 1885 English translation of Henri Frédéric Amiel's *Journal Intime,* in an 1886 review by Walter Pater of Amiel's *Journal,* and again in an 1887 essay about Amiel by Matthew Arnold—and Wilde is probably quoting it from one of these sources.

80. A poetic retraction of a former statement—that is, *The Tempest* is a recantation of the realism corrupting Shakespeare's earlier works.

81. "they have neither aspirations nor aspirates" added 1891.

"What is true about the drama and the novel is no less true about those arts that we call the decorative arts. The whole history of these arts in Europe is the record of the struggle between Orientalism, with its frank rejection of imitation, its love of artistic convention, its dislike to the actual representation of any object in Nature, and our own imitative spirit. Wherever the former has been paramount, as in Byzantium, Sicily, and Spain, by actual contact, or in the rest of Europe by the influence of the Crusades, we have had beautiful and imaginative work in which the visible things of life are transmuted into artistic conventions, and the things that Life has not are invented and fashioned for her delight. But wherever we have returned to Life and Nature, our work has always become vulgar, common, and uninteresting. Modern tapestry, with its aerial effects, its elaborate perspective, its broad expanses of waste sky, its faithful and laborious realism, has no beauty whatsoever. The pictorial glass of Germany is absolutely detestable. We are beginning to weave possible carpets in England, but only because we have returned to the method and spirit of the East. Our rugs and carpets of twenty years ago, with their solemn depressing truths, their inane worship of Nature, their sordid reproductions of visible objects, have become, even to the Philistine, a source of laughter. A cultured Mahomedan[82] once remarked to us, 'You Christians are so occupied in misinterpreting the fourth commandment that you have never thought of making an artistic application of the second.'[83] He was perfectly right, and the

82. A Muslim
83. The fourth of the Ten Commandments enjoins Judeo-Christians to "keep the sabbath day, to sanctify it." The second forbids making "any

whole truth of the matter is this: The proper school to learn art in is not Life but Art."

And now let me read you a passage which seems to me to settle the question very completely.[84]

"It was not always thus. . . . [I]n the published speeches of Cicero and the biographies of Suetonius . . . in the *Lives of the Saints;* in Froissart and Sir Thomas Malory; in the travels of Marco Polo . . . in the autobiography of Benvenuto Cellini; in the memoirs of Casanova; in Defoe's *History of the Plague;* in Boswell's *Life of Johnson;* in Napoleon's despatches, and in the works of our own Carlyle, whose *French Revolution* is one of the most fascinating historical novels ever written,[85] facts are either kept in their proper subordinate position, or else entirely excluded on the general ground of dulness. Now, everything is changed. Facts are not merely finding a footing-place in history, but they are usurping the domain of Fancy, and have invaded the kingdom of Romance. Their chilling touch is over everything. They are vulgarising mankind. The crude commercialism of America, its materialising spirit, its indifference to the poetical side of things, and its lack of imagination and of high, unattainable ideals, are entirely due to that country having adopted for its national

---

graven image, or any likeness of any thing that is in heaven above, or that is in the earth beneath." Islam similarly prohibits representations of both heavenly and living creatures, with the result that Islamic art has traditionally developed along abstract and purely decorative lines.

84. In 1891 Wilde substituted "seems to me to settle the question very completely" for "deals with the commonplace character of our literature."

85. In 1891 Wilde substituted "historical novels" for "historical romances."

hero, a man, who according to his own confession, was incapable of telling a lie, and it is not too much to say that the story of George Washington and the cherry-tree has done more harm, and in a shorter space of time, than any other moral tale in the whole of literature."[86]

Cyril. My dear boy!

Vivian. I assure you it is the case, and the amusing part of the whole thing is that the story of the cherry-tree is an absolute myth. However, you must not think that I am too despondent about the artistic future of America or of our own country. Listen to this:—"That some change will take place before this century has drawn to its close, we have no doubt whatsoever. Bored by the tedious and improving conversation of those who have neither the wit to exaggerate nor the genius to romance, tired of the intelligent person whose reminiscences are always based upon memory, whose statements are invariably limited by probability, and who is at any time liable to be corroborated by the merest Philistine who happens

86. "The cherry tree myth is the most well-known and longest enduring legend about George Washington. In the original story, when Washington was six years old, he received a hatchet as a gift and damaged his father's cherry tree. When his father discovered what he had done, he became angry and confronted him. Young George bravely said, 'I cannot tell a lie . . . I did cut it with my hatchet.' Washington's father embraced him and rejoiced that his son's honesty was worth more than a thousand trees. Ironically, this iconic story about the value of honesty was invented by one of Washington's first biographers, an itinerant minister and bookseller named Mason Locke Weems" (Digital Encyclopedia of George Washington: https://www.mountvernon.org/library/digitalhistory/digital-encyclopedia/article/cherry-tree-myth/).

to be present, society sooner or later must return to its lost leader, the cultured and fascinating liar. Who he was who first, without ever having gone out to the rude chase, told the wondering cavemen at sunset how he had dragged the Megatherium from the purple darkness of its jasper cave,[87] or slain the Mammoth in single combat and brought back its gilded tusks, we cannot tell, and not one of our modern anthropologists, with all their much-boasted science, has had the ordinary courage to tell us. Whatever was his name or race, he was certainly the true founder of social intercourse. For the aim of the liar is simply to charm, to delight, to give pleasure. He is the very basis of civilized society, and without him a dinner party, even at the mansions of the great,[88] is as dull as a lecture at the Royal Society or a debate at the Incorporated Authors, or one of Mr. Burnand's farcical comedies.[89]

"Nor will he be welcomed by society alone. Art, breaking from the prison-house of realism, will run to greet him, and will kiss his false, beautiful lips, knowing that he alone is in possession of the great secret of all her manifestations, the secret that Truth is entirely and absolutely a matter of style; while Life—poor, probable, uninteresting human life—tired

87. A *megatherium*, meaning "great beast," was a hairy giant sloth, roughly the size of an elephant, that lived in prehistoric times.

88. See p. 68 and p. 195 above.

89. *The Royal Society of London for Improving Natural Knowledge,* known simply as the *Royal Society;* or *The Royal Society of Literature;* the *Incorporated Society of Authors,* now known simply as the *Society of Authors;* the comic writer F. C. Burnand, who was the editor of *Punch,* authored some fifty-five farcical stage comedies, including *The Colonel* (1881), in which Wilde himself was mercilessly mocked. Wilde added "or one of Mr. Burnand's farcical comedies" to this sentence in 1891.

of repeating herself for the benefit of Mr. Herbert Spencer,[90] scientific historians, and the compilers of statistics in general, will follow meekly after him, and try to reproduce, in her own simple and untutored way, some of the marvels of which he talks.

"No doubt there will always be critics who, like a recent writer in the *Saturday Review,*[91] will gravely censure the teller of fairy tales for his defective knowledge of natural history, who will measure imaginative work by their own lack of any imaginative faculty, and who will hold up their ink-stained hands in horror if some honest gentleman, who has never been farther than the yew-trees of his own garden, pens a fascinating book of travels like Sir John Mandeville,[92] or, like great Raleigh, writes a whole history of the world,[93] without

90. Herbert Spencer (1820–1903), biologist, pioneering sociologist, and social Darwinist. Spencer was much admired in his day and is still famous for inventing the phrase "survival of the fittest." Wilde's Oxford notebooks demonstrate the profound effect Spencer had on Wilde's thinking about human and cultural history.

91. Wilde is alluding to an unsigned review, by Alexander Ross, of his own fairy-tale collection *The Happy Prince and Other Tales* that had appeared in *The Saturday Review of Politics, Literature, Science and Art*, a weekly review, on October 20, 1888. In his review, Ross had remarked that in his fairy tale "The Nightingale and The Rose," Wilde's "artistic sense has stumbled a little along with his natural history" (rpr. in *Oscar Wilde: The Critical Heritage,* ed. Karl Beckson [New York: Routledge and Kegan Paul, 1970], 62).

92. *The Travels of Sir John Mandeville*, owned by Wilde and recommended in "To Read, or Not to Read," below.

93. *A History of the World* (1614), written and published while Sir Walter Raleigh was imprisoned in the Tower of London for alleged conspiracy, during the reign of James I.

knowing anything whatsoever about the past. To excuse themselves they will try and shelter under the shield of him who made Prospero the magician, and gave him Caliban and Ariel as his servants, who heard the Tritons blowing their horns round the coral reefs of the Enchanted Isle, and the fairies singing to each other in a wood near Athens, who led the phantom kings in dim procession across the misty Scottish heath, and hid Hecate in a cave with the weird sisters.[94] They will call upon Shakespeare—they always do—and will quote that hackneyed passage about Art holding the mirror up to Nature, forgetting that this unfortunate aphorism is deliberately said by Hamlet in order to convince the bystanders of his absolute insanity in all art-matters."[95]

Cyril. Ahem! Another cigarette, please.

Vivian. My dear fellow, whatever you may say, it is merely a dramatic utterance, and no more represents Shakespeare's real views upon art than the speeches of Iago represent his real views upon morals. But let me get to the end of the passage:

"Art finds her own perfection within, and not outside of, herself.[96] She is not to be judged by any external standard of resemblance. She is a veil, rather than a mirror. She has flowers

94. Wilde is alluding to Shakespeare's *The Tempest, A Midsummer Night's Dream*, and *Macbeth*.

95. The "purpose of playing," Hamlet tells a troupe of traveling actors in *Hamlet*, is "to hold as 'twere the mirror up to nature; to show virtue her own feature, scorn her own image, and the very age and body of the time his form and pressure."

96. An echo of James McNeill Whistler's contention that Art "is . . . selfishly occupied with her own perfection only—having no desire to

that no forests know of, birds that no woodland possesses. She makes and unmakes many worlds, and can draw the moon from heaven with a scarlet thread.[97] Hers are the 'forms more real than living man,'[98] and hers the great archetypes of which things that have existence are but unfinished copies.[99] Nature has, in her eyes, no laws, no uniformity. She can work miracles at her will, and when she calls monsters from the deep they come. She can bid the almond tree blossom in winter, and send the snow upon the ripe cornfield. At her word the frost lays its silver finger on the burning mouth of June, and the winged lions creep out from the hollows of the Lydian hills. The dryads peer from the thicket as she passes by, and the brown fauns smile strangely at her when she comes near them. She has hawk-faced gods that worship her, and the centaurs gallop at her side."[100]

---

teach—seeking and finding the beautiful in all conditions, and in all times" ("Mr. Whistler's 'Ten O'Clock,'" in Whistler, *The Gentle Art*, 136).

97. As Horst Schroeder observes, the concluding phrase is an allusion to the Thessalian witches of classical antiquity. See too Wilde's "The Fisherman and His Soul," where the witch boasts "with a wheel I can draw the Moon from heaven" (Wilde, *The Short Stories of Oscar Wilde*, 237).

98. Percy Bysshe Shelley, *Prometheus Unbound*, 1:748.

99. An allusion to Plato's theory of forms, according to which truth and reality reside not in perceptible, material things but in the ideas or "great archetypes" of which they are but impoverished copies. As Guy points out, Wilde is rewriting Plato here, since art, in Plato's view, divorces its beholder from true being, rather than providing greater access to it.

100. Wilde refers here and in the previous sentence to the fantastical beings—griffins, dryads, fauns, hawk-faced gods, centaurs—of Greek mythology.

Cyril. I like that. I can see it. Is that the end?[101]

Vivian. No. There is one more passage, but it is purely practical. It simply suggests some methods by which we could revive this lost art of Lying.

Cyril. Well, before you read it to me, I should like to ask you a question. What do you mean by saying that life, "poor, probable, uninteresting human life," will try to reproduce the marvels of art? I can quite understand your objection to art being treated as a mirror. You think it would reduce genius to the position of a cracked looking-glass. But you don't mean to say that you seriously believe that Life imitates Art, that Life in fact is the mirror, and Art the reality?

Vivian. Certainly I do. Paradox though it may seem—and paradoxes are always dangerous things—it is none the less true that Life imitates Art far more than Art imitates Life. We have all seen in our own day in England how a certain curious and fascinating type of beauty, invented and emphasized by two imaginative painters,[102] has so influenced Life that whenever one goes to a private view or to an artistic salon one sees, here the mystic eyes of Rossetti's dream, the long ivory

101. "I like that. I can see it" added 1891, when Wilde also deleted "of this dangerous article" after "the end."

102. Wilde is referring to the painters Dante Gabriel Rossetti and Edward Burne-Jones, as Vivian's ensuing comments make clear. *The Golden Stairs* (1880, not "Golden Stair") and *Laus Veneris* (1873–1875, *not* "Laus Amoris") are paintings by Burne-Jones: "the passion-pale face of Andromeda" refers to Burne-Jones's paintings *The Rock of Doom* (1885–1888) and *The Doom Fulfilled* (1884–1885); "the thin hands and lithe beauty of the Vivien in 'Merlin's Dream'" refers to Burne-Jones's painting *The Beguiling of Merlin* (1877).

throat, the strange square-cut jaw, the loosened shadowy hair that he so ardently loved, there the sweet maidenhood of "The Golden Stair," the blossom-like mouth and weary loveliness of the "Laus Amoris," the passion-pale face of Andromeda, the thin hands and lithe beauty of the Vivien in "Merlin's Dream." And it has always been so. A great artist invents a type, and Life tries to copy it, to reproduce it in a popular form, like an enterprising publisher. Neither Holbein nor Vandyck found in England what they have given us.[103] They brought their types with them, and Life with her keen imitative faculty set herself to supply the master with models. The Greeks, with their quick artistic instinct, understood this, and set in the bride's chamber the statue of Hermes or of Apollo,[104] that she might bear children as lovely as the works of art that she looked at in her rapture or her pain. They knew that Life gains from Art not merely spirituality, depth of thought and feeling, soul-turmoil or soul-peace, but that she can form herself on the very lines and colours of art, and can reproduce the dignity of Pheidias as well as the grace of Praxiteles.[105] Hence came their objection to realism. They disliked it on purely social grounds. They felt that it inevitably makes people ugly, and they were perfectly right. We try to improve the conditions of the race by means of good air, free sunlight, wholesome water, and hideous bare buildings for the better

103. Hans Holbein the Younger (see n.60 above) and Anthony van Dyke (1599–1614), court painters respectively to Henry VIII and Charles I, both of Continental origin.

104. In Greek statuary, both idealized types of male beauty.

105. Pheidias (c. 490–c. 430 BCE) and Praxiteles (c. 400–330 BCE) were arguably the two greatest sculptors of Greek antiquity.

housing of the lower orders. But these things merely produce health, they do not produce beauty. For this, Art is required, and the true disciples of the great artist are not his studio-imitators, but those who become like his works of art, be they plastic as in Greek days, or pictorial as in modern times; in a word, Life is Art's best, Art's only pupil.

As it is with the visible arts, so it is with literature. The most obvious and the vulgarest form in which this is shown is in the case of the silly boys who, after reading the adventures of Jack Sheppard or Dick Turpin, pillage the stalls of unfortunate apple-women, break into sweet-shops at night, and alarm old gentlemen who are returning home from the city by leaping out on them in suburban lanes, with black masks and unloaded revolvers.[106] This interesting phenomenon, which always occurs after the appearance of a new edition of either of the books I have alluded to, is usually attributed to the influence of literature on the imagination. But this is a mistake. The imagination is essentially creative and always seeks for a new form. The boy-burglar is simply the inevitable result of life's imitative instinct. He is Fact, occupied as Fact usually is, with trying to reproduce Fiction, and what we see in him is repeated on an extended scale throughout the whole of life. Schopenhauer has analyzed the pessimism that characterizes

106. Jack Sheppard (1702–1724) and Dick Turpin (1705–1739) were notorious English thieves, the former a four-time prison escapee, the latter a highwayman. They became folk heroes in their own short lifetimes and died by public execution. Their "adventures" were immortalized and glamorized in broadsheets, penny dreadfuls, prints, plays, and the immensely popular early novels of William Harrison Ainsworth (1805–1882).

modern thought,[107] but Hamlet invented it. The world has become sad because a puppet was once melancholy. The Nihilist, that strange martyr who has no faith, who goes to the stake without enthusiasm, and dies for what he does not believe in, is a purely literary product. He was invented by Tourgenieff, and completed by Dostoieffski.[108] Robespierre came out of the pages of Rousseau[109] as surely as the People's Palace rose out of the *debris* of a novel.[110] Literature always anticipates life. It does not copy it, but moulds it to its purpose. The nineteenth century, as we know it, is largely an invention of Balzac. Our Luciens de Rubempré, our Rastignacs, and De Marsays made their first appearance on the stage of the *Comédie Humaine*.[111] We are merely carrying out, with footnotes and unnecessary additions, the whim or fancy or creative vision of a great novelist. I once asked a lady, who knew Thackeray intimately, whether he had had any model

107. Arthur Schopenhauer (1788–1860), whose pessimistic treatise *The World as Will and Idea* (1819) was fashionable with British intellectuals after its translation into English in the mid-1880s.

108. Ivan Turgenev (1818–1883) and Fyodor Dostoevsky (1821–1881).

109. Maximilian Robespierre (1758–1794), the violent French revolutionary, was inspired by the writings of the social philosopher Jean-Jacques Rousseau (1718–1778).

110. The "People's Palace" in the Mile End Road, containing auditoria, art galleries, a library, reading rooms, and classrooms, was an educational and cultural center for working class inhabitants of London's impoverished East End. It was inspired by the "Palace of Delight" in Walter Besant's novel *All Sorts and Conditions of Men* (1882).

111. For *La Comédie Humaine,* see p. 161, n.39 above, and for Lucien de Rubempré see n.58 above. De Rubempré, Eugène de Rastignac, and Henri de Marsay are characters who reappear throughout Balzac's saga.

for Becky Sharp.[112] She told me that Becky was an invention, but that the idea of the character had been partly suggested by a governess who lived in the neighborhood of Kensington Square, and was the companion of a very selfish and rich old woman. I inquired what became of the governess, and she replied that, oddly enough, some years after the appearance of *Vanity Fair,* she ran away with the nephew of the lady with whom she was living, and for a short time made a great splash in society, quite in Mrs. Rawdon Crawley's style, and entirely by Mrs. Rawdon Crawley's methods. Ultimately she came to grief, disappeared to the Continent, and used to be occasionally seen at Monte Carlo and other gambling places. The noble gentleman from whom the same great sentimentalist drew Colonel Newcome died, a few months after *The Newcomes* had reached a fourth edition, with the word "Adsum" on his lips.[113] Shortly after Mr. Stevenson published his curious psychological story of transformation,[114] a friend of mine, called Mr. Hyde, was in the north of London, and being anxious to get to a railway station, he took what he thought would be a short cut, lost his way, and found himself in a network of mean, evil-looking streets. Feeling rather nervous he began to walk extremely fast, when suddenly out of an archway ran a child right between his legs. It fell on the pavement, he tripped over it, and trampled upon it.

112. The heroine of Thackeray's *Vanity Fair*, who marries Rawdon Crawley midway through the novel.

113. Colonel Newcome, in Thackeray's *The Newcomes* (1853–1855), dies in the final chapter with the word "Adsum" (meaning "I am present") on his lips, as Vivian implies.

114. Robert Louis Stevenson, *The Strange Case of Dr. Jekyll and Mr. Hyde* (1886)

Being of course very much frightened and a little hurt, it began to scream, and in a few seconds the whole street was full of rough people who came pouring out of the houses like ants. They surrounded him, and asked him his name. He was just about to give it when he suddenly remembered the opening incident in Mr. Stevenson's story. He was so filled with horror at having realized in his own person that terrible and well-written scene, and at having done accidentally, though in fact, what the Mr. Hyde of fiction had done with deliberate intent, that he ran away as hard as he could go. He was, however, very closely followed, and finally he took refuge in a surgery, the door of which happened to be open, where he explained to a young assistant, who happened to be there, exactly what had occurred. The humanitarian crowd were induced to go away on his giving them a small sum of money, and as soon as the coast was clear he left. As he passed out, the name on the brass door-plate of the surgery caught his eye. It was "Jekyll." At least it should have been.[115]

Here the imitation, as far as it went, was of course accidental. In the following case the imitation was self-conscious. In the year 1879, just after I had left Oxford, I met at a reception at the house of one of the Foreign Ministers[116] a woman of very curious exotic beauty. We became great friends, and were constantly together.[117] And yet what interested most in her was, not her beauty, but her character, her entire vague-

115. "At least it should have been" added 1891.
116. Ambassadors.
117. This sentence added 1891, together with small changes to the previous sentence.

ness of character.[118] She seemed to have no personality at all, but simply the possibility of many types. Sometimes she would give herself up entirely to art, turn her drawing-room into a studio, and spend two or three days a week at picture-galleries or museums. Then she would take to attending race-meetings, wear the most horsey clothes, and talk about nothing but betting. She abandoned religion for mesmerism, mesmerism for politics, and politics for the melodramatic excitements of philanthropy.[119] In fact, she was a kind of Proteus, and as much a failure in all her transformations as was that wondrous sea-god when Odysseus laid hold of him.[120] One day a serial began in one of the French magazines. At that time I used to read serial stories, and I well remember the shock of surprise I felt when I came to the description of the heroine. She was so like my friend that I brought her the magazine, and she recognized herself in it immediately, and seemed fascinated by the resemblance. I should tell you, by the way, that the story was translated from some dead Russian writer, so that the author had not taken his type from my friend. Well, to put the matter briefly, some months afterwards I was in Venice, and finding the magazine in the reading-room of the hotel, I took it up casually to see what had become of the heroine. It was a most piteous tale, as the girl had ended by running away with a man absolutely inferior to her, not merely in social station, but in character and

118. "not her beauty, but her character" added 1891; also "strange vagueness" altered to "entire vagueness."

119. This sentence, as well as "In fact" in the next, added 1891.

120. Proteus was a sea god with the magical capacity to change shape. In the *Odyssey*, Menelaus, not Odysseus, forced Proteus to change back into his true shape.

intellect also. I wrote to my friend that evening about my views on John Bellini, and the admirable ices at Florio's,[121] and the artistic value of gondolas, but added a postscript to the effect that her double in the story had behaved in a very silly manner. I don't know why I added that, but I remember I had a sort of dread over me that she might do the same thing. Before my letter had reached her, she had run away with a man who deserted her in six months. I saw her in 1884 in Paris, where she was living with her mother, and I asked her whether the story had had anything to do with her action. She told me that she had felt an absolutely irresistible impulse to follow the heroine step by step in her strange and fatal progress, and that it was with a feeling of real terror that she had looked forward to the last few chapters of the story. When they appeared, it seemed to her that she was compelled to reproduce them in life, and she did so. It was a most clear example of this imitative instinct of which I was speaking, and an extremely tragic one.

However, I do not wish to dwell any further upon individual instances. Personal experience is a most vicious and limited circle. All that I desire to point out is the general principle that Life imitates Art far more than Art imitates Life, and I feel sure that if you think seriously about it you will find that it is true. Life holds the mirror up to Art, and either reproduces some strange type imagined by painter or sculptor, or realizes in fact what has been dreamed in fiction. Scientifically speaking, the basis of life—the energy of life, as

121. Giovanni Bellini (c. 1430–1516), Venetian painter; Cafe Florian, founded 1720, reputedly the oldest cafe in the world, situated in St. Mark's Square, Venice.

Aristotle would call it[122]—is simply the desire for expression, and Art is always presenting various forms through which this expression can be attained. Life seizes on them and uses them, even if they be to her own hurt. Young men have committed suicide because Rolla did so, have died by their own hand because by his own hand Werther died.[123] Think of what we owe to the imitation of Christ, of what we owe to the imitation of Caesar.

Cyril. The theory is certainly a very curious one,[124] but to make it complete you must show that Nature, no less than Life, is an imitation of Art. Are you prepared to prove that?

Vivian. My dear fellow, I am prepared to prove anything.

Cyril. Nature follows the landscape painter, then, and takes her effects from him?

Vivian. Certainly. Where, if not from the Impressionists, do we get those wonderful brown fogs that come creeping down our streets, blurring the gas-lamps and changing the houses into monstrous shadows? To whom, if not to them and their

122. "The energy of the mind is the essence of life" (Aristotle, *Metaphysics*, Book 11). Aristotle (384–322 BCE) was the first authority to employ the term *energeia* from which the modern word "energy" is derived.

123. Rolla and Werther are the suicidal heroes, respectively, of Alfred de Musset's *Rolla* (1833) and Johann Wolfgang von Goethe's *The Sorrows of Young Werther* (1774).

124. The following eight hundred words, in which Vivian shows he is "prepared to prove anything" by discoursing on how Nature imitates Art, up to Cyril's important utterance, "You have proved it to my dissatisfaction, which is better," weren't present in the first publication of "The Decay of Lying." They were longest single addition made for the 1891 text.

James McNeill Whistler, *Nocturne: The Thames at Battersea.* Lithotint print, 1878. "Where, if not from the Impressionists," asks Vivian rhetorically in "The Decay of Lying," "do we get those wonderful brown fogs that come creeping down our streets, blurring the gas-lamps and changing the houses into monstrous shadows? To whom, if not to them and their master, do we owe the lovely silver mists that brood over our river, and turn to faint forms of fading grace curved bridge and swaying barge?"

master, do we owe the lovely silver mists that brood over our river, and turn to faint forms of fading grace curved bridge and swaying barge?[125] The extraordinary change that has taken place in the climate of London during the last ten years

125. "their master" alludes to James McNeill Whistler, who at the time of writing was closely allied in the public's mind with the French impressionists. Wilde is here invoking Whistler's Nocturnes, in which Whistler frequently depicts London's River Thames at twilight.

is entirely due to a particular school of Art. You smile. Consider the matter from a scientific or a metaphysical point of view, and you will find that I am right. For what is Nature? Nature is no great mother who has borne us. She is our creation. It is in our brain that she quickens to life. Things are because we see them, and what we see, and how we see it, depends on the Arts that have influenced us. To look at a thing is very different from seeing a thing. One does not see anything until one sees its beauty. Then, and then only, does it come into existence. At present, people see fogs, not because there are fogs, but because poets and painters have taught them the mysterious loveliness of such effects. There may have been fogs for centuries in London. I dare say there were. But no one saw them, and so we do not know anything about them. They did not exist till Art had invented them. Now, it must be admitted, fogs are carried to excess. They have become the mere mannerism of a clique, and the exaggerated realism of their method gives dull people bronchitis. Where the cultured catch an effect, the uncultured catch cold. And so, let us be humane, and invite Art to turn her wonderful eyes elsewhere. She has done so already, indeed. That white quivering sunlight that one sees now in France, with its strange blotches of mauve, and its restless violet shadows, is her latest fancy, and, on the whole, Nature reproduces it quite admirably. Where she used to give us Corots and Daubignys, she gives us now exquisite Monets and entrancing Pisaros.[126]

---

126. For Corot, see n.5 above, and for Monet, see introduction, p. 16 above. Like Corot, Charles-François Daubigny (1817–1878) was a mid-Victorian landscape painter; and like Monet, Camille Pissarro (not *Pisaro*) (1830–1903) was a leading Impressionist *plein air* painter.

Indeed there are moments, rare, it is true, but still to be observed from time to time, when Nature becomes absolutely modern. Of course she is not always to be relied upon. The fact is that she is in this unfortunate position. Art creates an incomparable and unique effect, and, having done so, passes on to other things. Nature, upon the other hand, forgetting that imitation can be made the sincerest form of insult, keeps on repeating this effect until we all become absolutely wearied of it. Nobody of any real culture, for instance, ever talks nowadays about the beauty of a sunset. Sunsets are quite old-fashioned. They belong to the time when Turner was the last note in art. To admire them is a distinct sign of provincialism of temperament. Upon the other hand they go on. Yesterday evening Mrs. Arundel insisted on my going to the window, and looking at the glorious sky, as she called it. Of course I had to look at it. She is one of those absurdly pretty Philistines to whom one can deny nothing. And what was it? It was simply a very second-rate Turner, a Turner of a bad period, with all the painter's worst faults exaggerated and over-emphasized. Of course, I am quite ready to admit that Life very often commits the same error. She produces her false Renés and her sham Vautrins, just as Nature gives us, on one day a doubtful Cuyp, and on another a more than questionable Rousseau.[127] Still, Nature irritates one more when she does things of that kind. It seems so stupid, so obvious, so unnecessary. A false Vautrin might be delightful. A doubtful Cuyp is unbearable. However, I don't want to be too hard on

127. René is the fictional hero of Chateaubriand's novella *René* (1802). For Vautrin, see p. 161, n.39 above. Aelbert Cuyp (1620–1691) and Théodore Rousseau (1812–1867) were landscape painters.

Nature. I wish the Channel, especially at Hastings, did not look quite so often like a Henry Moore,[128] grey pearl with yellow lights, but then, when Art is more varied, Nature will, no doubt, be more varied also. That she imitates Art, I don't think even her worst enemy would deny now. It is the one thing that keeps her in touch with civilized man. But have I proved my theory to your satisfaction?

Cyril. You have proved it to my dissatisfaction, which is better. But even admitting this strange imitative instinct in Life and Nature,[129] surely you would acknowledge that Art expresses the temper of its age, the spirit of its time, the moral and social conditions that surround it, and under whose influence it is produced.

Vivian. Certainly not! Art never expresses anything but itself. This is the principle of my new aesthetics; and it is this, more than that vital connection between form and substance, on which Mr. Pater dwells, that makes music the type of all the arts.[130] Of course, nations and individuals, with that healthy natural vanity which is the secret of life, are always under the impression that it is of them that the Muses are talking, always trying to find in the calm dignity of imaginative art some mirror of their own turbid passions, always forgetting that

128. Henry Moore, R. A. (1831–1895), the foremost British marine painter of his day.

129. "and Nature" added 1891.

130. In his essay "Style" (1888) Walter Pater calls music "the ideal of all art whatever, precisely because in it, it is impossible to distinguish the form from the substance or matter, the subject from the expression." See too p. 356, n.7 below, for Pater's earlier formulation that "all art aspires to the condition of music."

the singer of life is not Apollo, but Marsyas.[131] Remote from reality, and with her eyes turned away from the shadows of the cave,[132] Art reveals her own perfection, and the wondering crowd that watches the opening of the marvellous, many-petalled rose fancies that it is its own history that is being told to it, its own spirit that is finding expression in a new form. But it is not so. The highest art rejects the burden of the human spirit, and gains more from a new medium or a fresh material than she does from any enthusiasm for art, or from any lofty passion, or from any great awakening of the human consciousness. She develops purely on her own lines. She is not symbolic of any age. It is the ages that are her symbols.

131. According to Greek myth, Apollo, the god of music and poetry, flayed alive the faun Marsyas (often credited with inventing the flute) after vanquishing him in a contest of musicianship adjudicated by the Muses, who stipulated that the contest's winner might do what he liked with the loser. Wilde writes in *De Profundis*: "Marsyas had no more song, the Greeks said. Apollo had been victor. The lyre had vanquished the reed. But perhaps the Greeks were mistaken. I hear in much modern Art the cry of Marsyas. It is bitter in Baudelaire, sweet and plaintive in Lamartine, mystic in Verlaine. It is in the deferred resolutions of Chopin's music. It is in the discontent that haunts the recurrent faces of Burne-Jones's women. Even Matthew Arnold . . . has not a little of it" (Wilde, *Annotated Prison Writings*, 233). Wilde went on to liken himself to Marsyas; and for Wilde's description of his own poem *The Ballad of Reading Gaol* as "a song of Marsyas, not a song of Apollo," see *The Complete Letters of Oscar Wilde*, ed. Merlin Holland and Rupert Hart-Davis [New York: Henry Holt, 2000], 1035.

132. An allusion to, as well as a rejection of, Plato's myth of the cave, in which Plato likens men to primitive cave-dwellers preoccupied with their own shadows in the firelight. Rather than attending to the light source behind them, Plato maintains, men face the inner walls of their cave and see only the flickering images of their own shadows projected there.

Even those who hold that Art is representative of time and place and people, cannot help admitting that the more imitative an art is, the less it represents to us the spirit of its age. The evil faces of the Roman emperors look out at us from the foul porphyry and spotted jasper in which the realistic artists of the day delighted to work, and we fancy that in those cruel lips and heavy sensual jaws we can find the secret of the ruin of the Empire. But it was not so. The vices of Tiberius could not destroy that supreme civilization, any more than the virtues of the Antonines could save it.[133] It fell for other, for less interesting reasons. The sibyls and prophets of the Sistine may indeed serve to interpret for some that new birth of the emancipated spirit that we call the Renaissance;[134] but what do the drunken boors and brawling peasants of Dutch

133. Julius Caesar Augustus Tiberius (b. 42 BCE) ruled as emperor of Rome from 14 CE to 37 CE, although in 26 CE he abruptly retired to Capri, where he set aside a suite of rooms in which to pursue "the vices he had so long struggled to conceal" (Suetonius, *Lives of the Caesars*, tr. Catharine Edwards [Oxford: Oxford Univ. Press, 2000], 118). According to Suetonius, the bedrooms, each decked out with lewd paintings and sculptures, were adjacent to a "library . . . equipped with the works of Elephantis, so that an illustration of the required position would always be available if anyone needed guidance" (119). Elephantis was a Greek woman poet whose works (now lost) apparently described numerous different modes of sexual coition. The Antonines were four relatively benevolent Roman Emperors—Antoninus Pius, Marcus Aurelius, Lucius Verus, and Commodus—who ruled from 138 to 193 CE. According to Edward Gibbon, the Antonine dynasty represents a period when "the Roman Empire was governed by absolute power, under the guidance of wisdom and virtue."

134. Wilde alludes to Michelangelo's frescos on the ceiling of the Sistine Chapel.

art tell us about the great soul of Holland? The more abstract, the more ideal an art is, the more it reveals to us the temper of its age. If we wish to understand a nation by means of its art, let us look at its architecture or its music.

Cyril. I quite agree with you there. The spirit of an age may be best expressed in the abstract ideal arts, for the spirit itself is abstract and ideal. Upon the other hand, for the visible aspect of an age, for its look, as the phrase goes, we must surely go to the arts of imitation.

Vivian. I don't think so. After all, what the imitative arts really give us are merely the various styles of particular artists, or of certain schools of artists. Surely you don't imagine that the people of the Middle Ages bore any resemblance at all to the figures on mediaeval stained glass, or in mediaeval stone and wood carving, or on mediaeval metalwork, or tapestries, or illuminated MSS. They were probably very ordinary-looking people, with nothing grotesque, or remarkable, or fantastic in their appearance. The Middle Ages, as we know them in art, are simply a definite form of style, and there is no reason at all why an artist with this style should not be produced in the nineteenth century. No great artist ever sees things as they really are. If he did, he would cease to be an artist. Take an example from our own day. I know that you are fond of Japanese things.[135] Now, do you really imagine that the Japanese people, as they are presented to us in art, have any existence? If you do, you have never understood Japanese art at all. The

135. For the Victorian cult of Japonisme—vividly on display in James McNeill Whistler's *The Princess From the Land of Porcelain* (1863–1865), *The Peacock Room* (1876–1877), and in Aubrey Beardsley's "pictures" to the first English translation (1894) of Wilde's play *Salomé*—see p. 74, n.3 above.

Japanese people are the deliberate self-conscious creation of certain individual artists. If you set a picture by Hokusai, or Hokkei, or any of the great native painters, beside a real Japanese gentleman or lady, you will see that there is not the slightest resemblance between them.[136] The actual people who live in Japan are not unlike the general run of English people; that is to say, they are extremely commonplace, and have nothing curious or extraordinary about them. In fact the whole of Japan is a pure invention. There is no such country, there are no such people. One of our most charming painters went recently to the Land of the Chrysanthemum in the foolish hope of seeing the Japanese.[137] All he saw, all he had

136. Although he doesn't name them, Lord Henry Wotton is probably thinking of Katsushika Hokusai (1760–1849) and Totoya Hokkei (1780–1850), the two Japanese Edo-period artists named here by Vivian, when, at the start of Wilde's novel *The Picture of Dorian Gray*, the "gleam" of the laburnum blossoms, the "flame-like beauty" of its branches, and the "fantastic shadows" of birds in flight remind him—in a clear instance of life imitating art—of "those pallid jade-faced painters who, in an art that is necessarily immobile, seek to convey the sense of swiftness and motion" (Wilde, *The Picture of Dorian Gray: An Annotated, Uncensored Edition*, ed. Frankel [Cambridge, MA: The Belknap Press of Harvard Univ. Press, 2011], 67). Wilde would have been familiar with Hokusai and Hokkei from important studies of *Japonisme* such as Rutherford Alcock's *Art and Art Industries in Japan* (which he owned), William Anderson's *Pictorial Arts of Japan*, Marcus Huish's *Japan and Its Art*, and the short-lived periodical *Artistic Japan*, published monthly, with tipped-in, high-quality color reproductions of Japanese prints, from 1888 to 1891. It is likely that Wilde attended the exhibition of Hokusai's drawings and prints held at the Fine Art Society in 1890.

137. The painter-etcher Mortimer Menpes, a close friend of Wilde's and godfather to one of his children, visited Japan in 1887. He exhibited

the chance of painting, were a few lanterns and some fans. He was quite unable to discover the inhabitants, as his delightful exhibition at Messrs. Dowdeswell's Gallery showed only too well. He did not know that the Japanese people are, as I have said, simply a mode of style, an exquisite fancy of art. And so, if you desire to see a Japanese effect, you will not behave like a tourist and go to Tokio.[138] On the contrary, you will stay at home and steep yourself in the work of certain Japanese artists, and then, when you have absorbed the spirit of their style, and caught their imaginative manner of vision, you will go some afternoon and sit in the Park or stroll down Piccadilly, and if you cannot see an absolutely Japanese effect there, you will not see it anywhere. Or, to return again to the past, take the Greeks. Do you think that Greek art ever tells us what the Greek people were like? Do you believe that the Athenian women were like the stately dignified figures of the Parthenon frieze, or like those marvellous goddesses who sat in the triangular pediments of the same building? If you judge from the art, they certainly were so. But read an authority, like Aristophanes for instance. You will find that the Athenian ladies laced tightly, wore high-heeled shoes, dyed their hair yellow, painted and rouged their faces, and were exactly like any silly fashionable or fallen creature of our own day.[139] The fact is that we look back on

the paintings and etchings resulting from the trip at Dowdeswell's Gallery, in New Bond Street, the following year.

138. This sentence, together with the next and the opening phrase of the one ensuing, from "And so" to "to return again to the past," added 1891.

139. As Josephine Guy suggests, Wilde is probably thinking here of the description of Athenian women in Aristophanes's bawdy comedy

the ages entirely through the medium of Art, and Art, very fortunately, has never once told us the truth.

Cyril. But modern portraits by English painters, what of them? Surely they are like the people they pretend to represent?

Vivian. Quite so. They are so like them that a hundred years from now no one will believe in them. The only portraits that one believes in are portraits where there is very little of the sitter and a very great deal of the artist. Holbein's drawings of the men and women of his time impress us with a sense of their absolute reality.[140] But this is simply because Holbein compelled life to accept his conditions, to restrain itself within his limitations, to reproduce his type, and to appear as he wished it to appear. It is style that makes us believe in a thing—nothing but style. Most of our modern portrait painters are doomed to absolute oblivion. They never paint what they see. They paint what the public sees, and the public never sees anything.

Cyril. Well, after that I think I should like to hear the end of your article.

Vivian. With pleasure. Whether it will do any good I really cannot say. Ours is certainly the dullest and most prosaic century possible. Why, even Sleep has played us false, and has

---

Lysistrata as "trimmed and bedizened in . . . saffron silks," with "finical shoes," "paints and perfumes," and "robes of gauze." Aubrey Beardsley's infamous illustrations to *Lysistrata* include depictions of the Athenian women based on these descriptions.

140. See n.60 above

closed up the gates of ivory, and opened the gates of horn.[141] The dreams of the great middle classes of this country, as recorded in Mr. Myers's two bulky volumes on the subject and in the Transactions of the Psychical Society, are the most depressing things that I have ever read.[142] There is not even a fine nightmare among them. They are commonplace, sordid, and tedious. As for the Church I cannot conceive anything better for the culture of a country than the presence in it of a body of men whose duty it is to believe in the supernatural, to perform daily miracles, and to keep alive that mythopoeic[143] faculty which is so essential for the imagination. But in the English Church a man succeeds, not through his capacity for belief, but through his capacity for disbelief. Ours is the only Church where the sceptic stands at the altar, and where St. Thomas is regarded as the ideal apostle.[144] Many a worthy clergyman, who passes his life in admirable works of kindly charity, lives and dies unnoticed and unknown; but it is sufficient for some shallow uneducated passman[145] out of

141. In Greek mythology, the gates of ivory are the gates though which fictitious and deceptive dreams emerge. By contrast, dreams "that come through the gate of polished horn bring true things to pass, when any mortal sees them" (*The Odyssey*).

142. Frederick Myers (1843–1910) was a pioneering psychologist, occultist, and president of the Society for Psychical Research, which he cofounded in 1882. His two-volume *Phantasms of the Living* (1886), cowritten with Edmund Gurney and Frank Podmore, was an important precursor to Freud's *The Interpretation of Dreams*.

143. Mythmaking.

144. According to John 20:24–29, the apostle Saint Thomas doubted Christ's resurrection and demanded to feel Christ's wounds before being convinced.

145. For a *passman,* see p. 159, n.36 above.

either University[146] to get up in his pulpit and express his doubts about Noah's ark, or Balaam's ass, or Jonah and the whale, for half of London to flock to hear him, and to sit openmouthed in rapt admiration at his superb intellect. The growth of common-sense in the English Church is a thing very much to be regretted. It is really a degrading concession to a low form of realism. It is silly, too.[147] It springs from an entire ignorance of psychology. Man can believe the impossible, but man can never believe the improbable. However, I must read the end of my article:—

"What we have to do, what at any rate it is our duty to do, is to revive this old art of Lying. Much of course may be done, in the way of educating the public, by amateurs in the domestic circle, at literary lunches, and at afternoon teas. But this is merely the light and graceful side of lying, such as was probably heard at Cretan dinner parties.[148] There are many other forms. Lying for the sake of gaining some immediate personal advantage, for instance—lying with a moral purpose, as it is usually called—though of late it has been rather looked down upon, was extremely popular with the antique world. Athena laughs when Odysseus tells her 'his words of sly devising,' as Mr. William Morris phrases it,[149] and the glory

146. Cambridge and Oxford were widely considered the only universities fit for Victorian gentlemen, despite the growth of new metropolitan and provincial universities.

147. This sentence and the next two, from "It is silly" to "the improbable," added 1891.

148. The Cretan philosopher Epimenides (c. 600 BCE) proclaimed paradoxically that "all Cretans are liars."

149. When Odysseus attempts to deceive Pallas Athena about his identity, upon arriving back in Ithaca, the latter smiles and remarks "Ah,

of mendacity illumines the pale brow of the stainless hero of Euripidean tragedy,[150] and sets amongst the noble women of the past the young bride of one of Horace's most exquisite odes.[151] Later on, what at first had been merely a natural instinct was elevated into a self-conscious science. Elaborate rules were laid down for the guidance of mankind, and an important school of literature grew up round the subject. Indeed, when one remembers the excellent philosophical treatise of Sanchez on the whole question, one cannot help regretting that no one has ever thought of publishing a cheap and condensed edition of the works of that great casuist.[152]

---

cunning were he and shifty, who thee should overbear / In guilefulness . . . / And thy words of sly devising" (*The Odyssey of Homer: Done into English Verse*, tr. William Morris [London: Reeves and Turner, 1887], 13.l.291–295)

150. In Euripedes's tragedy *Ion*, the hero promises his mother that he will "bury all of it in darkness" if she only tells him who his father truly is. When she answers that he was fathered by Apollo, not by her husband Xouthos—and is confirmed in this statement by the goddess Athena—Ion promises to hide the truth, and to maintain Xouthos's belief in his paternity, in order that he may assume the mantle of ruler of Athens.

151. In Greek mythology, the daughters of Danaus were made to marry the fifty sons of Danaus's twin brother Aegyptus, a mythical king of Egypt. All but one of them, Hypermestra, killed their husbands on their wedding night and were thereafter condemned to spend eternity carrying water in a perforated urn. In his ode about this myth, the Latin poet Horace writes "The only one of their number worthy of the marriage torch was magnificently deceitful towards her scheming father, a girl who won everlasting fame" (Odes III.11, in Horace, *Odes and Epodes* ed. and tr. Niall Rudd [Cambridge, MA: Harvard Univ. Press, 2004], 175)

152. A *casuist* is a theologian who studies doubtful questions of duty, conduct, and belief. Wilde alludes to *Quod Nihil Scitur* (*That Nothing Is Known*), written in 1576 by the Portuguese philosopher Francisco Sanches,

A short primer, 'When to Lie and How,' if brought out in an attractive and not too expensive a form, would no doubt command a large sale, and would prove of real practical service to many earnest and deep-thinking people. Lying for the sake of the improvement of the young, which is the basis of home education, still lingers among us, and its advantages are so admirably set forth in the early books of Plato's *Republic* that it is unnecessary to dwell upon them here.[153] It is a mode of lying for which all good mothers have peculiar capabilities, but it is capable of still further development, and has been sadly overlooked by the School Board. Lying for the sake of a monthly salary is of course well known in Fleet Street,[154] and the profession of a political leader-writer is not without its advantages. But it is said to be a somewhat dull occupation, and it certainly does not lead to much beyond a kind of ostentatious obscurity. The only form of lying that is absolutely beyond reproach is Lying for its own sake, and the highest development of this is, as we have already pointed out, Lying in Art. Just as those who do not love Plato more than Truth cannot pass beyond the threshold of the Academe, so those who do not love Beauty more than Truth never know the inmost shrine of Art. The solid stolid

---

in which Sanches argues that perfect knowledge is unattainable and that man's senses restrict him to a knowledge of appearances only, never of real substances.

153. Vivian refers to books 2 and 3 of Plato's *Republic*, particularly to Socrates's formulation of the "useful" lie, when "we make falsehood as much like truth as we can, and so turn it to account" (*The Portable Plato*, ed. Scott Buchanan [New York: Penguin, 1977], 361).

154. English journalism was synonymous with London's Fleet Street, where England's popular newspapers were housed.

British intellect lies in the desert sands like the Sphinx in Flaubert's marvellous tale, and fantasy, *La Chimère,* dances round it, and calls to it with her false, flute-toned voice.[155] It may not hear her now, but surely some day, when we are all bored to death with the commonplace character of modern fiction, it will hearken to her and try to borrow her wings.

"And when that day dawns, or sunset reddens, how joyous we shall all be! Facts will be regarded as discreditable, Truth will be found mourning over her fetters, and Romance, with her temper of wonder, will return to the land. The very aspect of the world will change to our startled eyes. Out of the sea will rise Behemoth and Leviathan, and sail round the high-pooped galleys, as they do on the delightful maps of those ages when books on geography were actually readable.[156] Dragons will wander about the waste places, and the phoenix will soar from her nest of fire into the air. We shall lay our hands upon the basilisk, and see the jewel in the toad's head. Champing his gilded oats, the Hippogriff will stand in our stalls, and over our heads will float the Blue Bird singing of beautiful and impossible things, of things that are lovely and that never happen, of things that are not and that should be. But before this comes to pass we must cultivate the lost art of Lying."

155. In Gustave Flaubert's "marvellous" novel *The Temptation of St. Anthony* (1874), the father of monasticism and hermit, St. Anthony of Egypt, is severely tested by a vision of, amongst others, the Chimera (in Greek mythology, a fire-breathing female monster) and the Sphinx.

156. Behemoth and Leviathan are a large mythical beast and a sea monster, respectively, mentioned in Job 40:15–24. Leviathan has become synonymous with any large sea monster or whale. Renaissance maps often incorporated icons of spouting whales and sailing galleys.

Cyril. Then we must certainly cultivate it at once. But in order to avoid making any error I want you to tell me briefly the doctrines of the new aesthetics.

Vivian. Briefly, then, they are these. Art never expresses anything but itself. It has an independent life, just as Thought has, and develops purely on its own lines. It is not necessarily realistic in an age of realism, nor spiritual in an age of faith. So far from being the creation of its time, it is usually in direct opposition to it, and the only history that it preserves for us is the history of its own progress. Sometimes it returns upon its footsteps, and revives some antique form, as happened in the archaistic movement of late Greek Art, and in the pre-Raphaelite movement of our own day. At other times it entirely anticipates its age, and produces in one century work that it takes another century to understand, to appreciate, and to enjoy. In no case does it reproduce its age. To pass from the art of a time to the time itself is the great mistake that all historians commit.

The second doctrine is this. All bad art comes from returning to Life and Nature, and elevating them into ideals. Life and Nature may sometimes be used as part of Art's rough material, but before they are of any real service to art they must be translated into artistic conventions. The moment Art surrenders its imaginative medium it surrenders everything. As a method Realism is a complete failure, and the two things that every artist should avoid are modernity of form and modernity of subject-matter. To us, who live in the nineteenth century, any century is a suitable subject for art except our own. The only beautiful things are the things that do not concern us. It is, to have the pleasure of quoting myself, exactly because Hecuba is nothing to us that her sorrows are so suitable a motive for a tragedy. Besides, it is only the modern that ever becomes old-fashioned. M. Zola sits down to give us a picture of the Second Empire.[157] Who cares for the Second Empire now? It is out of date. Life goes faster than Realism, but Romanticism is always in front of Life.

The third doctrine is that Life imitates Art far more than Art imitates Life. This results not merely from Life's imitative instinct, but from the fact that the self-conscious aim of Life is simply to find expression, and that Art offers it certain beautiful forms through which it may realize that energy. It is a theory that has never been put forward before, but it is extremely fruitful, and throws an entirely new light upon the history of Art.

It follows, as a corollary from this, that external Nature also imitates Art. The only effects that she can show us are effects that we have already seen through poetry, or in paintings. This is the secret of Nature's charm, as well as the explanation of Nature's weakness.[158]

The final revelation is that Lying, the telling of beautiful untrue things, is the proper aim of Art. But of this I think I have spoken at sufficient length. And now let us go out on the terrace, where "droops the milk-white peacock like a ghost," while the evening star "washes the dusk with silver."[159]

157. See nn. 24, 25, and 28 above. France's Second Empire, under the Bonapartist regime of Napoleon III, lasted from 1852 to 1870.

158. This short paragraph added 1891.

159. "Now droops the milk-white peacock like a ghost. / And like a ghost she glimmers on to me" (Tennyson, *The Princess*); "Speak silence with thy glimmering eyes, / And wash the dusk with silver" (Blake, "To The Evening Star").

At twilight nature becomes a wonderfully suggestive effect, and is not without loveliness, though perhaps its chief use is to illustrate quotations from the poets. Come! We have talked long enough.

Pen Pencil and Poison: A Study in Green[†]

It has constantly been made a subject of reproach against artists and men of letters that they are lacking in wholeness and completeness of nature. As a rule this must necessarily be so. That very

† Wilde's memoir of the writer, artist, forger, and murderer Thomas Griffiths Wainewright (1794–1847) is his most important meditation on the congruity of art and crime, as well as an argument for the irrelevance of moral considerations in appreciating art. It was inspired partly by Swinburne, who had remarked of Wainewright, in *William Blake: A Critical Study* (1866), "with pen, with palette, or with poison, his hand was never a mere craftsman's." It implicitly takes issue with Thomas Carlyle, who had remarked without irony in *On Heroes, Hero-Worship, and the Heroic* that "I have no notion of a truly great man that could not be all sorts of men" and, more specifically, that "the man-of-letters . . . is, in various respects, a very singular phenomenon. . . . Few shapes of Heroism can be more unexpected." Wilde drew heavily from *Essays and Criticisms by Thomas Griffiths Wainewright*, ed. W. Carew Hazlitt (1880), as he acknowledges at the memoir's conclusion. However, Wilde departs dramatically from Hazlitt by depicting Wainewright as an apostle of art for art's sake. First published, signed, with the subtitle "A Study" in Jan. 1889 in *Fortnightly Review* (where it was preceded and followed by literary essays penned by Swinburne and John Addington Symonds respectively), the memoir was extensively revised for republication in *Intentions* (1891), where it appeared with its present, more Whistleresque subtitle. The *Intentions* version is printed here. For the subtitle's debt to Whistler's paintings, see Nicholas Frankel, *Oscar Wilde's Decorated Books* (Ann Arbor: Univ. of Michigan Press, 2000), 99.

concentration of vision and intensity of purpose which is the characteristic of the artistic temperament is in itself a mode of limitation. To those who are pre-occupied with the beauty of form nothing else seems of much importance. Yet there are many exceptions to this rule. Rubens served as ambassador, and Goethe as state councillor, and Milton as Latin secretary to Cromwell.[160] Sophocles held civic office in his own city; the humorists, essayists, and novelists of modern America seem to desire nothing better than to become the diplomatic representatives of their country;[161] and Charles Lamb's friend, Thomas Griffiths Wainewright, the subject of this brief memoir, though of an extremely artistic temperament, followed many masters other than art, being not merely a poet and a painter, an art-critic, an antiquarian, and a writer of prose, an amateur of

160. During lengthy stays at the courts of Philip IV of Spain and Charles I of England, the artist Peter Paul Rubens (1577–1640) combined the roles of painter and diplomat; the poet Johann Wolfgang von Goethe was a councillor at the court of Karl August of Saxe-Weimar; following Parliament's victory under Oliver Cromwell in the English Civil War, the poet John Milton was appointed Secretary for Foreign Tongues in March 1649. Though Milton's main task was to compose the English Republic's foreign correspondence in Latin, he also produced propaganda for Cromwell's regime and served as a censor.

161. The playwright Sophocles (c. 496–406 BCE) was elected a general in or around 441 BCE, and seven years before his death, he was one of ten elders appointed by the city of Athens to a committee of public safety, with responsibility for saving the Athenian regime following its disastrous incursion into Syracuse. See Ruth Scodel, "Sophocles' Biography" and Robin Osborne, "What Was Sophocles' Own Political Position?" in *A Companion to Sophocles,* ed. Kirk Ormand (Oxford: Wiley-Blackwell, 2012), 25–37 and 271–273. The writers Washington Irving, Nathaniel Hawthorne, William Dean Howells, Bret Harte, and James Russell Lowell were all diplomatic representatives of the United States.

Thomas Griffiths Wainewright, *Portrait of a Young Man (Self-Portrait)*. c. 1825. Pencil and watercolor on paper.

beautiful things, and a dilettante of things delightful, but also a forger of no mean or ordinary capabilities, and as a subtle and secret poisoner almost without rival in this or any age.

This remarkable man, so powerful with "pen, pencil, and poison," as a great poet of our own day has finely said of him,[162] was born at Chiswick, in 1794. His father was the son of a distinguished solicitor

162. See headnote p. 245 above

of Gray's Inn and Hatton Garden.[163] His mother was the daughter of the celebrated Dr. Griffiths, the editor and founder of the *Monthly Review*, the partner in another literary speculation of Thomas Davies, that famous bookseller of whom Johnson said that he was not a bookseller, but "a gentleman who dealt in books," the friend of Goldsmith and Wedgwood, and one of the most well-known men of his day.[164] Mrs. Wainewright died, in giving him birth, at the early age of twenty-one, and an obituary notice in the *Gentleman's Magazine* tells us of her "amiable disposition and numerous accomplishments," and adds somewhat quaintly that "she is supposed to have understood the writings of Mr. Locke as well as perhaps any person of either sex now living."[165] His father did not long survive his young wife, and the little child seems to have

163. In Wainewright's day, Chiswick was a village on the north bank of the River Thames, about fifteen miles southwest of central London, though its population grew tenfold in the nineteenth century and it is now part of the London metropolis. Gray's Inn is one of four Inns of Court in the city of London, where barristers train and practice (see n.17 above); the district of Hatton Garden, famous for its jewelers, is located nearby.

164. As well as founding and editing the influential *Monthly Review*, Ralph Griffiths, LLD (1720–1803) was the publisher of John Cleland's *Fanny Hill* (1749). Thomas Davies (1712–1785), a friend of the playwright Oliver Goldsmith as well as of the pottery manufacturer Josiah Wedgwood, was a publisher, bookseller, and actor of wide repute. Wilde follows Hazlitt in attributing the remark "not a bookseller, but a gentleman dealing in books" to Dr. Johnson, although an earlier source (John Nichols, *Literary Anecdotes of the Eighteenth Century* [1812–1815]) attributes the remark to Thomas Campbell instead.

165. *Gentleman's Magazine* (October 1784): 965. The brief obituary is reprinted in its entirety in Hazlitt's introduction to *Essays and Criticisms*, xiii. John Locke is the grandfather of British empiricist philosophy.

been brought up by his grandfather, and, on the death of the latter in 1803, by his uncle George Edward Griffiths, whom he subsequently poisoned. His boyhood was passed at Linden House, Turnham Green,[166] one of those many fine Georgian mansions that have unfortunately disappeared before the inroads of the sub-urban builder, and to its lovely gardens and well-timbered park he owed that simple and impassioned love of nature which never left him all through his life, and which made him so peculiarly sus-ceptible to the spiritual influences of Wordsworth's poetry. He went to school at Charles Burney's academy at Hammersmith.[167] Mr. Burney was the son of the historian of music,[168] and the near kinsman of the artistic lad who was destined to turn out his most remarkable pupil. He seems to have been a man of a good deal of culture, and in after years Mr. Wainewright often spoke of him with much affection as a philosopher, an archaeologist, and an admirable teacher who, while he valued the intellectual side of education, did not forget the importance of early moral training. It was under Mr. Burney that he first developed his talent as an artist, and Mr. Hazlitt[169] tells us that a drawing-book which he

166. Turnham Green, just north of Chiswick, was an outlying rural district of London, though as Wilde acknowledges, it had been subsumed into London's suburbia by Wilde's day.

167. Charles Burney (1757–1817) was a distinguished Classical scholar who opened his own school at Hammersmith in 1786. Wilde distorts Hazlitt in stating that Wainewright was schooled at Hammersmith: Hazlitt locates Burney's Academy "at Hammersmith or Greenwich" (*Essays and Criticisms*, xviii). In fact, Wainewright was schooled at Greenwich, in southeast London, where Burney had moved his academy in 1793.

168. Dr. Charles Burney (1726–1814), distinguished musical historian.

169. William Carew Hazlitt (1834–1913), Wilde's principal source for facts about Wainewright's life and writings, not to be confused with his

used at school is still extant, and displays great talent and natural feeling. Indeed, painting was the first art that fascinated him. It was not till much later that he sought to find expression by pen or poison.

Before this, however, he seems to have been carried away by boyish dreams of the romance and chivalry of a soldier's life, and to have become a young guardsman. But the reckless dissipated life of his companions failed to satisfy the refined artistic temperament of one who was made for other things. In a short time he wearied of the service. "Art," he tells us, in words that still move many by their ardent sincerity and strange fervour, "Art touched her renegade; by her pure and high influences the noisome mists were purged; my feelings, parched, hot, and tarnished, were renovated with cool, fresh bloom, simple, beautiful to the simple-hearted."[170] But Art was not the only cause of the change. "The writings of Wordsworth," he goes on to say, "did much towards calming the confusing whirl necessarily incident to sudden mutations. I wept over them tears of happiness and gratitude."[171] He accordingly left the army, with its rough barrack-life and coarse mess-room tittle-tattle, and returned to Linden House, full of this new-born enthusiasm for culture. A severe illness, in which, to use his own words, he was "broken like a vessel of clay,"[172] prostrated him for a time. His delicately strung organization, however indifferent it

more famous grandfather William Hazlitt, Wainewright's contemporary, whom Wilde refers to simply as "Hazlitt."

170. Wainewright, "Janus Weatherbound; or the Weathercock Steadfast for Lack of Oil," *London Magazine,* Jan. 1823, rpt. in *Essays and Criticisms,* ed. Hazlitt, 305. Wilde has subtly altered Wainewright's awkward phrase "a cool fresh bloom, childly, simple, beautiful to the simple-hearted" (*sic*).

171. Wainewright, "Janus Weatherbound," 305

172. Wainewright, "Janus Weatherbound," 305

might have been to inflicting pain on others, was itself most keenly sensitive to pain. He shrank from suffering as a thing that mars and maims human life, and seems to have wandered through that terrible valley of melancholia from which so many great, perhaps greater, spirits have never emerged. But he was young—only twenty-five years of age—and he soon passed out of the "dead black waters," as he called them,[173] into the larger air of humanistic culture. As he was recovering from the illness that had led him almost to the gates of death, he conceived the idea of taking up literature as an art. "I said with John Woodvill," he cries, "It were a life of gods to dwell in such an element," to see, and hear, and write brave things:—

> "These high and gusty relishes of life
> Have no allayings of mortality."[174]

It is impossible not to feel that in this passage we have the utterance of a man who had a true passion for letters. "To see, and hear, and write brave things,"[175] this was his aim.

Scott, the editor of the *London Magazine*,[176] struck by the young man's genius, or under the influence of the strange fascination that

---

173. Wainewright, "Janus Weatherbound," 306.

174. Wainewright, "Janus Weatherbound," 307. Wainewright is here quoting from Charles Lamb's dramatic poem *John Woodvil* (misspelled by Hazlitt as "Woodvill").

175. Wainewright, "Janus Weatherbound," 307.

176. John Scott (1783–1821) was founding editor of the *London Magazine*, a major organ of Romantic-era prose. The magazine flourished briefly—but very successfully at first—from 1820–1829. Besides Wainewright and Lamb, it provided a forum for William Wordsworth, John Keats, William Hazlitt, Thomas Carlyle, and John Clare among others.

THE CRITICAL WRITINGS OF OSCAR WILDE

he exercised on every one who knew him, invited him to write a series of articles on artistic subjects, and under a series of fanciful pseudonyms he began to contribute to the literature of his day. *Janus Weathercock, Egomet Bonmot,* and *Van Vinkvooms,* were some of the grotesque masks under which he chose to hide his seriousness, or to reveal his levity. [177] A mask tells us more than a face. These disguises intensified his personality. In an incredibly short time he seems to have made his mark. Charles Lamb speaks of "kind, light-hearted Wainewright," whose prose is "capital."[178] We hear of him entertaining Macready, John Forster, Maginn, Talfourd, Sir Wentworth Dilke, the poet John Clare, and others, at a *petit-diner.*[179] Like Disraeli, he determined to startle the town as a dandy,[180]

177. In 1891 Wilde revised this sentence heavily, although he failed to correct his misreading of Wainewright's pseudonym "Vinkbooms," and also added the two sentences that immediately follow it. The revised and added sentences closely echo Wilde's notions that "insincerity. . . . is merely a method by which we can multiply our personalities" (Wilde, *The Picture of Dorian Gray: An Annotated, Uncensored Edition,* 203) and that "Man is least himself when he talks in his own person. Give him a mask and he will tell you the truth" (Wilde, *Criticism,* 185). As he had written in "The Decay of Lying," "what is interesting about people in good society . . . is the mask that each one of them wears, not the reality that lies behind the mask" (p. 199 above).

178. Lamb, quoted in Hazlitt's introduction to *Essays and Criticisms,* xxx–xxxi.

179. John Forster, William McGinn, Sir Thomas Noon Talfourd, Charles Wentworth Dilke, and John Clare were all eminent literary men. William Macready, the preeminent tragic actor of his day, was their close associate. A *petit-diner* is an informal dinner.

180. The novelist and politician Benjamin Disraeli, later prime minister of Britain, dressed as a dandy in order to "startle the town" in the early years of his career.

and his beautiful rings, his antique cameo breast-pin, and his pale lemon-coloured kid gloves, were well known, and indeed were regarded by Hazlitt as being the signs of a new manner in literature: while his rich curly hair, fine eyes, and exquisite white hands gave him the dangerous and delightful distinction of being different from others. There was something in him of Balzac's Lucien de Rubempré. At times he reminds us of Julien Sorel.[181] De Quincey saw him once. It was at a dinner at Charles Lamb's. "Amongst the company, all literary men, sat a murderer," he tells us, and he goes on to describe how on that day he had been ill, and had hated the face of man and woman, and yet found himself looking with intellectual interest across the table at the young writer beneath whose affectations of manner there seemed to him to lie so much unaffected sensibility, and speculates on "what sudden growth of another interest" would have changed his mood, had he known of what terrible sin the guest to whom Lamb paid so much attention was even then guilty.[182]

His life-work falls naturally under the three heads suggested by Mr. Swinburne, and it may be partly admitted that, if we set aside his achievements in the sphere of poison, what he has actually left to us hardly justifies his reputation.[183]

181. For Lucien de Rubembré, see n.58 above. Julien Sorel is the hero of Stendhal's 1830 novel *Le Rouge et Le Noir* (The Red and The Black).

182. The last three sentences of this paragraph added 1891. The direct quotations are from Thomas De Quincey's essay "Charles Lamb," in his *Biographical Essays* (Boston: Ticknor and Fields, 1861), 206–208, although De Quincey states that the dinner party took place "at the house of Messrs. Taylor & Hessey, the publishers" (206).

183. For "the three heads suggested by Mr. Swinburne," see headnote p. 245 above. In the 1889 version, this witty paragraph began, "It must be admitted that his literary work hardly justifies his reputation" before

But then it is only the Philistine who seeks to estimate a personality by the vulgar test of production.[184] This young dandy sought to be somebody, rather than to do something. He recognized that Life itself is an art, and has its modes of style no less than the arts that seek to express it. Nor is his work without interest. We hear of William Blake stopping in the Royal Academy before one of his pictures and pronouncing it to be "very fine."[185] His essays are prefiguring of much that has since been realized. He seems to have anticipated some of those accidents of modern culture that are regarded by many as true essentials. He writes about La Gioconda, and early French poets and the Italian Renaissance. He loves Greek gems, and Persian carpets, and Elizabethan translations of *Cupid and Psyche,* and the *Hypnerotomachia,* and bookbindings, and early editions, and wide-margined proofs. He is keenly sensitive to the value of beautiful surroundings, and never wearies of describing to us the rooms in which he lived, or would have liked to live.[186] He had that curious love of green, which in individuals is always the sign of a subtle artistic temperament, and in nations is said to denote a laxity, if not a decadence of

---

continuing (with no paragraph break) with the sentences that make up the next paragraph in the present (1891) version.

184. For "Philistine," see p. 43, n.2 and p. 115, n.5 above

185. This sentence and the next two added 1891.

186. In Wilde's account, Wainewright shares many interests in common with the aesthetes of the 1880s and 1890s, especially Walter Pater, the fountainhead of late-Victorian aesthetic thought. In *The Renaissance*, Pater had written memorably about Leonardo's *La Gioconda*, the Italian Renaissance, and early French romances; and Pater's meditation "The Child in The House" includes a description of the rooms in which he had grown up.

morals.[187] Like Baudelaire he was extremely fond of cats, and with Gautier, he was fascinated by that "sweet marble monster" of both sexes that we can still see at Florence and in the Louvre.[188]

There is of course much in his descriptions, and his suggestions for decoration, that shows that he did not entirely free himself from the false taste of his time. But it is clear that he was one of the first to recognize what is, indeed, the very keynote of aesthetic eclecticism, I mean the true harmony of all really beautiful things irrespective of age or place, of school or manner.[189] He saw that in decorating a room, which is to be, not a room for show, but a room to live in, we should never aim at any archaeological reconstruction of the past, nor burden ourselves with any fanciful necessity

187. Wilde was famous for his love of "artistic" green—and following Robert Hichens's thinly veiled satire *The Green Carnation* (1894), he was virtually synonymous with the specially dyed green carnation he wore in his buttonhole to the opening of *Lady Windermere's Fan*.

188. Baudelaire's *Les Fleurs du Mal* (Flowers of Evil) contains several cat poems; Gautier's fascination with the Borghese Hermaphroditus, a marble statue depicting the twin-sexed god Hermaphroditus, is evident from his poem "Contralto," which appeared in his collection *Emaux et Camées*. Percy Bysshe Shelley, from whom Wilde quotes here, had referred to the statue as "that sweet marble monster of both sexes" in his "Studies for 'Epipsychidion.'" Wilde would also have known Swinburne's poem "Hermaphroditus," immortalizing the statue for English-language readers. Copies of the statue are housed in the Louvre in Paris, and in the Villa Borghese at Florence. But Wilde is describing his own fascinations here as much as Wainewright's: Wilde's poem *The Sphinx* was partly inspired by Baudelaire's cat poems, while the Borghese Hermaphroditus features briefly in *Dorian Gray* too.

189. Wilde implies that Wainewright was a forerunner of ideas about decoration and beauty that Wilde himself later laid out in his lectures "The House Beautiful" and "The Decorative Arts," as well as in the dialogues "The Decay of Lying" and "The Critic as Artist."

for historical accuracy. In this artistic perception he was perfectly right. All beautiful things belong to the same age.

And so, in his own library, as he describes it, we find the delicate fictile vase of the Greek, with its exquisitely painted figures and the faint ΚΑΛΟΣ finely traced upon its side,[190] and behind it hangs an engraving of the "Delphic Sibyl" of Michael Angelo, or of the "Pastoral" of Giorgione. Here is a bit of Florentine majolica, and here a rude lamp from some old Roman tomb. On the table lies a book of Hours, "cased in a cover of solid silver gilt, wrought with quaint devices and studded with small brilliants and rubies," and close by it "squats a little ugly monster, a Lar, perhaps, dug up in the sunny fields of corn-bearing Sicily."[191] Some dark antique bronzes contrast "with the pale gleam of two noble *Christi Crucifixi,* one carved in ivory, the other moulded in wax."[192] He has his trays of Tassie's gems,[193] his tiny Louis-Quatorze *bonbonnière* with a miniature by Petitot,[194] his highly prized "brown-biscuit teapots,

---

190. ΚΑΛΟΣ means "beautiful." *Fictile* means "made of clay." Wilde here closely follows Wainewright's own description of his library, in "Van Vinkbooms: His Dogmas for Dilettanti" (in *Essays and Criticisms,* ed. Hazlitt, 209–234), with its "fictile vase" (222) and engravings of the "Delphic Sybil" and "Pastorale" of Michelangelo and Giorgione respectively (224 and 227).

191. Wainewright, "Van Vinkbooms," 222. A *Lar* is a Roman household god.

192. Wainewright, "Van Vinkbooms," 223–224.

193. Gems engraved and adorned by the Scottish jeweler James Tassie (1735–1799).

194. A small reticule for keeping sweets or *bonbons,* dating from the period of Louis XIV, incorporating a miniature painted portrait in enamel by Jean-Louis Petitot (1607–1691).

filagree-worked," his citron morocco letter-case, and his "pomona-green" chair.[195]

One can fancy him lying there in the midst of his books and casts and engravings, a true virtuoso, a subtle connoisseur, turning over his fine collection of Marc Antonios, and his Turner's "Liber Studiorum," of which he was a warm admirer, or examining with a magnifier some of his antique gems and cameos, "the head of Alexander on an onyx of two strata," or "that superb *altissimo relievo* on cornelian, Jupiter Aegiochus."[196] He was always a great amateur[197] of engravings, and gives some very useful suggestions as to the best means of forming a collection. Indeed, while fully appreciating modern art, he never lost sight of the importance of reproductions of the great masterpieces of the past, and all that he says about the value of plaster casts is quite admirable.

As an art-critic he concerned himself primarily with the complex impressions produced by a work of art, and certainly the first

195. Wainewright, "Van Vinkbooms," 221, 234.

196. Wainewright, "Van Vinkbooms," 212, 223. Marcantonio Raimondi (c. 1480–c. 1543) engraved fine reproductions of paintings by Raphael and Giulio Romano. *Liber Studiorum,* a collection of seventy prints produced between 1807–1819 in homage to *Liber Veritas* by the French landscape painter Claude Lorraine, has been called Turner's "personal manifesto of his ambitions for landscape art" (Tate Online); Wainewright meticulously examines cameos painted on onyx and cornelian, depicting Alexander the Great and the Roman god Jupiter respectively; cornelian, mentioned fleetingly in *The Picture of Dorian Gray* as possessing the power to appease anger, is a translucent, orange, semi-precious stone; *altissimo relievo,* meaning "highest relief," is a sculptural technique whereby an image is carved with maximum possible projection from its ground or backdrop, thereby providing it with the air of depth or three-dimensionality.

197. Lover or connoisseur, from the Latin *amare* ("to love").

step in aesthetic criticism is to realize one's own impressions.[198] He cared nothing for abstract discussions on the nature of the Beautiful,[199] and the historical method, which has since yielded such rich fruit, did not belong to his day, but he never lost sight of the great truth that Art's first appeal is neither to the intellect nor to the emotions, but purely to the artistic temperament, and he more than once points out that this temperament, this "taste," as he calls it, being unconsciously guided and made perfect by frequent contact with the best work, becomes in the end a form of right judgment.[200] Of course there are fashions in art just as there are fashions in dress, and perhaps none of us can ever quite free ourselves from the influence of custom and the influence of novelty. He certainly could not, and he frankly acknowledges how difficult it is to form

198. In "Janus Weathercock's Reasons Against Writing An Account of 'The Exhibition,'" Wainewright had declared that criticism is "neither more nor less than a genuine exposition of the impressions by a given subject on a tasteful mind" (*Essays and Criticisms,* ed. Hazlitt, 246). But as Guy has observed, Wilde is deliberately recouching Wainewright's ideas in terms that echo Walter Pater's famous aesthetic declaration, in his preface to *The Renaissance,* that "the first step towards seeing one's object as it really is, is to know one's own impression as it really is, to discriminate it, to realise it distinctly."

199. Cf. Pater: "What is important . . . is not that the critic should possess a correct abstract definition of beauty for the intellect, but a certain kind of temperament, the power of being deeply moved by the presence of beautiful objects" (Pater, Preface to *The Renaissance*, ed. Donald L. Hill [Berkeley: Univ. of California Press, 1980], xxi).

200. An echo of Matthew Arnold, who had declared, in his preface to *Literature and Dogma* (1873), that "culture implies not only knowledge but right tact and justness of judgement" and, in *Culture and Anarchy* (see p. 115, n.5 above), that "culture is *to know the best that has been thought and said in the world.*"

any fair estimate of contemporary work. But, on the whole, his taste was good and sound. He admired Turner and Constable at a time when they were not so much thought of as they are now, and saw that for the highest landscape art we require more than "mere industry and accurate transcription."[201] Of Crome's "Heath Scene near Norwich" he remarks that it shows "how much a subtle observation of the elements, in their wild moods, does for a most uninteresting flat,"[202] and of the popular type of landscape of his day he says that it is "simply an enumeration of hill and dale, stumps of trees, shrubs, water, meadows, cottages, and houses; little more than topography, a kind of pictorial map-work; in which rainbows, showers, mists, haloes, large beams shooting through rifted clouds, storms, starlight, all the most valued materials of the real painter, are not."[203] He had a thorough dislike of what is obvious or commonplace in art, and while he was charmed to entertain Wilkie at dinner, he cared as little for Sir David's pictures as he did for Mr. Crabbe's poems. With the imitative and realistic tendencies of his day he had no sympathy, and he tells us frankly that his great admiration for Fuseli was largely due to the fact that the little Swiss did not consider it necessary that an artist should only paint what he sees. The qualities that he sought for in a picture were composition, beauty and dignity of line, richness of colour, and imaginative power. Upon the other hand, he was not a doctrinaire.

201. Wainewright, "Exhibition of the Royal Academy," rpt. in *Essays and Criticisms,* 154. Wilde has misquoted Wainewright's phrase "mere industry and servile transcription."

202. Wainewright, "The British Institution," rpt. in *Essays and Criticisms,* 121.

203. Wainewright, "The British Institution," 116. Wilde has subtly altered this quotation by inserting "simply" and substituting "stumps" for "clumps."

"I hold that no work of art can be tried otherwise than by laws deduced from itself: whether or not it be consistent with itself is the question."[204] This is one of his excellent aphorisms. And in criticising painters so different as Landseer and Martin, Stothard and Etty, he shows that, to use a phrase now classical, he is trying "to see the object as in itself it really is."[205]

However, as I pointed out before, he never feels quite at his ease in his criticisms of contemporary work. "The present," he says, "is about as agreeable a confusion to me as Ariosto on the first perusal. . . . Modern things dazzle me. I must look at them through Time's telescope. Elia complains that to him the merit of a MS. poem is uncertain; 'print,' as he excellently says, 'settles it.' Fifty years' toning does the same thing to a picture."[206] He is happier when he is writing about Watteau and Lancret, about Rubens and Giorgione, about Rembrandt, Correggio, and Michael Angelo; happiest of all when he is writing about Greek things. What is Gothic touched him very little, but classical art and the art of the Renaissance were always dear to him. He saw what our English school could gain from a study of Greek models, and never wearies

204. Wainewright, "Janus Weathercock's Reasons," 261–222. Wilde has subtly altered this quotation by substituting "art" for "ability," by changing Wainewright's punctuation slightly, and also by inserting "is the question" at the end of the quote.

205. Wilde is invoking Matthew Arnold's influential definition of criticism, first given in "On Translating Homer" and famously repeated in "The Function of Criticism at the Present Time." For Walter Pater's reformulation of Arnold's notion, see p. 30, n.9 above. For Wilde's own engagement with (and ultimate rejection of) Arnold's notion, see "The Critic as Artist" below, esp. pp. 307–308.

206. Wainwright, "Exhibition of the Royal Academy," rpt. in *Essays and Criticisms*, 145, 143. Wilde has made changes to Wainewright's own wording. Elia was the pen name of Charles Lamb.

of pointing out to the young student the artistic possibilities that lie dormant in Hellenic marbles and Hellenic methods of work. In his judgments on the great Italian Masters, says De Quincey, "There seemed a tone of sincerity and of native sensibility, as in one who spoke for himself, and was not merely a copier from books." The highest praise that we can give to him is that he tried to revive style as a conscious tradition. But he saw that no amount of art-lectures or art congresses, or "plans for advancing the fine arts," will ever produce this result.[207] The people, he says very wisely, and in the true spirit of Toynbee Hall, must always have "the best models constantly before their eyes."[208]

As is to be expected from one who was a painter, he is often extremely technical in his art criticisms. Of Tintoret's "St. George delivering the Egyptian Princess from the Dragon" he remarks:—

"The robe of Sabra, warmly glazed with Prussian blue, is relieved from the pale greenish background by a vermilion scarf; and the full hues of both are beautifully echoed, as it were, in a lower key by the purple-lake coloured stuffs and bluish iron armour of the saint, besides an ample balance to the vivid azure drapery on the foreground in the indigo shades of the wild wood surrounding the castle."[209]

And elsewhere he talks learnedly of "a delicate Schiavone, various as a tulip-bed, with rich broken tints," of "a glowing portrait,

207. Wainewright, "Van Vinkbooms," 185
208. Wainewright, "Van Vinkbooms," 185. For Toynbee Hall, see p. 139, n.4 above.
209. Wainewright, "Van Vinkbooms," 180.

remarkable for *morbidezza,* by the scarce Moroni," and of another picture being "pulpy in the carnations."[210]

But, as a rule, he deals with his impressions of the work as an artistic whole, and tries to translate those impressions into words, to give, as it were, the literary equivalent for the imaginative and mental effect. He was one of the first to develop what has been called the art-literature of the nineteenth century, that form of literature which has found in Mr. Ruskin and Mr. Browning its two most perfect exponents.[211] His description of Lancret's *Repas Italien,* in which "a dark-haired girl, 'amorous of mischief,' lies on the daisy-powdered grass,"[212] is in some respects very charming.

210. Wainewright, "Janus Weathercock's Reasons," 255, 261. Andrea Schiavone (c. 1510–1563) was a Mannerist painter of the Italian Renaissance. Wilde has corrected Wainewright's spelling of "Morone" to "Moroni," probably on the assumption that Wainewright meant the Italian Renaissance portrait painter Giambattista Moroni (1520–1578). However, Schroeder speculates that Wainewright was referring to the earlier Italian Mannerist Domenico Morone (c. 1442–1518), whose paintings, although not portraits, are indeed scarce. In art criticism, *morbidezza* means "lifelike delicacy in flesh tints" (OED).

211. Wilde is alluding to an address on "Modern Art and Modern Life" by the statesman Sir George Otto Trevelyan, delivered in March 1887 at the opening of an art exhibition at St. Jude's School, Whitechapel, in which Trevelyan declared that "the passing generation will be famous throughout all time as the great age of art literature. In other countries, and in former days, art criticism indeed existed as a science, or a semi-science, but it was reserved tor two great Englishmen, for Ruskin and Robert Browning, to paint in glowing colours the relation between art and all that is interesting and beautiful in books and nature, history and manners" (rpt. in *Sydney Morning Herald,* May 23, 1887, 5). Wilde had previously cited Trevelyan's remarks approvingly in an 1888 book review.

212. Wainewright, "Sentimentalities on the Fine Arts, No. 2," rpt. in *Essays and Criticisms,* 28. Wilde has substituted "lies on" for Wainewright's

Here is his account of "The Crucifixion," by Rembrandt. It is extremely characteristic of his style:—

"Darkness—sooty, portentous darkness—shrouds the whole scene: only above the accursed wood, as if through a horrid rift in the murky ceiling, a rainy deluge—'sleety-flaw, discoloured water'—streams down amain, spreading a grisly spectral light, even more horrible than that palpable night. Already the Earth pants thick and fast! the darkened Cross trembles! the winds are dropt—the air is stagnant—a muttering rumble growls underneath their feet, and some of that miserable crowd begin to fly down the hill. The horses snuff the coming terror, and become unmanageable through fear. The moment rapidly approaches when, nearly torn asunder by His own weight, fainting with loss of blood, which now runs in narrower rivulets from His slit veins, His temples and breast drowned in sweat, and His black tongue parched with the fiery death-fever, Jesus cried, 'I thirst.' The deadly vinegar is elevated to Him.

"His head sinks, and the sacred corpse 'swings senseless of the cross.' A sheet of vermilion flame shoots sheer through the air and vanishes; the rocks of Carmel and Lebanon cleave asunder; the sea rolls on high from the sands its black weltering waves. Earth yawns, and the graves give up their dwellers. The dead and the living are mingled together in unnatural conjunction and hurry through the holy city. New prodigies await them there. The veil of the temple—the unpierceable veil—is rent asunder from top to bottom, and that

---

"curled on." Nicolas Lancret (1690–1743), a French genre painter, was the best-known practitioner of the *fête galante*.

dreaded recess containing the Hebrew mysteries—the fatal ark with the tables and seven-branched candelabrum—is disclosed by the light of unearthly flames to the God-deserted multitude.

"Rembrandt never *painted* this sketch, and he was quite right. It would have lost nearly all its charms in losing that perplexing veil of indistinctness which affords such ample range wherein the doubting imagination may speculate. At present it is like a thing in another world. A dark gulf is betwixt us. It is not tangible by the body. We can only approach it in the spirit."[213]

In this passage, written, the author tells us, "in awe and reverence,"[214] there is much that is terrible, and very much that is quite horrible, but it is not without a certain crude form of power, or, at any rate, a certain crude violence of words, a quality which this age should highly appreciate, as it is its chief defect. It is pleasanter, however, to pass to this description of Giulio Romano's "Cephalus and Procris":—

"We should read Moschus's lament for Bion, the sweet shepherd, before looking at this picture, or study the picture as a preparation for the lament. We have nearly the same images in both. For either victim the high groves and forest dells murmur; the flowers exhale sad perfume from their buds; the nightingale mourns on the craggy lands, and the swallow in the long-winding vales; 'the satyrs, too, and fauns dark-veiled

213. Wainewright, "Sentimentalities on the Fine Arts, No. 3," 53–54, original quotation slightly altered by Wilde.
214. Wainewright, "Sentimentalities on the Fine Arts, No. 3," 52.

groan,' and the fountain nymphs within the wood melt into tearful waters. The sheep and goats leave their pasture; and oreads, 'who love to scale the most inaccessible tops of all up-rightest rocks,' hurry down from the song of their wind-courting pines; while the dryads bend from the branches of the meeting trees, and the rivers moan for white Procris, 'with many-sobbing streams,'

"Filling the far-seen ocean with a voice."

The golden bees are silent on the thymy Hymettus; and the knelling horn of Aurora's lore no more shall scatter away the cold twilight on the top of Hymettus. The foreground of our subject is a grassy sunburnt bank, broken into swells and hollows like waves (a sort of land-breakers), rendered more uneven by many foot-tripping roots and stumps of trees stocked untimely by the axe, which are again throwing out light green shoots. This bank rises rather suddenly on the right to a clustering grove, penetrable to no star, at the entrance of which sits the stunned Thessalian king, holding between his knees that ivory-bright body which was, but an instant agone, parting the rough boughs with her smooth forehead, and treading alike on thorns and flowers with jealousy-stung foot—now helpless, heavy, void of all motion, save when the breeze lifts her thick hair in mockery.

"From between the closely-neighboured boles astonished nymphs press forward with loud cries—

"And deerskin-vested satyrs, crowned with ivy twists,
    advance:
And put strange pity in their horned countenance."

"Laelaps lies beneath, and shows by his panting the rapid pace of death. On the other side of the group, Virtuous Love with 'vans dejected' holds forth the arrow to an approaching troop of sylvan people, fauns, rams, goats, satyrs, and satyr-mothers, pressing their children tighter with their fearful hands, who hurry along from the left in a sunken path between the foreground and a rocky wall, on whose lowest ridge a brook-guardian pours from her urn her grief-telling waters. Above and more remote than the Ephidryad, another female, rending her locks, appears among the vine-festooned pillars of an unshorn grove. The centre of the picture is filled by shady meadows, sinking down to a river-mouth; beyond is 'the vast strength of the ocean stream,' from whose floor the extinguisher of stars, rosy Aurora, drives furiously up her brine-washed steeds to behold the death-pangs of her rival."[215]

Were this description carefully rewritten, it would be quite admirable. The conception of making a prose-poem out of paint is excellent. Much of the best modern literature springs from the same aim. In a very ugly and sensible age, the arts borrow, not from life, but from each other.[216]

His sympathies, too, were wonderfully varied. In everything connected with the stage, for instance, he was always extremely interested, and strongly upheld the necessity for archaeological ac-

215. Wainewright, "Van Vinkbooms, No. 2," 203–206. "Filling the far-seen ocean with a voice" derives from Leigh Hunt's poem "On the Death of Bion, the Herdsman of Love"; Hunt's authorship was acknowledged, directly following this quotation, in Wainewright's original essay.

216. This paragraph and the first sentence of the next added 1891.

curacy in costume and scene-painting. "In art," he says in one of his essays, "whatever is worth doing at all is worth doing well;"[217] and he points out that once we allow the intrusion of anachronisms, it becomes difficult to say where the line is to be drawn. In literature, again, like Lord Beaconsfield on a famous occasion, he was "on the side of the angels."[218] He was one of the first to admire Keats and Shelley—"the tremulously-sensitive and poetical Shelley," as he calls him.[219] His admiration for Wordsworth was sincere and profound. He thoroughly appreciated William Blake.[220] One of the best copies of the "Songs of Innocence and Experience" that is now in existence was wrought specially for him. He loved Alain Chartier, and Ronsard, and the Elizabethan dramatists, and Chaucer and Chapman, and Petrarch. And to him all the arts were one. "Our critics," he remarks with much wisdom, "seem hardly aware of the identity of the primal seeds of poetry and painting, nor that any true advancement in the serious study of one art cogenerates a proportionate perfection in the other;"[221] and he says elsewhere that if a man who does not admire Michael Angelo talks of his love for Milton, he is deceiving either himself or

217. "Wainewright, "Janus's Jumble," rpt. in *Essays and Criticisms*, 82. Wainewright's observation, although proverbial, is not original. It was made originally by the fourth Earl of Chesterfield (1694–1773).

218. Benjamin Disraeli, first Earl of Beaconsfield, when asked for his reaction to Darwin's *Origin of the Species*, replied, "The question is this: is man an ape or an angel? I . . . am on the side of the angels."

219. Wainewright, "The Delicate Intricacies," rpt. in *Essays and Criticisms*, 271.

220. This sentence and the next added 1891.

221. Wainewright, "Janus Weathercock; or, The Weathercock Steadfast for Lack of Oil," 314–315.

his listeners.[222] To his fellow-contributors in the *London Magazine* he was always most generous, and praises Barry Cornwall, Allan Cunningham, Hazlitt, Elton, and Leigh Hunt without anything of the malice of a friend. Some of his sketches of Charles Lamb are admirable in their way, and, with the art of the true comedian, borrow their style from their subject:—

"What can I say of thee more than all know? that thou hadst the gaiety of a boy with the knowledge of a man: as gentle a heart as ever sent tears to the eyes.

"How wittily would he mistake your meaning, and put in a conceit most seasonably out of season. His talk without affectation was compressed, like his beloved Elizabethans, even unto obscurity. Like grains of fine gold, his sentences would beat out into whole sheets. He had small mercy on spurious fame, and a caustic observation on the *fashion for men of genius* was a standing dish. Sir Thomas Browne was a 'bosom cronie' of his; so was Burton, and old Fuller. In his amorous vein he dallied with that peerless Duchess of many-folio odour; and with the heyday comedies of Beaumont and Fletcher he induced light dreams. He would deliver critical touches on these, like one inspired, but it was good to let him choose his own game; if another began even on the acknowledged pets he was liable to interrupt, or rather append, in a mode difficult to define whether as misapprehensive or mischievous. One night at C____'s, the above dramatic partners were the temporary subject of chat. Mr. X. commended the passion and haughty style of a tragedy (I don't know which of them), but was instantly taken up by Elia, who told him

222. Wainewright, "Janus Weathercock," 314–315.

'*That* was nothing; the lyrics were the high things—the lyrics!'"[223]

One side of his literary career deserves especial notice. Modern journalism may be said to owe almost as much to him as to any man of the early part of this century. He was the pioneer of Asiatic prose, and delighted in pictorial epithets and pompous exaggerations. To have a style so gorgeous that it conceals the subject is one of the highest achievements of an important and much admired school of Fleet-Street leader-writers, and this school *Janus Weathercock* may be said to have invented.[224] He also saw that it was quite easy by continued reiteration to make the public interested in his own personality, and in his purely journalistic articles this extraordinary young man tells the world what he had for dinner, where he gets his clothes, what wines he likes, and in what state of health he is, just as if he were writing weekly notes for some popular newspaper of our own time. This being the least valuable side of his work, is the one that has had the most obvious influence. A publicist, now-a-days, is a man who bores the community with the details of the illegalities of his private life.[225]

Like most artificial people he had a great love of nature. "I hold three things in high estimation," he says somewhere: "to sit lazily on an eminence that commands a rich prospect; to be shadowed by thick trees while the sun shines around me; and to enjoy solitude with the consciousness of neighbourhood. The country gives

223. Wainewright, "Janus Weathercock," 320–322; Wilde has compressed and repunctuated this extract considerably.

224. For Fleet Street, see n.154 above.

225. This sentence added 1891.

them all to me."[226] He writes about his wandering over fragrant furze and heath repeating Collins's "Ode to Evening," just to catch the fine quality of the moment; about smothering his face "in a watery bed of cowslips, wet with May-dews;"[227] and about the pleasure of seeing the sweet-breathed kine "pass slowly homeward through the twilight," and hearing "the distant clank of the sheep-bell."[228] One phrase of his, "the polyanthus glowed in its cold bed of earth, like a solitary picture of Giorgione on a dark oaken panel,"[229] is curiously characteristic of his temperament, and this passage is rather pretty in its way—

"The short tender grass was covered with marguerites—'such that men called *daisies* in our town'—thick as stars on a summer's night. The harsh caw of the busy rooks came pleasantly mellowed from a high dusky grove of elms at some distance off, and at intervals was heard the voice of a boy scaring away the birds from the newly-sown seeds. The blue depths were the colour of the darkest ultramarine; not a cloud streaked the calm aether; only round the horizon's edge streamed a light, warm film of misty vapour, against which the near village with its ancient stone church showed sharply out with blinding whiteness. I thought of Wordsworth's 'Lines written in March.'"[230]

226. Wainewright, "Van Vinkbooms,"167. Wilde has made subtle changes to the original quotation.

227. Wainewright, "Janus's Jumble," 63.

228. Wainewright, "The British Institution," 118.

229. Wainewright, "Sentimentalities on the Fine Arts, No. 3," 35, original quotation slightly altered by Wilde.

230. Wainewright, "Sentimentalities on the Fine Arts, No. 3," 36.

However, we must not forget that the cultivated young man who penned these lines, and who was so susceptible to Wordsworthian influences, was also, as I said at the beginning of this memoir, one of the most subtle and secret poisoners of this or any age. How he first became fascinated by this strange sin he does not tell us, and the diary in which he carefully noted the results of his terrible experiments and the methods that he adopted, has unfortunately been lost to us. Even in later days, too, he was always reticent on the matter, and preferred to speak about "The Excursion," and the "Poems founded on the Affections."[231] There is no doubt, however, that the poison that he used was strychnine.[232] In one of the beautiful rings of which he was so proud, and which served to show off the fine modelling of his delicate ivory hands, he used to carry crystals of the Indian *nux vomica,* a poison, one of his biographers tells us, "nearly tasteless, difficult of discovery, and capable of almost infinite dilution."[233] His murders, says De Quincey, were more than were ever made known judicially. This is no doubt so, and some of them are worthy of mention. His first victim was his uncle,

231. This sentence added 1891.

232. A colorless, crystalline alkaloid, often used as a pesticide for small mammals and birds. Strychnine causes muscular convulsions and eventually death through asphyxia or sheer exhaustion.

233. Hazlitt, introduction to *Essays and Criticisms,* lxviii. *Nux vomica,* a borrowing from Latin meaning "vomit-inducing nut," refers to the highly poisonous seeds of the tree *Strychnos nux-vomica,* native to southern Asia, which contain strychnine. Compare with Wilde's description, in his story "Lord Arthur Savile's Crime," of the properties of the poison *aconitine:* "swift—indeed, almost immediate, in its effect—perfectly painless, and . . . not by any means unpalatable."

Mr. Thomas Griffiths.[234] He poisoned him in 1829 to gain possession of Linden House, a place to which he had always been very
much attached. In the August of the next year he poisoned
Mrs. Abercrombie, his wife's mother, and in the following December he poisoned the lovely Helen Abercrombie, his sister-
in-law. Why he murdered Mrs. Abercrombie is not ascertained. It
may have been for a caprice, or to quicken some hideous sense of
power that was in him, or because she suspected something, or for
no reason.[235] But the murder of Helen Abercrombie was carried
out by himself and his wife for the sake of a sum of about 18,000*l.*
for which they had insured her life in various offices. The circumstances were as follows. On the 12th of December, he and his wife
and child came up to London from Linden House, and took lodgings at No. 12, Conduit Street, Regent Street. With them were the
two sisters, Helen and Madeleine Abercrombie. On the evening
of the 14th they all went to the play, and at supper that night Helen
sickened. The next day she was extremely ill, and Dr. Locock,
of Hanover Square, was called in to attend her. She lived till
Monday, the 20th, when, after the doctor's morning visit, Mr. and
Mrs. Wainewright brought her some poisoned jelly, and then went
out for a walk. When they returned Helen Abercrombie was dead.
She was about twenty years of age, a tall graceful girl with fair
hair. A very charming red-chalk drawing of her by her brother-
in-law is still in existence, and shows how much his style as an artist
was influenced by Sir Thomas Lawrence, a painter for whose work
he had always entertained a great admiration. De Quincey says

234. An error. Wilde means Wainewright's uncle George Edward Griffiths. In the sentences that follow, Wilde has silently altered the spelling
of "Abercromby," in his source text, to "Abercrombie."

235. This sentence added 1891.

HELEN FRANCES PHŒBE ABERCROMBY.

FROM AN ORIGINAL DRAWING
BY T.G.WAINEWRIGHT.

Thomas Griffiths Wainewright, chalk portrait of his sister-in-law Helen Abercromby, nearly a decade before he murdered her in 1830. "A very charming red-
chalk drawing of her by her brother-in-law is still in existence," Wilde calmly
states, "and shows how much his style as an artist was influenced by Sir Thomas
Lawrence."

that Mrs. Wainewright was not really privy to the murder.[236] Let us hope that she was not. Sin should be solitary, and have no accomplices.

The insurance companies, suspecting the real facts of the case, declined to pay the policy on the technical ground of misrepresentation and want of interest, and, with curious courage, the poisoner entered an action in the Court of Chancery against the Imperial, it being agreed that one decision should govern all the cases.[237] The trial, however, did not come on for five years, when, after one disagreement, a verdict was ultimately given in the companies' favour. The judge on the occasion was Lord Abinger. *Egomet Bonmot* was represented by Mr. Erie and Sir William Follet, and the Attorney-General and Sir Frederick Pollock appeared for the other side. The plaintiff, unfortunately, was unable to be present at either of the trials. The refusal of the companies to give him the 18,000*l.* had placed him in a position of most painful pecuniary embarrassment. Indeed, a few months after the murder of Helen Abercrombie, he had actually been arrested for debt in the streets of London while he was serenading the pretty daughter of one of his friends. This difficulty was got over at the time, but shortly afterwards he thought it better to go abroad till he could come to some practical arrangement with his creditors. He accordingly went to Boulogne on a visit to the father of the young lady in question, and while he was there induced him to insure his life with the

236. This sentence and the next two added 1891.

237. The Court of Chancery, famously mocked by Dickens in *Bleak House* for its slow pace and arcane procedures, was a court in England and Wales with jurisdiction over all matters of equity, including disputes over trusts, estates, and wills. It was dissolved in 1873, to be replaced by the Chancery Division of the High Courts of Justice. The *Imperial* was an insurance company ("The Imperial Life Office").

Pelican Company[238] for 3,000*l*. As soon as the necessary formalities had been gone through and the policy executed, he dropped some crystals of strychnine into his coffee as they sat together one evening after dinner. He himself did not gain any monetary advantage by doing this. His aim was simply to revenge himself on the first office that had refused to pay him the price of his sin. His friend died the next day in his presence, and he left Boulogne at once for a sketching tour through the most picturesque parts of Brittany, and was for some time the guest of an old French gentleman, who had a beautiful country house at St. Omer. From this he moved to Paris, where he remained for several years, living in luxury, some say, while others talk of his "skulking with poison in his pocket, and being dreaded by all who knew him."[239] In 1837 he returned to England privately. Some strange mad fascination brought him back. He followed a woman whom he loved.

It was the month of June, and he was staying at one of the hotels in Covent Garden. His sitting room was on the ground floor, and he prudently kept the blinds down for fear of being seen. Thirteen years before, when he was making his fine collection of majolica and Marc Antonios, he had forged the names of his trustees to a power of attorney, which enabled him to get possession of some of the money which he had inherited from his mother, and had brought into marriage settlement. He knew that this forgery had been discovered, and that by returning to England he

238. "The Pelican is one of the four offices still remaining which were transacting life business before the close of the last century. . . . The Pelican heads a class by itself, as being the oldest proprietary company, established for the purpose of doing life business only" (*Bankers' Magazine* 52 [1891]: 662).

239. Quotation untraced.

was imperilling his life. Yet he returned. Should one wonder?[240] It was said that the woman was very beautiful. Besides, she did not love him.

It was by a mere accident that he was discovered. A noise in the street attracted his attention, and, in his artistic interest in modern life, he pushed aside the blind for a moment. Some one outside called out "That's Wainewright, the Bank-forger." It was Forrester, the Bow Street runner.[241]

On the 5th of July he was brought up at the Old Bailey.[242] The following report of the proceedings appeared in the *Times:*—

"Before Mr. Justice Vaughan and Mr. Baron Alderson, Thomas Griffiths Wainewright, aged forty-two, a man of gentlemanly appearance, wearing mustachios, was indicted for forging and uttering a certain power of attorney for 2,239*l.,* with intent to defraud the Governor and Company of the Bank of England.

"There were five indictments against the prisoner, to all of which he pleaded not guilty, when he was arraigned before Mr. Serjeant Arabin in the course of the morning. On being brought before the judges, however, he begged to be allowed to withdraw the former plea, and then pleaded guilty to two of the indictments, which were not of a capital nature.

"The counsel for the Bank having explained that there were three other indictments, but that the Bank did not desire to

240. This sentence and the next two added 1891.
241. The Bow Street Runners, a rudimentary police force established in London in 1749, were the forerunners of London's Metropolitan Police, established in 1829. The Bow Street unit remained active till 1839.
242. London's—and England's—central criminal court, where Wilde was himself tried and convicted in 1895.

shed blood, the plea of guilty on the two minor charges was recorded, and the prisoner at the close of the session sentenced by the Recorder to transportation for life."[243]

He was taken back to Newgate,[244] preparatory to his removal to the colonies. In a fanciful passage in one of his early essays he had fancied himself "lying in Horsemonger Gaol under sentence of death"[245] for having been unable to resist the temptation of stealing some Marc Antonios from the British Museum in order to complete his collection. The sentence now passed on him was to a man of his culture a form of death. He complained bitterly of it to his friends, and pointed out, with a good deal of reason, some people may fancy, that the money was practically his own, having come to him from his mother, and that the forgery, such as it was, had been committed thirteen years before, which to use his own phrase, was at least a *circonstance attenuante*.[246] The permanence of personality is a very subtle metaphysical problem, and certainly the English law solves the question in an extremely rough-and-ready manner. There is, however, something dramatic in the fact that this heavy punishment was inflicted on him for what, if we remember his fatal influence on the prose of modern journalism, was certainly not the worst of all his sins.

243. Wilde's quotation from *The Times,* like much else in his account of Wainewright's criminal career, is taken directly from Hazlitt's introduction to *Essays and Criticisms* (lxiii).

244. At the time of Wainewright's conviction, Newgate Prison was London's main prison. It appears in many of Dickens's novels.

245. Wainewright, "Janus Weathercock's Reasons," 250. Foreshadowing the title of his 1898 poem *The Ballad of Reading Gaol*, Wilde has altered Wainewright's spelling of "jail" to the more antiquated "gaol."

246. Extenuating circumstance.

While he was in gaol, Dickens, Macready, and Hablot Browne came across him by chance.[247] They had been going over the prisons of London, searching for artistic effects, and in Newgate they suddenly caught sight of Wainewright. He met them with a defiant stare, Forster tells us, but Macready was "horrified to recognize a man familiarly known to him in former years, and at whose table he had dined."[248]

Others had more curiosity, and his cell was for some time a kind of fashionable lounge. Many men of letters went down to visit their old literary comrade. But he was no longer the kind light-hearted Janus[249] whom Charles Lamb admired. He seems to have grown quite cynical.

To the agent of an insurance company who was visiting him one afternoon, and thought he would improve the occasion by pointing out that, after all crime was a bad speculation, he replied: "Sir, you City men enter on your speculations and take the chances of them. Some of your speculations succeed, some fail. Mine happen to have failed, yours happen to have succeeded. That is the only difference, sir, between my visitor and me. But, sir, I will tell you one thing in which I have succeeded to the last. I have been determined through life to hold the position of a gentleman. I have always done so. I do so still. It is the custom of this place that each of the inmates of a cell shall take his morning's turn of sweeping it out. I occupy a cell

247. Charles Dickens was good friends at this time with the actor William Macready (1793–1873), as well as with Hablot Knight Brown (1815–1882), who illustrated ten of Dickens's novels under the pen name "Phiz."

248. John Forster, *The Life of Charles Dickens, Vol. 1* (Leipzig: Tauchnitz, 1872), 230, quoted in Hazlitt, introduction to *Essays and Criticisms*, lxv.

249. Janus, the Roman god of gates and doors, possessed two faces, each looking in opposite directions.

with a bricklayer and a sweep, but they never offer me the broom!"[250] When a friend reproached him with the murder of Helen Abercrombie he shrugged his shoulders and said, "Yes; it was a dreadful thing to do, but she had very thick ankles."[251]

From Newgate he was brought to the hulks at Portsmouth,[252] and sent from there in the *Susan* to Van Diemen's Land[253] along with three hundred other convicts. The voyage seems to have been most distasteful to him, and in a letter written to a friend he spoke bitterly about the ignominy of "the companion of poets and artists" being compelled to associate with "country bumpkins."[254] The phrase that he applies to his companions need not surprise us.[255] Crime in England is rarely the result of sin. It is nearly always the result of starvation. There was probably no one on board in whom he would have found a sympathetic listener, or even a psychologically interesting nature.

His love of art, however, never deserted him. At Hobart Town[256] he started a studio, and returned to sketching and portrait-painting,

250. Quoted in Hazlitt, introduction to *Essays and Criticisms*, lxxi.

251. Wilde's adaptation of Wainewright's reply, when asked how he could have had the barbarity to kill so trusting and innocent a woman as Abercromby, "Upon my soul, I don't know, unless it was because she had such thick legs" (quoted in Hazlitt, introduction to *Essays and Criticisms*, lxix).

252. Prison ships, moored at Portsmouth.

253. Colonial name for the island of Tasmania, off the coast of New South Wales, in Australia. In 1803 the island was colonised by the British as a penal colony.

254. Quoted by Hazlitt, introduction to *Essays and Criticisms*, lxxii–lxxiii. Wilde has altered the quotation very slightly.

255. This sentence and the next three added 1891.

256. Hobart Town (now Hobart) was the principal city of Van Diemen's Land (see n.253 above).

and his conversation and manners seem not to have lost their charm. Nor did he give up his habit of poisoning, and there are two cases on record in which he tried to make away with people who had offended him. But his hand seems to have lost its cunning. Both of his attempts were complete failures, and in 1844, being thoroughly dissatisfied with Tasmanian society, he presented a memorial to the governor of the settlement, Sir John Eardley Wilmot, praying for a ticket-of-leave.[257] In it he speaks of himself as being "tormented by ideas struggling for outward form and realization, barred up from increase of knowledge, and deprived of the exercise of profitable or even of decorous speech." His request, however, was refused, and the associate of Coleridge consoled himself by making those marvellous *Paradis Artificiels* whose secret is only known to the eaters of opium.[258] In 1852 he died of apoplexy,

257. A document of parole issued to transported convicts who had served part of their sentence in the penal colonies of Australia and shown they could now be trusted with some freedoms. Once granted a ticket of leave, a convict was permitted to seek employment within a specified district, but could not leave that district without the permission of the government or the district's resident magistrate. Any permitted change of employer or district was recorded on the ticket. Ticket-of-leave men were permitted to marry, to bring their families from Britain, and to acquire property, but they were not permitted to carry firearms or board a ship. They were often required to repay the cost of their original passage to the penal colony. A convict who observed the conditions of his ticket-of-leave until the completion of one-half of his sentence was entitled to a conditional pardon, which removed all restrictions except the right to leave the colony.

258. "The associate . . . eaters of opium" substituted in 1891 for "he consoled himself with opium-eating."

his sole living companion being a cat, for which he had evinced an extraordinary affection.[259]

His crimes seem to have had an important effect upon his art.[260] They gave a strong personality to his style, a quality that his early work certainly lacked. In a note to the *Life of Dickens*, Forster mentions that in 1847 Lady Blessington received from her brother, Major Power, who held a military appointment at Hobart Town, an oil portrait of a young lady from his clever brush; and it is said that "he had contrived to put the expression of his own wickedness into the portrait of a nice, kind-hearted girl."[261] M. Zola, in one of his novels, tells us of a young man who, having committed a murder, takes to art, and paints greenish impressionist portraits of perfectly respectable people, all of which bear a curious resemblance to his victim.[262] The development of Mr. Wainewright's style seems to me far more subtle and suggestive. One can fancy an intense personality being created out of sin.[263]

259. Wilde here distorts his source, Hazlitt, who was unsure of the date of Wainewright's death and states only that Wainewright died "about the year 1852" (introduction to *Essays and Criticism,* lxxvi). In a footnote, Hazlitt elaborated that Wainewright's death took place "in all probability, between 1847 and 1852." In fact, Wainewright is now known to have died in 1847.

260. "an important effect" substituted in 1891 for "a curious effect."

261. After citing this unattributed quotation, which he had taken verbatim from Forster's *Life of Dickens,* Hazlitt adds, "On the other hand, none of the artist's personal character seems to have been transfused into the portraits of the two Abercrombys" (lxxvii, n.1).

262. An allusion to Zola's novel *Thérèse Raquin.*

263. A direct foreshadowing of Wilde's novel *The Picture of Dorian Gray,* as well as of Wilde's own "sinful" career. "Sin," Wilde remarks in

This strange and fascinating figure that for a few years dazzled literary London, and made so brilliant a *debut* in life and letters, is undoubtedly a most interesting study. Mr. W. Carew Hazlitt, his latest biographer, to whom I am indebted for many of the facts contained in this memoir, and whose little book is, indeed, quite invaluable in its way, is of opinion that his love of art and nature was a mere pretence and assumption, and others have denied to him all literary power. This seems to me a shallow, or at least a mistaken, view. The fact of a man being a poisoner is nothing against his prose. The domestic virtues are not the true basis of art, though they may serve as an excellent advertisement for second-rate artists.[264] It is possible that De Quincey exaggerated his critical powers, and I cannot help saying again that there is much in his published works that is too familiar, too common, too journalistic, in the bad sense of that bad word. Here and there he is distinctly vulgar in expression, and he is always lacking in the self-restraint of the true artist. But for some of his faults we must blame the time in which he lived, and, after all, prose that Charles Lamb thought "capital" has no small historic interest. That he had a sincere love of art and nature seems to me quite certain. There is no essential incongruity between crime and culture. We cannot re-write the whole of history for the purpose of gratifying our moral sense of what should be.

Of course, he is far too close to our own time for us to be able to form any purely artistic judgment about him. It is impossible not to feel a strong prejudice against a man who might have poi-

---

"The Critic as Artist," "is an essential element of progress. Without it the world would stagnate, or grow old, or become colourless" (p. 300 below).

264. "second-rate artists" substituted in 1891 for "art."

soned Lord Tennyson, or Mr. Gladstone, or the Master of Balliol.[265] But had the man worn a costume and spoken a language different from our own, had he lived in imperial Rome, or at the time of the Italian Renaissance, or in Spain in the seventeenth century, or in any land or any century but this century and this land, we would be quite able to arrive at a perfectly unprejudiced estimate of his position and value. I know that there are many historians, or at least writers on historical subjects, who still think it necessary to apply moral judgments to history, and who distribute their praise or blame with the solemn complacency of a successful schoolmaster. This, however, is a foolish habit, and merely shows that the moral instinct can be brought to such a pitch of perfection that it will make its appearance wherever it is not required. Nobody with the true historical sense ever dreams of blaming Nero, or scolding Tiberius or censuring Caesar Borgia.[266] These personages

265. The classicist and educational reformer Benjamin Jowett (1817–1893) was the master of Balliol College, Oxford, from 1870 until his death. Along with the poet laureate, Alfred Lord Tennyson (1809–1892) and the four-time prime minister William Ewart Gladstone (1809–1898), he was one of the paragons of Victorian Britain.

266. Historical personages synonymous with depravity and violent excess. Nero and Tiberius were among the most sexually depraved of Roman emperors. They feature again in *The Picture of Dorian Gray* when Dorian Gray feels that the lives of "those strange terrible people who had passed across the stage of the world, and made sin so marvellous, and evil so full of wonder, . . . had been his own" (Wilde, *The Picture of Dorian Gray: An Annotated, Uncensored Edition,* 206). The Italian Renaissance duke Cesare Borgia, son of Pope Alexander VI (both of whom also feature in *The Picture of Dorian Gray),* relinquished the office of Roman Catholic cardinal in order to become commander of the Papal Armies. He remains infamous for his cruelty and ruthlessness.

have become like the puppets of a play. They may fill us with terror, or horror, or wonder, but they do not harm us. They are not in immediate relation to us. We have nothing to fear from them. They have passed into the sphere of art and of science, and neither art nor science knows anything of moral approval or disapproval. And so it may be some day with Charles Lamb's friend. At present I feel that he is just a little too modern to be treated in that fine spirit of disinterested curiosity to which we owe so many charming studies of the great criminals of the Italian Renaissance from the pens of Mr. John Addington Symonds, Miss A. Mary F. Robinson, Miss Vernon Lee, and other distinguished writers.[267] However, Art has not forgotten him. He is the hero of Dickens's *Hunted Down,* the Varney of Bulwer's *Lucretia;* and it is gratifying to note that fiction has paid some homage to one who was so powerful with "pen, pencil, and poison." To be suggestive for fiction is to be of more importance than a fact.[268]

267. "from the pens of . . . distinguished writers" added 1891. Wilde is thinking of *The Age of the Despots* (1886), the final volume of Symonds's multivolume *The Renaissance in Italy* (1875–1886); A. Mary F. Robinson, *The End of the Middle Ages* (London: T. Fisher Unwin, 1889); and Vernon Lee [Violet Paget], *Euphorion: Being Studies of the Antique and the Medieval in the Renaissance* (2nd ed. rev. London: T. Fisher Unwin, 1885). All three influenced the detailed allusions to Renaissance criminality and debauchery that Wilde incorporated into the central chapter of *The Picture of Dorian Gray,* where Wilde's eponymous protagonist reads with fascination of "those whom Lust and Blood and Weariness . . . made monstrous or mad" and learns to "look on evil simply as a mode through which he could realize his conception of the beautiful" (Wilde, *The Picture of Dorian Gray: An Annotated, Uncensored Edition,* 208–210).

268. The memoir's important concluding sentence added 1891.

From "The Critic as Artist: With Some Remarks on the Importance of Doing Nothing"[†]

After a brief, witty digression about the joys of reading autobiographies and the value of "mere egotism" in literature, the opening pages of Wilde's dialogue (omitted here in the interests of brevity) settle quickly into an intricate debate between Ernest and Gilbert about the value of criticism. "Why cannot the artist be left alone," asks Ernest, "to create a new world if he wishes it, or, if not, to shadow forth the world which we

† First published, signed, in two separate parts, in the July and September 1890 numbers of *Nineteenth Century*, under the title "The True Function and Value of Criticism." The dialogue was extensively revised and retitled "The Critic as Artist" when republished in *Intentions* in 1891. The extract from part one given here is from the *Intentions* text. Wilde's subtitle (part of the main title in 1890) echoes his endorsements, in "A Chinese Sage," of "the great creed of inaction" and of Chuang Tzǔ's notion that "the best action is that which is never done" (p. 79 and p. 80 above). In both 1890 and 1891 versions, Wilde gave part two of the dialogue a different, companion subtitle: "With some remarks upon the importance of discussing everything." For the dialogue form, see headnote pp. 184–185 above.

Wilde's original title suggests that he wanted "The Critic as Artist" to be understood as a reply to Matthew Arnold's influential essay "The Function of Criticism at the Present Time" (1865), where, despite maintaining that British culture would be rejuvenated by a development of the critical spirit and by a disinterested "free play of the mind on all subjects which it touches," Arnold had accepted "as a general proposition, that the critical faculty is lower than the inventive." But as Wilde's later title indicates, "The Critic as Artist" also demands to be understood as a reposte to Wilde's onetime friend and nemesis, the artist James McNeill Whistler, who had set the cultural authority of the critic back immeasurably, while simultaneously asserting the autonomy of the artist, when he had successfully sued the critic John Ruskin for libel in 1878 (see introduction). For Wilde's earlier demurral at Whistler's claim in his "Ten O'Clock" lecture, that, as Wilde put it, "only a painter may be a judge of painting," see p. 48 above.

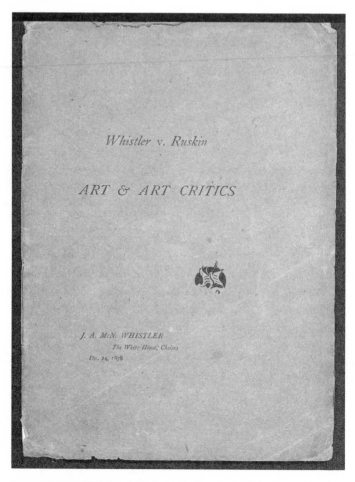

Whistler v. Ruskin

ART & ART CRITICS

J. A. McN. WHISTLER
The White House, Chelsea
Dec. 24, 1878

James McNeill Whistler, *Whistler v. Ruskin, Art and Art Critics* (London: Chatto and Windus, 1878), front paper wrapper. Whistler formalized his enmity towards critics in this pamphlet, and his legal victory over the critic John Ruskin in the libel trial that preceded it represented the triumph of art over criticism. Over a decade later, Wilde's dialogue "The Critic as Artist" redressed the balance and proved the culminating event in the decade-long battle of wits between Wilde and the famously cantankerous painter.

already know, and of which, I fancy, we would each one of us be wearied if Art, with her fine spirit of choice and deliberate instinct of selection, did not, as it were, purify it for us, and give to it a momentary perfection [?] . . . Why should the artist be troubled by the shrill clamour of criticism? Why should those who cannot create take upon themselves to estimate the value of creative work?"

Ernest supports these questions with an impassioned disquisition upon the creative powers of the Greek visual artist and artisan, particularly the sculptor, potter, and jeweler, and then by asserting that "in the best days of art there were no art critics . . . The Greeks had no art critics." This assertion—which closely echoes James McNeill Whistler's assertion, in his "Ten O'Clock" lecture, that when "Greece was in its splendor . . . Art reigned supreme . . . and there was no meddling from the outsider"[269]*—prompts Gilbert to instance Aristotle and Plato as proofs that "the Greeks were a nation of art critics, and . . . they invented the criticism of art, just as they invented the criticism of everything else." The extract that follows elucidates the grounds of Gilbert's reply.*

A Dialogue: Part 1
Scene: The Library Of A House in Piccadilly, Overlooking the Green Park
Persons: Gilbert and Ernest[270]

269. Whistler, "Ten O'Clock," 141. Gilbert's response to Ernest's observation that "in the best days of art there were no art critics"—"I seem to have heard that observation before. . . . It has all the vitality of error, and all the tediousness of an old friend"—is implicitly a recognition that Ernest is espousing ideas previously voiced by Wilde's "old friend" Whistler.

270. There has been much inconclusive speculation about Wilde's choice of names for his two imaginary interlocutors. His use of "Ernest" to designate the more serious and conservative of the two anticipates his use of this name in *The Importance of Being Earnest,* and perhaps also Mrs. Allonby's critique, in *A Woman of No Importance,* of her husband Ernest, whose chin is "too square," who "has got no conversation at all," and who is "absolutely uninteresting" because he speaks only what is "perfectly true."

Gilbert. . . . Whatever, in fact, is modern in our life we owe to the Greeks. Whatever is an anachronism is due to medievalism. It is the Greeks who have given us the whole system of art-criticism,[271] and how fine their critical instinct was, may be seen from the fact that the material they criticised with most care was, as I have already said, language.[272] For the material that painter or sculptor uses is meagre in comparison with that of words. Words have not merely music as sweet as that of viol and lute, colour as rich and vivid as any that makes lovely for us the canvas of the Venetian or the Spaniard, and plastic form no less sure and certain than that which reveals itself in marble or in bronze, but thought and passion and spirituality are theirs also, are theirs indeed alone.[273] If the Greeks had criticised nothing but language, they would still have been the great art-critics of the world. To know the

271. Gilbert's contentions here echo and extend the closing remarks in Wilde's undergraduate thesis, "The Rise of Historical Criticism" (1878), where, after tracing the genesis of the critical spirit in Ancient Greece, Wilde argues "The only spirit which is entirely removed from us is the medieval; the Greek spirit is essentially modern. . . . Across the drear wastes of a thousand years the Greek and the modern spirit join hands." For Wilde's concept of *art-criticism,* see n.320 below.

272. Gilbert had earlier remarked that the Greeks "elaborated the criticism of language . . . to a point to which we, with our accentual system of reasonable or emotional emphasis, can barely if at all attain. . . . Their test was always the spoken word in its musical and metrical relations" (Wilde, *Criticism,* 137).

273. cf. "Words! Mere words! . . . [W]hat a subtle magic there was in them! They seemed to be able to give a plastic form to formless things, and to have a music of their own as sweet as that of viol or of lute" (Wilde, *The Picture of Dorian Gray: An Annotated, Uncensored Edition,* 96).

principles of the highest art, is to know the principles of all
the arts.

But I see that the moon is hiding behind a sulphur-coloured
cloud. Out of a tawny mane of drift she gleams like a lion's
eye. She is afraid that I will talk to you of Lucian and Long-
inus, of Quinctilian and Dionysius, of Pliny and Fronto and
Pausanias,[274] of all those who in the antique world wrote or
lectured upon art-matters. She need not be afraid. I am tired

---

274. These Greek and Roman rhetoricians had all featured in Wilde's undergraduate education, and Wilde has learned their lessons
well. Lucian (c. 120–c. 180 CE), a Greek satirist and sophist, was the
author of *How to Write History*, among numerous other works; Long-
inus is the name generally given for the author of the oft-anthologized
first-century critical treatise *On the Sublime*, although little is known
about him, and his authorship remains a matter of dispute; Quintilian
(c. 35–c. 100 CE), still sometimes spelt "Quinctilian" (as here), the
founder of a Roman school of rhetoric, where Pliny the Younger was
his student, wrote *The Education of An Orator*, parts of which may be
based on an earlier text, now lost, titled *On the Causes of Corrupted
Eloquence*; Dionysius refers either to Dionysius Thrax (c. 170–c. 90 BCE),
author of the earliest extant Greek manuscript on grammar, the *Art of
Grammar*, or to Dionysius of Helicarnassus (fl. c. 25 BCE), coiner of
the phrase "the style is the man" and author of *On The Arrangement of
Words* and other works on oratory and writing; Pliny the Younger
(c. 61–c. 112 CE), was a prominent Roman orator and politician whose
sole surviving oration, a Panegyric to Trajan, offers a masterclass in
how one speaks to and about power; Fronto (c. 100–c. 166 CE), the
leading orator of his day, was the rhetoric tutor of the future emperors
Marcus Aurelius and Lucius Verus; Pausanius (fl. c. 160 CE) was a Greek
travel writer, whose *Descriptions of Greece* is noted for its varied rhe-
torical styles.

of my expedition into the dim, dull abyss of facts. There is nothing left for me now but the divine μονόκρονος ἡδονή[275] of another cigarette. Cigarettes have at least the charm of leaving one unsatisfied.

Ernest. Try one of mine. They are rather good. I get them direct from Cairo. The only use of our *attachés* is that they supply their friends with excellent tobacco. And as the moon has hidden herself, let us talk a little longer. I am quite ready to admit that I was wrong in what I said about the Greeks. They were, as you have pointed out, a nation of art-critics. I acknowledge it, and I feel a little sorry for them. For the creative faculty is higher than the critical. There is really no comparison between them.

Gilbert. The antithesis between them is entirely arbitrary. Without the critical faculty, there is no artistic creation at all,[276] worthy of the name. You spoke a little while ago of that fine spirit of choice and delicate instinct of selection by which the artist realizes life for us, and gives to it a momentary perfection. Well, that spirit of choice, that subtle tact of omission, is really the critical faculty in one of its most characteristic moods, and no one who does not possess this critical faculty can create anything at all in art. Arnold's definition of literature as a criticism of life, was not very felicitous in form,[277] but it showed how keenly he

275. Momentary pleasure.
276. A riposte to Matthew Arnold's claim that "the critical power is of lower rank than the creative."
277. "The end and aim of all literature," Matthew Arnold declared, is "nothing but . . . a criticism of life" ("Joubert" [1865], in his *Lectures and*

recognised the importance of the critical element in all creative work.

Ernest. I should have said that great artists worked unconsciously, that they were "wiser than they knew," as, I think, Emerson remarks somewhere.[278]

Gilbert. It is really not so, Ernest. All fine imaginative work is self-conscious and deliberate. No poet sings because he must sing. At least, no great poet does. A great poet sings because he chooses to sing. It is so now, and it has always been so. We are sometimes apt to think that the voices that sounded at the dawn of poetry were simpler, fresher, and more natural than ours, and that the world which the early poets looked at, and through which they walked, had a kind of poetical quality of its own, and could pass almost without changing into song. The snow lies thick now upon Olympus, and its steep scarped sides are bleak and barren, but once, we fancy, the white feet of the Muses brushed the dew from the anemones in the morning, and at evening came Apollo to sing to the shepherds in the vale.[279] But in this we are merely lending to other ages what we desire, or think we desire, for our own. Our historical sense is at fault. Every century that produces poetry is, so far, an artificial century, and the work that seems to us to be the most natural and simple product of its time is always the result of the

Essays in Criticism, ed. R. H. Super [Ann Arbor: Univ. Michigan Press, 1962], 209).

278. Emerson remarks "We are wiser than we know" in his essay "The Over-Soul," and that "Few men are wiser than they know" in "Compensation."

279. See n.69 above.

291

most self-conscious effort. Believe me, Ernest, there is no fine art without self-consciousness, and self-consciousness and the critical spirit are one.

Ernest. I see what you mean, and there is much in it. But surely you would admit that the great poems of the early world, the primitive, anonymous collective poems, were the result of the imagination of races, rather than of the imagination of individuals?

Gilbert. Not when they became poetry. Not when they received a beautiful form. For there is no art where there is no style, and no style where there is no unity, and unity is of the individual. No doubt Homer had old ballads and stories to deal with, as Shakespeare had chronicles and plays and novels from which to work, but they were merely his rough material. He took them, and shaped them into song. They become his, because he made them lovely. They were built out of music,

> And so not built at all,
> And therefore built for ever.[280]

The longer one studies life and literature, the more strongly one feels that behind everything that is wonderful stands the individual, and that it is not the moment that makes the man, but the man who creates the age. Indeed, I am inclined to think that each myth and legend that seems to us to spring

---

280. Wilde is slightly misquoting Merlin's account, in Tennyson's *Idylls of the King*, of how fairy kings and queens built the city of Camelot: "The city is built / To music, therefore never built at all, / And therefore built for ever" (*The Idylls of the King*, 2.273–274).

out of the wonder, or terror, or fancy of tribe and nation, was in its origin the invention of one single mind. The curiously limited number of the myths seems to me to point to this conclusion. But we must not go off into questions of comparative mythology. We must keep to criticism. And what I want to point out is this. An age that has no criticism is either an age in which art is immobile, hieratic, and confined to the reproduction of formal types, or an age that possesses no art at all. There have been critical ages that have not been creative, in the ordinary sense of the word, ages in which the spirit of man has sought to set in order the treasures of his treasure-house, to separate the gold from the silver, and the silver from the lead, to count over the jewels, and to give names to the pearls. But there has never been a creative age that has not been critical also. For it is the critical faculty that invents fresh forms. The tendency of creation is to repeat itself. It is to the critical instinct that we owe each new school that springs up, each new mould that art finds ready to its hand. There is really not a single form that art now uses that does not come to us from the critical spirit of Alexandria, where these forms were either stereotyped, or invented, or made perfect.[281] I say Alexandria, not merely because it was

281. Wilde's eulogy to the critical spirit of Alexandria represents a considerable change of heart. In his undergraduate thesis "The Rise of Historical Criticism" (1878) he had written that "the founding of that city of Alexandria, in which Western and Eastern thought met with such strange result to both, diverted the critical tendencies of the Greek spirit into questions of grammar, philology and the like. The narrow, artificial atmosphere of that University town (as we may call it) was fatal to the development of that independent and speculative spirit of research which strikes out new methods of inquiry and of which historical criticism is

there that the Greek spirit became most self-conscious, and indeed ultimately expired in scepticism and theology, but because it was to that city, and not to Athens, that Rome turned for her models, and it was through the survival, such as it was, of the Latin language that culture lived at all. When, at the Renaissance, Greek literature dawned upon Europe, the soil had been in some measure prepared for it. But, to get rid of the details of history, which are always wearisome and usually inaccurate, let us say generally, that the forms of art have been due to the Greek critical spirit. To it we owe the epic, the lyric, the entire drama in every one of its developments, including burlesque, the idyll, the romantic novel, the novel of adventure, the essay, the dialogue, the oration, the lecture, for which perhaps we should not forgive them, and the epigram, in all the wide meaning of that word.[282] In fact, we

one. The Alexandrines combined a great love of learning with an ignorance of the true principles of research, an enthusiastic spirit for accumulating materials with a wonderful incapacity to use them." (Wilde, *Criticism,* 42).

282. In Ancient Greece, the *epigram* was a "short direct poem" expressing "one single thought . . . rather more intellectual and analytical than lyrical and passionate; the thought is usually voiced as a comment on a new and symbolic situation—the death of a friend, the breaking of a lover's vow, the dedication of an offering, the sudden realization of some incongruity or some beauty" (*Oxford Classical Dictionary*). In Roman times, "even among the Greeks, [epigrams] assumed a greater variety of aspect, and were employed as the vehicle of satire or ridicule, as a means of producing hilarity and mirth. A good many of the epigrammatists flourished in or after the age of Martial, and may have followed or co-operated with him to produce this change of style." (Lord Neaves, *The Greek Anthology* [Philadelphia: Lippincott, 1874], 14). Present-day knowledge of classical epigrams derives almost entirely from *The Greek Anthology*—

owe it everything, except the sonnet, to which, however, some curious parallels of thought-movement may be traced in the Anthology, American journalism, to which no parallel can be found anywhere, and the ballad in sham Scotch dialect, which one of our most industrious writers has recently proposed should be made the basis for a final and unanimous effort on the part of our second-rate poets to make themselves really romantic.[283] Each new school, as it appears, cries out against criticism, but it is to the critical faculty in man that it owes its origin. The mere creative instinct does not innovate, but reproduces.

Ernest. You have been talking of criticism as an essential part of the creative spirit, and I now fully accept your theory. But what of criticism outside creation? I have a foolish habit of

referred to by Wilde as "the *Anthology*" in the next sentence—the name generally given to an anthology of thousands of such epigrams that has descended from classical times. See p. 333, n.6 and headnote, p. 351 below.

283. In *Romantic Ballads and Poems of Phantasy* (1888), the Scottish poet William Sharp asserted that "there is a Romantic Revival imminent in our poetic literature" and that "our poets, especially those of the youngest generation, will shortly turn towards the 'ballad' as a poetic vehicle." Sharp disparaged those who "would prefer a dexterously-turned triolet to such apparently uncouth measures as . . . the ballad of 'Clerk Saunders' [or] who would rather listen to the drawing-room music of the Villanelle than to the wild harp-playing by the mill-dams o' Binnorie or the sough of the night-wind o'er drumly Annan Water." Wilde had taken issue with Sharp's views on the use of Scotch dialect once before, when reviewing Sharp's book for *Woman's World*: "our language is not likely to be permanently enriched by such words as 'weet,' 'saut,' 'blawing,' and 'snawing'" ("A Note On Some Modern Poets" [1888], rpt. in Wilde, *Journalism,* ed. John Stokes and Mark Turner, vol. 7 of *The Complete Works of Oscar Wilde* [Oxford: Oxford Univ. Press, 2013], 116).

reading periodicals, and it seems to me that most modern criticism is perfectly valueless.

Gilbert. So is most modern creative work also. Mediocrity weighing mediocrity in the balance, and incompetence applauding its brother—that is the spectacle which the artistic activity of England affords us from time to time. And yet, I feel I am a little unfair in this matter. As a rule, the critics— I speak, of course, of the higher class, of those in fact who write for the sixpenny papers—are far more cultured than the people whose work they are called upon to review. This is, indeed, only what one would expect, for criticism demands infinitely more cultivation than creation does.

Ernest. Really?

Gilbert. Certainly. Anybody can write a three-volumed novel.[284] It merely requires an absolute ignorance of both life

284. The witless, prudish Miss Prism is the author of a three-volume novel of "more than usually revolting sentimentality" in Wilde's *The Importance of Being Earnest*. Single-volume novels were still a comparative rarity when "The Critic as Artist" was first published. Novels were typically (and expensively) published in three volumes, with a view to their acquisition by circulating libraries, which would in turn lend out one volume at a time for a fee. The largest and most successful such library, Mudie's Select Library, dominated the book market and acted as an unofficial censor by refusing to acquire novels that did not adhere to the strictest moral, social, and sexual conventions. However, one year before the periodical publication of "The Critic as Artist," Wilde noted that "the influence of Mudie on literature, the baneful influence of the circulating library, is clearly on the wane. The gain to literature is incalculable. English novels were becoming very tedious with their three volumes of padding—at least, the second volume was always padding—and

and literature. The difficulty that I should fancy the reviewer feels is the difficulty of sustaining any standard. Where there is no style a standard must be impossible. The poor reviewers are apparently reduced to be the reporters of the police-court of literature, the chroniclers of the doings of the habitual criminals of art. It is sometimes said of them that they do not read all through the works they are called upon to criticise. They do not. Or at least they should not. If they did so, they would become confirmed misanthropes, or, if I may borrow a phrase from one of the pretty Newnham graduates, confirmed womanthropes for the rest of their lives.[285] Nor is it necessary. To know the vintage and quality of a wine one need not drink the whole cask. It must be perfectly easy in half an hour to say whether a book is worth anything or worth nothing. Ten minutes are really sufficient, if one has the instinct for form. Who wants to wade through a dull volume? One tastes it, and that is quite enough—more than enough, I should imagine. I am aware that there are many honest workers in painting as well as in literature who object to criticism entirely. They are quite right. Their work stands in no intellectual relation to their age. It brings us no new element of pleasure. It suggests no fresh departure of thought,

---

extremely indigestible" ("Some Literary Notes" [January 1889], rpt. in Wilde, *Journalism*, vol. 7, 146)

285. For Newnham, see p. 57, n.6 above. A *womanthrope,* coined from a humorous blend of "woman" and "misanthrope," is a hater of women or *misogynist.* Wilde uses the term again in *The Importance of Being Earnest*, where Canon Chasuble winces at "so neologistic a phrase." However, George Otto Trevelyan records encountering it "in a novel by a female hand" as early as 1863 ("Letters of a Competition Wallah," *Macmillans Magazine* 8 [July 1863]: 202–203).

or passion, or beauty. It should not be spoken of. It should be left to the oblivion that it deserves.

Ernest. But, my dear fellow—excuse me for interrupting you—you seem to me to be allowing your passion for criticism to lead you a great deal too far. For, after all, even you must admit that it is much more difficult to do a thing than to talk about it.

Gilbert. More difficult to do a thing than to talk about it? Not at all. That is a gross popular error. It is very much more difficult to talk about a thing than to do it. In the sphere of actual life that is of course obvious. Anybody can make history. Only a great man can write it. There is no mode of action, no form of emotion, that we do not share with the lower animals. It is only by language that we rise above them, or above each other—by language, which is the parent, and not the child, of thought. Action, indeed, is always easy, and when presented to us in its most aggravated, because most continuous form, which I take to be that of real industry, becomes simply the refuge of people who have nothing whatsoever to do. No, Ernest, don't talk about action. It is a blind thing dependent on external influences, and moved by an impulse of whose nature it is unconscious. It is a thing incomplete in its essence, because limited by accident, and ignorant of its direction, being always at variance with its aim. Its basis is the lack of imagination. It is the last resource of those who know not how to dream.[286]

286. Compare with Chuang Tzǔ's notion that "the divine man ignores action" (p. 84 above); see too Wilde's references to "the *reductio ad*

Ernest. Gilbert, you treat the world as if it were a crystal ball. You hold it in your hand, and reverse it to please a wilful fancy. You do nothing but rewrite history.

Gilbert. The one duty we owe to history is to rewrite it. That is not the least of the tasks in store for the critical spirit. When we have fully discovered the scientific laws that govern life, we shall realize that the one person who has more illusions than the dreamer is the man of action. He, indeed, knows neither the origin of his deeds nor their results. From the field in which he thought that he had sown thorns, we have gathered our vintage, and the fig-tree that he planted for our pleasure is as barren as the thistle, and more bitter.[287] It is because Humanity has never known where it was going that it has been able to find its way.

Ernest. You think, then, that in the sphere of action a conscious aim is a delusion?

Gilbert. It is worse than a delusion. If we lived long enough to see the results of our actions it may be that those who call themselves good would be sickened with a dull remorse, and

---

absurdam of practice" (p. 190 above) and "the importance of doing nothing" (p. 285 and headnote above).

287. An amalgam of Job 24:6 (the poor "gather the vintage of the wicked") and Matthew 7:16–17: "By their fruits ye shall know them. Do men gather grapes of thorns, or figs of thistles? Even so every good tree bringeth forth good fruit, but the corrupt tree bringeth forth evil fruit." Wilde had previously quoted from Matthew 7:16 in "Mr. Whistler's Ten O'Clock" (see p. 47 above), and he would quote the same gospel verse again when composing *De Profundis*, asking "who knew better than [Christ] that . . . one cannot gather grapes off thorns or figs from thistles?" (Wilde, *Annotated Prison Writings*, 207).

those whom the world calls evil stirred by a noble joy. Each little thing that we do passes into the great machine of life, which may grind our virtues to powder and make them worthless, or transform our sins into elements of a new civilization, more marvellous and more splendid than any that has gone before. But men are the slaves of words. They rage against Materialism, as they call it, forgetting that there has been no material improvement that has not spiritualized the world, and that there have been few, if any, spiritual awakenings that have not wasted the world's faculties in barren hopes, and fruitless aspirations, and empty or trammelling creeds. What is termed Sin is an essential element of progress. Without it the world would stagnate, or grow old, or become colourless. By its curiosity, Sin increases the experience of the race. Through its intensified assertion of individualism, it saves us from monotony of type. In its rejection of the current notions about morality, it is one with the higher ethics. And as for the virtues! What are the virtues? Nature, M. Renan tells us, cares little about chastity,[288] and it may be that it is to the shame of the Magdalen, and not to their own purity, that the Lucretias of modern life owe their freedom from stain.[289] Charity, as even those of whose religion it makes a

288. The French historian and philologist Ernest Renan (1823–1892) declared in his *Souvenirs d'enfance et de jeunesse* (Memories of Childhood and Youth, 1883) that "la nature ne tient pas du tout à ce que l'homme soit chaste." Matthew Arnold had previously cited and translated this remark, as "Nature cares nothing for chastity," in his essay "Numbers or, The Majority and The Remnant" (1884; rpt. in his *Discourses in America* [1885]).

289. Mary Magdalen was the most important woman among Christ's disciples and also the first witness to his resurrection. She is generally

formal part have been compelled to acknowledge, creates a multitude of evils.[290] The mere existence of conscience, that faculty of which people prate so much nowadays, and are so ignorantly proud, is a sign of our imperfect development. It must be merged in instinct before we become fine. Self-denial is simply a method by which man arrests his progress, and self-sacrifice a survival of the mutilation of the savage, part of that old worship of pain which is so terrible a factor in the history of the world, and which even now makes its victims day by day, and has its altars in the land. Virtues! Who knows what the virtues are? Not you. Not I. Not anyone. It is well for our vanity that we slay the criminal, for if we suffered him to live he might show us what we had gained by his crime. It is well for his peace that the saint goes to his martyrdom. He is spared the sight of the horror of his harvest.

---

understood to have been a prostitute reclaimed from sin by virtue of penitence, then elevated to the sainthood in consequence. However, Luke 8:2 states only that she was a woman whom Christ cured of "evil spirits" and "from whom seven demons had gone out." By Wilde's day, a magdalen was any penitent prostitute or "fallen" woman who sought to renounce her past life. According to the Roman historian Livy, Lucretia (died c. 508 BCE), the beautiful and chaste wife of a Roman nobleman, committed suicide following her rape by a son of the last king of Rome, thereby precipitating the fall of the monarchy and the rise of the Roman Republic. Her name is now proverbial for the chaste, faithful wife. Her story, which fascinated Chaucer and Shakespeare among others, features prominently in Renaissance literature and art.

290. An adaptation of 1 Peter 4:8, which declares that "charity covers a multitude of sins." For Wilde's reworking of this witticism in "The Soul of Man Under Socialism," see p. 148 above.

Ernest. Gilbert, you sound too harsh a note. Let us go back to the more gracious fields of literature. What was it you said? That it was more difficult to talk about a thing than to do it?

Gilbert. (after a pause). Yes: I believe I ventured upon that simple truth. Surely you see now that I am right? When man acts he is a puppet. When he describes he is a poet. The whole secret lies in that. It was easy enough on the sandy plains by windy Ilion to send the notched arrow from the painted bow, or to hurl against the shield of hide and flame-like brass the long ash-handled spear.[291] It was easy for the adulterous queen to spread the Tyrian carpets for her lord, and then, as he lay couched in the marble bath, to throw over his head the purple net, and call to her smooth-faced lover to stab through the meshes at the heart that should have broken at Aulis. For Antigone even, with Death waiting for her as her bridegroom, it was easy to pass through the tainted air at noon, and climb the hill, and strew with kindly earth the wretched naked corse that had no tomb. But what of those who wrote about

291. "Windy Ilion" is a set collocation in Homer's *Iliad* (3.305, 8.499, 13.724, 23.64) for the plains by the Scamander River where the Trojan War was fought. See, too, Tennyson's allusion to the "ringing plains of windy Troy" in his poem "Ulysses." Wilde is invoking Homer's own descriptive epithets to imply that Greek heroism is an effect of Homeric language or artistry. Similarly in the next two sentences, Wilde implies that Clytemnestra's villainy (together with her lover Aegisthus, she purportedly murdered her husband Agamemnon upon his return from the Trojan Wars, whence he had set sail from the port city of Aulis, after sacrificing their daughter Iphigenia to ensure favorable winds) is an effect of Aeschylus's language in *Agamemnon*; and Antigone's bravery in burying her brother's corpse an effect of Sophocles's language in *Antigone*.

these things? What of those who gave them reality, and made them live for ever? Are they not greater than the men and women they sing of?. . . . What is action? It dies at the moment of its energy. It is a base concession to fact. The world is made by the singer for the dreamer. . . .

. . . . Movement, that problem of the visible arts, can be truly realized by Literature alone. It is Literature that shows us the body in its swiftness and the soul in its unrest.

Ernest. Yes; I see now what you mean. But, surely, the higher you place the creative artist, the lower must the critic rank.

Gilbert. Why so?

Ernest. Because the best that he can give us will be but an echo of rich music, a dim shadow of clear-outlined form. It may, indeed, be that life is chaos, as you tell me that it is; that its martyrdoms are mean and its heroisms ignoble; and that it is the function of Literature to recreate, from the rough material of actual existence, a new world that will be more marvellous, more enduring, and more true than the world that common eyes look upon, and through which common natures seek to realise their perfection. But surely, if this new world has been made by the spirit and touch of a great artist, it will be a thing so complete and perfect that there will be nothing left for the critic to do. I quite understand now, and indeed admit most readily, that it is far more difficult to talk about a thing than to do it. But it seems to me that this sound and sensible maxim, which is really extremely soothing to one's feelings, and should be adopted as its motto by every Academy of Literature all over the world, applies only to the relations that exist between Art and Life, and not to any relations that there may be between Art and Criticism.

Gilbert. But, surely, Criticism is itself an art. And just as artistic creation implies the working of the critical faculty, and, indeed, without it cannot be said to exist at all, so Criticism is really creative in the highest sense of the word. Criticism, in fact, is both creative and independent.

Ernest. Independent?

Gilbert. Yes; independent. Criticism is no more to be judged by any low standard of imitation or resemblance than is the work of poet or sculptor. The critic occupies the same relation to the work of art he criticises that the artist does to the visible world of form and colour, or the unseen world of passion and of thought. He does not even require for the perfection of his art the finest materials. Anything will serve his purpose. And just as out of the sordid and sentimental amours of the silly wife of a small country-doctor in the squalid village of Yonville-l'Abbaye, near Rouen, Gustave Flaubert was able to create a classic, and make a masterpiece of style,[292] so, from subjects of little or of no importance, such as the pictures in this year's Royal Academy, or in any year's Royal Academy for that matter, Mr. Lewis Morris's poems, M. Ohnet's novels, or the plays of Mr. Henry Arthur Jones,[293] the true critic can, if it be his pleasure so to direct

292. Wilde is alluding to Flaubert's *Madame Bovary.* In 1891 Wilde substituted "style" for the earlier version's "form."

293. In the 1890 serial version of "The Critic as Artist," the plays of Henry Arthur Jones (1851–1929) were omitted from this list, which included instead Adelphi melodramas and the novels of William Dean

or waste his faculty of contemplation, produce work that will be flawless in beauty and instinct[294] with intellectual subtlety. Why not? Dulness is always an irresistible temptation for brilliancy, and stupidity is the permanent *Bestia Trionfans* that calls wisdom from its cave.[295] To an artist so creative as the critic, what does subject-matter signify? No more and no less than it does to the novelist and the painter. Like them, he can find his motives everywhere. Treatment is the test. There is nothing that has not in it suggestion or challenge.

Ernest. But is Criticism really a creative art?

Gilbert. Why should it not be? It works with materials, and puts them into a form that is at once new and delightful. What more can one say of poetry? Indeed, I would call criticism a creation within a creation. For just as the great art-

---

Howells (1837–1920). By classing Royal Academy paintings as "subjects of little or no importance," alongside Jones's melodramas, the sub-Tennysonian poetry of Lewis Morris (1833–1907), and novels by the French writer Georges Ohnet (1848–1918), Wilde pointedly criticizes the British cultural establishment of his day.

294. *Instinct* (adj.) means imbued. In 1891 Wilde substituted "flawless in beauty" for the earlier version's "flawless in style."

295. Wilde is alluding to *Spaccio de la bestia trionfante* (The Expulsion of the Triumphant Beast), by the Italian philosopher and theologian Giordano Bruno (1548–1600), as well as to Plato's Allegory of the Cave, in which wisdom is depicted as reluctantly leaving its primitive cave and slowly coming to see things as they really are. For Bruno, the "triumphant beast" is a metaphor for the dominion of sin over the divine part of the soul, although here Wilde allies it with the nameless "someone" who "drags" the seer from his cave, temporarily blinding him as he reluctantly makes his journey towards the light (Plato, *Republic*, bk. 7, 515c–517). Bruno's writings were popular with British intellectuals in the 1880s.

ists, from Homer and Aeschylus, down to Shakespeare and Keats, did not go directly to life for their subject-matter, but sought for it in myth, and legend, and ancient tale, so the critic deals with materials that others have, as it were, purified for him, and to which imaginative form and colour have been already added. Nay more, I would say that the highest Criticism, being the purest form of personal impression, is in its way more creative than creation, as it has least reference to any standard external to itself, and is, in fact, its own reason for existing, and, as the Greeks would put it, in itself, and to itself, an end. Certainly, it is never trammelled by any shackles of verisimilitude. No ignoble considerations of probability, that cowardly concession to the tedious repetitions of domestic or public life, affect it ever. One may appeal from fiction unto fact. But from the soul there is no appeal.

Ernest. From the soul?

Gilbert. Yes, from the soul. That is what the highest criticism really is, the record of one's own soul. It is more fascinating than history, as it is concerned simply with oneself. It is more delightful than philosophy, as its subject is concrete and not abstract, real and not vague. It is the only civilized form of autobiography, as it deals not with the events, but with the thoughts of one's life; not with life's physical accidents of deed or circumstance, but with the spiritual moods and imaginative passions of the mind. I am always amused by the silly vanity of those writers and artists of our day who seem to imagine that the primary function of the critic is to chatter about their second-rate work. The best that one can say of most modern creative art is that it is just a little less vulgar than reality, and so the critic, with his fine sense of distinction and sure instinct of delicate refinement, will prefer to look into the silver mirror or through the woven veil, and will turn his eyes away from the chaos and clamour of actual existence, though the mirror be tarnished and the veil be torn. His sole aim is to chronicle his own impressions. It is for him that pictures are painted, books written, and marble hewn into form.[296]

Ernest. I seem to have heard another theory of Criticism.

Gilbert. Yes: it has been said by one whose gracious memory we all revere, and the music of whose pipe once lured Proserpina from her Sicilian fields, and made those white feet stir, and not in vain, the Cumnor cowslips, that the proper aim of Criticism is to see the object as in itself it really is.[297] But

---

296. Wilde is heavily indebted to Walter Pater here: "What is this song or picture, this engaging personality presented in life or in a book, to *me*? What effect does it really produce on me? Does it give me pleasure? and if so, what sort or degree of pleasure? How is my nature modified by its presence, and under its influence? The answers to these questions are the original facts with which the aesthetic critic has to do . . . And he who experiences these impressions strongly, and drives directly at the discrimination and analysis of them, has no need to trouble himself with the abstract question what beauty is in itself, or what its exact relation to truth or experience" (preface to *The Renaissance,* xx).

297. In "The Function of Criticism at the Present Time" (1865), Matthew Arnold wrote, "It is the business of the critical power . . . 'to see the object as in itself it really is.'" In "Thyrsis," his elegy for Arthur Hugh Clough, Arnold wrote that although Proserpine (the Roman goddess of spring and fertility) "trod Sicilian fields" and "knew each lily white which Enna yields," she "never heard" of "our poor Thames"; "Her foot the Cumnor cowslips never stirr'd; / And we should tease her with our plaint in vain" (ll. 93–100). By including the phrase "not in vain," Wilde

this is a very serious error, and takes no cognizance of Criticism's most perfect form, which in its essence is purely subjective, and seeks to reveal its own secret and not the secret of another. For the highest Criticism deals with art not as expressive but as impressive purely.

Ernest. But is that really so?

Gilbert. Of course it is. Who cares whether Mr. Ruskin's views on Turner are sound or not?[298] What does it matter? That mighty and majestic prose of his, so fervid and so fiery-coloured in its noble eloquence, so rich in its elaborate symphonic music, so sure and certain, at its best, in subtle choice of word and epithet, is at least as great a work of art as any of those wonderful sunsets that bleach or rot on their corrupted canvases in England's Gallery;[299] greater indeed, one is apt to think at times, not merely because its equal beauty is more enduring, but on account of the fuller variety of its appeal, soul speaking to soul in those long-cadenced lines, not through form and colour alone, though through these, indeed, completely and without loss, but with intellectual and emotional utterance, with lofty passion and with loftier thought, with imaginative insight, and with poetic aim; greater, I always think, even as Literature is the greater art. Who, again, cares whether Mr. Pater has put into the portrait of Monna Lisa something that Lionardo never

underscores his differences with Arnold. Cumnor is a small village near Oxford.

298. See John Ruskin, *Modern Painters I*, vol. 3 of *The Works of John Ruskin*, ed. E. T. Cook and Alexander Wedderburn (London: George Allen, 1903), esp. p. 228ff.

299. England's National Gallery, located in London's Trafalgar Square.

dreamed of?[300] The painter may have been merely the slave of an archaic smile, as some have fancied, but whenever I pass into the cool galleries of the Palace of the Louvre, and stand before that strange figure "set in its marble chair in that cirque of fantastic rocks, as in some faint light under sea,"[301] I murmur to myself, "She is older than the rocks among which she sits; like the vampire, she has been dead many times, and learned the secrets of the grave; and has been a diver in deep seas, and keeps their fallen day about her; and trafficked for strange webs with Eastern merchants; and, as Leda, was the mother of Helen of Troy, and, as St. Anne, the mother of Mary; and all this has been to her but as the sound of lyres and flutes, and lives only in the delicacy with which it has moulded the changing lineaments, and tinged the eyelids and the hands."[302] And I say to my friend, "The presence that thus so strangely rose beside the waters is expressive of what in the ways of a thousand years man had come to desire;" and he answers me, "Hers is the head upon which all 'the ends of the world are come,' and the eyelids are a little weary."[303]

And so the picture becomes more wonderful to us than it really is, and reveals to us a secret of which, in truth, it knows nothing, and the music of the mystical prose is as sweet in our ears as was that flute-player's music that lent to the lips of La Gioconda those subtle and poisonous curves. Do you

300. See Pater, *The Renaissance*, 97–99. Like Wilde's spelling of *Mona Lisa* ("Monna Lisa") and *Leonardo* ("Lionardo"), the quotations that follow are taken directly from the 1873 version of Pater's text.

301. Pater, *The Renaissance*, 97.

302. Pater, *The Renaissance*, 99.

303. Pater, *The Renaissance*, 98. "The ends of the world are come" is Pater's quotation, from 1 Corinthians 10:11.

ask me what Lionardo would have said had anyone told him of this picture that "all the thoughts and experience of the world had etched and moulded there, in that which they had of power to refine and make expressive the outward form, the animalism of Greece, the lust of Rome, the reverie of the Middle Age with its spiritual ambition and imaginative loves, the return of the Pagan world, the sins of the Borgias?"[304] He would probably have answered that he had contemplated none of these things, but had concerned himself simply with certain arrangements of lines and masses, and with new and curious colour-harmonies of blue and green, and it is for this very reason that the criticism which I have quoted is criticism of the highest kind. It treats the work of art simply as a starting-point for a new creation. It does not confine itself—let us at least suppose so for the moment—to discovering the real intention of the artist and accepting that as final. And in this it is right, for the meaning of any beautiful created thing is, at least, as much in the soul of him who looks at it, as it was in his soul who wrought it. Nay, it is rather the beholder who lends to the beautiful thing its myriad meanings, and makes it marvellous for us, and sets it in some new relation to the age, so that it becomes a vital portion of our lives, and a symbol of what we pray for, or perhaps of what, having prayed for, we fear that we may receive. The longer I study, Ernest, the more clearly I see that the beauty of the visible arts is, as the beauty of music, impressive primarily, and that it may be marred, and indeed often is so, by any excess of intellectual intention on the part of the artist. For

304. Pater, *The Renaissance*, 98, except that Wilde has altered Pater's "has etched" and "has of power" to "had etched," "had of power," etc.

when the work is finished it has, as it were, an independent
life of its own, and may deliver a message far other than that
which was put into its lips to say.[305] Sometimes, when I listen
to the overture to *Tannhäuser,* I seem indeed to see that comely
knight treading delicately on the flower-strewn grass, and to
hear the voice of Venus calling to him from the caverned
hill.[306] But at other times it speaks to me of a thousand different things, of myself, it may be, and my own life, or of the
lives of others whom one has loved and grown weary of loving,
or of the passions that man has known, or of the passions
that man has not known, and so has sought for. To-night it
may fill one with that ἔρως τῶν ἀδυνάτων, that *Amour de
l'Impossible,*[307] which falls like a madness on many who think

305. Again Wilde is indebted to Walter Pater, who had said, in "The
School of Giorgione" (1877, added to *The Renaissance* in 1888), that "a
great picture has no more definite message for us than an accidental play
of sunlight and shadow for a few moments on the wall or floor" and "art
is always striving to be independent of the mere intelligence, to become
a matter of pure perception, to get rid of its responsibilities to its subject
or material" (Pater, *The Renaissance,* 104, 108).

306. An allusion to Richard Wagner's opera *Tannhäuser* (written
1843–1845), performed numerous times in London in the 1880s, in which
Wagner dramatized and scored the German legend of the knight Tannhäuser's infatuated love for the goddess Venus.

307. *Love of the impossible.* In an important letter to his undergraduate friend Harry Marillier, now widely seen as both a yearning love
letter and a coded expression of Wilde's homosexuality, Wilde writes,
"you too have that love of things impossible—ἔρως τῶν ἀδυνάτων—
l'amour de l'impossible (how do men name it?). . . . Our most fiery moments of ecstasy are merely shadows of what somewhere else we have
felt, or of what we long some day to feel" (*Complete Letters,* 272). For
an interpretation of these Greek and French phrases as expressions of

they live securely and out of reach of harm, so that they sicken suddenly with the poison of unlimited desire, and, in the infinite pursuit of what they may not obtain, grow faint and swoon or stumble. To-morrow, like the music of which Aristotle and Plato tell us, the noble Dorian music of the Greek, it may perform the office of a physician, and give us an anodyne against pain, and heal the spirit that is wounded, and "bring the soul into harmony with all right things."[308] And what is true about music is true about all the arts. Beauty has as many meanings as man has moods. Beauty is the symbol of symbols. Beauty reveals everything, because it expresses nothing. When it shows us itself, it shows us the whole fiery-coloured world.

Ernest. But is such work as you have talked about really criticism?

Gilbert. It is the highest Criticism, for it criticises not merely the individual work of art, but Beauty itself, and fills with

---

"a new sexual, intellectual, and artistic credo, . . . a pagan rejection of traditional concepts of love, monogamy, and fidelity, and a powerful affirmation of [Wilde's] intention to explore and experience his sexuality," see Neil McKenna, *The Secret Life of Oscar Wilde* (New York: Basic Books, 2005), 73–74.

308. Aristotle contends that "Dorian music is the gravest and manliest" in his *Politics*, bk. 8. In *Republic*, bk. 3, Plato similarly commends the Dorian as well as the Phyrgian musical mode as befitting "the utterances of men falling or succeeding, the temperate, the brave" (399c). "Bring the soul into harmony with all right things" is Wilde's variation on Plato's comment, in *Republic*, bk. 3, that "the influence that emanates from works of beauty . . . insensibly guide[s] [the young] "to likeness, to friendship, to harmony with beautiful reason" (401d).

wonder a form which the artist may have left void, or not understood, or understood incompletely.

Ernest. The highest Criticism, then, is more creative than creation, and the primary aim of the critic is to see the object as in itself it really is not; that is your theory, I believe?

Gilbert. Yes, that is my theory. To the critic the work of art is simply a suggestion for a new work of his own, that need not necessarily bear any obvious resemblance to the thing it criticises. The one characteristic of a beautiful form is that one can put into it whatever one wishes, and see in it whatever one chooses to see; and the Beauty, that gives to creation its universal and aesthetic element, makes the critic a creator in his turn, and whispers of a thousand different things which were not present in the mind of him who carved the statue or painted the panel or graved the gem. . . . .

From "The Truth of Masks: A Note on Illusion"†

In many of the somewhat violent attacks that have recently been made on that splendour of mounting which now characterizes our Shakespearian revivals in England, it seems to have been tacitly assumed by the critics that Shakespeare himself was more or less indifferent to the costume of his actors, and that, could he see

† First published, signed, in *Nineteenth Century,* May 1885, under the title "Shakespeare and Stage Costume." Wilde retitled and extensively revised the essay for republication in *Intentions* in 1891, when he added the present Whistleresque subtitle as well as the essay's final seven, paradoxical sentences. For Wilde's later distaste for the essay and his desire to replace it with "The Soul of Man" in a projected French translation of *Intentions,* see p. 184, headnote, above.

Mrs. Langtry's production of *Antony and Cleopatra*, he would probably say that the play, and the play only, is the thing, and that everything else is leather and prunella.[309] While, as regards any historical accuracy in dress, Lord Lytton, in an article in the *Nineteenth Century*, has laid it down as a dogma of art that archæology is entirely out of place in the presentation of any of Shakespeare's plays, and the attempt to introduce it one of the stupidest pedantries of an age of prigs.[310]

. . . . [A]s regards the theory that Shakespeare did not busy himself much about the costume-wardrobe of his theatre, anybody who cares to study Shakespeare's method will see that there is absolutely no dramatist of the French, English, or Athenian stage who relies so much for his illusionist[311] effects on the dress of his actors as Shakespeare does himself.

309. Wilde's friend, the actress Lillie Langtry (1853–1929), opened as Cleopatra in Lewis Wingfield's spectacular production *Antony and Cleopatra* at the Princess's Theatre in November 1890. In the 1885 version of "The Truth of Masks," Wilde had alluded here instead to both Henry Irving's 1882 production of *Much Ado about Nothing* and Wilson Barrett's 1884 production of *Hamlet*, but on revising the essay for *Intentions* he clearly felt that a reference to a more recent and topical Shakespeare production was necessary.

310. The statesman and writer Robert Bulwer-Lytton, first Earl of Lytton, had written that "the attempt to archaeologise the Shakespearean drama is one of the stupidest pedantries of an age of prigs" ("Miss Anderson's Juliet," *Nineteenth Century* 16 [December 1884]: 886, note 1). Wilde remained friendly with Lytton after publishing "Shakespeare and Stage Costume": shortly before Lytton's death, in November 1891, Wilde gave him an inscribed copy of *Intentions*; and in 1893 Wilde dedicated the first edition of *Lady Windermere's Fan* to Lytton's memory "in affection and admiration."

311. "illusionist" added in 1891.

Knowing how the artistic temperament is always fascinated by beauty of costume,[312] he constantly introduces into his plays masques and dances, purely for the sake of the pleasure which they give the eye; and we have still his stage-directions for the three great processions in *Henry the Eighth,* directions which are characterized by the most extraordinary elaborateness of detail down to the collars of S.S. and the pearls in Anne Boleyn's hair. Indeed it would be quite easy for a modern manager to reproduce these pageants absolutely as Shakespeare had them designed; and so accurate were they that one of the court officials of the time, writing an account of the last performance of the play at the Globe Theatre to a friend, actually complains of their realistic character, notably of the production on the stage of the Knights of the Garter in the robes and insignia of the order, as being calculated to bring ridicule on the real ceremonies; much in the same spirit in which the French Government, some time ago, prohibited that delightful actor, M. Christian,[313] from appearing in uniform, on the plea that it was prejudicial to the glory of the army that a colonel should be caricatured. And elsewhere the gorgeousness of apparel which distinguished the English stage under Shakespeare's influence was attacked by the contemporary critics, not as a rule, however, on the grounds of the democratic tendencies of realism, but usually on those moral grounds which are always the last refuge of people who have no sense of beauty.

The point, however, which I wish to emphasize is, not that Shakespeare appreciated the value of lovely costumes in adding

312. In 1891 Wilde substituted "the artistic temperament" for the earlier version's "the public."

313. Christian Perrin (1821–1889), French actor, known by his stage name of "Christian." He is buried near Wilde in Paris's Père Lachaise Cemetery.

picturesqueness to poetry, but that he saw how important costume is as a means of producing certain dramatic effects. Many of his plays, such as *Measure for Measure, Twelfth Night, The Two Gentleman of Verona, All's Well that Ends Well, Cymbeline,* and others, depend for their illusion[314] on the character of the various dresses worn by the hero or the heroine; the delightful scene in *Henry the Sixth,* on the modern miracles of healing by faith, loses all its point unless Gloster is in black and scarlet; and the *dénoûment* of the *Merry Wives of Windsor* hinges on the colour of Anne Page's gown. As for the uses Shakespeare makes of disguises the instances are almost number-less. Posthumus hides his passion under a peasant's garb, and Edgar his pride beneath an idiot's rags; Portia wears the apparel of a lawyer, and Rosalind is attired in "all points as a man"; the cloak-bag of Pisanio changes Imogen to the youth Fidele; Jessica flees from her father's house in boy's dress, and Julia ties up her yellow hair in fantastic love-knots, and dons hose and doublet; Henry the Eighth woos his lady as a shepherd, and Romeo his as a pilgrim; Prince Hal and Poins appear first as footpads in buckram suits, and then in white aprons and leather jerkins as the waiters in a tavern: and as for Falstaff, does he not come on as a highwayman, as an old woman, as Herne the Hunter, and as the clothes going to the laundry?

Nor are the examples of the employment of costume as a mode of intensifying dramatic situation less numerous. After slaughter of Duncan, Macbeth appears in his night-gown as if aroused from sleep; Timon ends in rags the play he had begun in splen-dour; Richard flatters the London citizens in a suit of mean and shabby armour, and, as soon as he has stepped in blood to the throne, marches through the streets in crown and George and

314. "for their illusion" substituted in 1891 for "entirely."

Garter; the climax of *The Tempest* is reached when Prospero, throwing off his enchanter's robes, sends Ariel for his hat and rapier, and reveals himself as the great Italian Duke; the very Ghost in *Hamlet* changes his mystical apparel to produce different effects; and as for Juliet, a modern playwright would probably have laid her out in her shroud, and made the scene a scene of horror merely, but Shakespeare arrays her in rich and gorgeous raiment, whose loveliness makes the vault "a feasting presence full of light," turns the tomb into a bridal chamber, and gives the cue and motive for Romeo's speech of the triumph of Beauty over Death.

Even small details of dress, such as the colour of a major-domo's stockings, the pattern on a wife's handkerchief, the sleeve of a young soldier, and a fashionable woman's bonnets, become in Shakespeare's hands points of actual dramatic importance, and by some of them the action of the play in question is conditioned absolutely. Many other dramatists have availed themselves of costume as a method of expressing directly to the audience the character of a person on his entrance, though hardly so brilliantly as Shakespeare has done in the case of the dandy Parolles, whose dress, by the way, only an archæologist can understand; the fun of a master and servant exchanging coats in presence of the audience, of ship-wrecked sailors squabbling over the division of a lot of fine clothes, and of a tinker dressed up like a duke while he is in his cups, may be regarded as part of that great career which costume has always played in comedy from the time of Aristophanes down to Mr. Gilbert; but nobody from the mere details of apparel and adornment has ever drawn such irony of contrast, such immediate and tragic effect, such pity and such pathos, as Shakespeare himself. . . .

. . . . Of the value of beautiful costume in creating an artistic temperament in the audience, and producing that joy in beauty for beauty's sake without which the great masterpieces of art can never be understood, I will not here speak; though it is worth while to notice how Shakespeare appreciated that side of the question in the production of his tragedies, acting them always by artificial light, and in a theatre hung with black; but what I have tried to point out is that archæology is not a pedantic method, but a method of artistic illusion,[315] and that costume is a means of displaying character without description, and of producing dramatic situations and dramatic effects. And I think it is a pity that so many critics should have set themselves to attack one of the most important movements on the modern stage before that movement has at all reached its proper perfection. That it will do so, however, I feel as certain as that we shall require from our dramatic critics in the future higher qualification than that they can remember Macready or have seen Benjamin Webster; we shall require of them indeed, that they cultivate a sense of beauty.[316] *Pour être plus difficile, la tâche n'en est que plus glorieuse.*[317] And if they will not encourage, at least they must not oppose, a movement of which Shakespeare of all dramatists would have most approved, for it has the illusion of truth for its method, and the illusion of beauty for its result.[318] Not that I agree with everything

315. In 1891 Wilde substituted "artistic illusion" for the earlier version's "realism."

316. The actor-managers William Macready (1793–1873) and Benjamin Webster (1797–1882).

317. "The task is only more glorious for being more difficult." Wilde is quoting from Charles Baudelaire's essay "On the Heroism of Modern Life."

318. In 1891, Wilde altered the last two clauses in this sentence, substituting "for it has Truth for its aim, and Beauty for its result" with "for it

that I have said in this essay.[319] There is much with which I entirely disagree. The essay simply represents an artistic standpoint,
and in aesthetic criticism attitude is everything. For in art there is
no such thing as a universal truth. A Truth in art is that whose
contradictory is also true. And just as it is only in art-criticism,
and through it, that we can apprehend the Platonic theory of ideas,
so it is only in art-criticism, and through it, that we can realize Hegel's system of contraries. The truths of metaphysics are the truths
of masks.[320]

---

has the illusion of truth for its method, and the illusion of beauty for its
result." The 1885 version of the essay ended at this point.

319. For Wilde's notion that "[t]he wise contradict themselves," see
p. 364 below. This sentence and the next six were added to the essay in
1891. As well as giving a powerful conclusion to "The Truth of Masks,"
they constitute an apt finale to *Intentions* as a whole, in which "The
Truth of Masks" was printed last.

320. By *art-criticism,* Wilde means criticism that is self-consciously
artistic in form as much as subject matter. Such criticism is not confined
to developments in visual art, although it is certainly alive to them and
often borrows from them, just as it borrows from poetry and music.
Above all, art-criticism is "never imitative," Wilde writes in "The Critic
as Artist"; through its "rejection of resemblance, [it] shows us . . . not
merely the meaning but also the mystery of Beauty, and, by transforming
each art into literature, [it] solves once for all the problem of Art's unity"
(Wilde, *Criticism,* 161). For Wilde's notion that "there are not many arts,
but one art merely: poem, picture and Parthenon, sonnet and statue–all
are in their essence the same and he who knows one knows all," see p. 48
above; and for his notion that criticism is "really a creative art," see pp.
305–313 above.

LETTERS TO THE PRESS

From "Woman's Dress"*

The "Girl Graduate"[1] . . . makes two points: that high heels are a necessity for any lady who wishes to keep her dress clean from the Stygian mud of our streets, and that without a tight corset 'the

---

* Extracted from a signed letter published on October 14, 1884, in the *Pall Mall Gazette*. Wilde's letter was a reply to two previous correspondents—the self-described "Girl Graduate" and Wentworth Huyshe, both of whom are invoked directly here by Wilde—who had taken issue with the *Gazette's* report, on October 2, of a lecture that Wilde had given on the subject of dress. These previous letters and the report of Wilde's lecture that had prompted them are reprinted in John Cooper, *Oscar Wilde on Dress* (Philadelphia: CSM Press, 2013), 133–145. First published under the title "Mr. Oscar Wilde on Woman's Dress," Wilde's letter was given the short title "Woman's Dress" (retained here) by his editor and executor Robert Ross when reprinted, eight years after Wilde's death, in *Miscellanies*, vol. 14 of *The Complete Works of Oscar Wilde* (London: Methuen, 1908). For the relation of Wilde's writings on dress to the broader dress reform movement of the late 1870s and 1880s, see headnote pp. 93–95 above.

1. By signing herself "the Girl Graduate," the anonymous female correspondent with whom Wilde here takes issue (see previous note) identifies herself as a recent graduate of one of only a small handful of British women's colleges that existed at the time, the most prominent of which were Newnham College and Girton College (both Cambridge), Lady Margaret Hall and Somerville Hall (both Oxford), and Bedford College (London). For Wilde's comment that "Girton and Newnham have rendered intellectual sympathy [between men and women] possible," see p. 57 above.

ordinary number of petticoats and etceteras' cannot be properly or conveniently held up.[2] Now, it is quite true that as long as the lower garments are suspended from the hips a corset is an absolute necessity; the mistake lies in not suspending all apparel from the shoulders. In the latter case a corset becomes useless, the body is left free and unconfined for respiration and motion, there is more health, and consequently more beauty. Indeed all the most ungainly and uncomfortable articles of dress that fashion has ever in her folly prescribed, not the tight corset merely, but the farthingale, the vertugadin, the hoop, the crinoline, and that modern monstrosity the so-called "dress improver" also, all of them have owed their origin to the same error, the error of not seeing that it is from the shoulders, and from the shoulders only, that all garments should be hung.[3]

And as regards high heels, I quite admit that some additional height to the shoe or boot is necessary if long gowns are to be worn in the street; but what I object to is that the height should be given to the heel only, and not to the sole of the foot also. The modern high-heeled boot is, in fact, merely the clog of the time of Henry VI,

2. *Etceteras* (Lat. meaning "the rest") was a term used in polite discourse as a "substitute for a suppressed substantive, generally a coarse or indelicate one. *spec. (plural)*, trousers" (OED). Wilde uses it as a substitute for *undergarments.*

3. A *farthingale* is "a frame-work of hoops, usually of whalebone, worked into some kind of cloth, formerly used for extending the skirts of women's dresses; a hooped petticoat" (OED), while a *vertugadin* (from the Spanish *verdugo,* meaning "green wood") is an older French term for the same thing. A *crinoline* is a reinforced petticoat or underskirt, made from "a stiff fabric made with a weft of horsehair and a warp of cotton or linen thread" (OED), while a *dress improver* is "a stuffed pad or wire frame worn below the waist under a woman's skirt to distend it; a bustle" (OED).

"In spite of all, some shape of beauty moves away the pall from our dark spirits."

KEATS.

Frontispiece to Mrs. H. R. Haweis, *The Art of Beauty*, 2nd ed. (London: Chatto and Windus, 1883). "The mistake lies in not suspending all apparel from the shoulders," Wilde writes in "Women's Dress": "in the latter case . . . the body is left free and unconfined . . . there is more health, and consequently more beauty." Wilde's ideas about women's dress were partly inspired by Haweis, a founder of the Rational Dress Society.

with the front prop left out, and its inevitable effect is to throw the body forward, to shorten the steps, and consequently to produce that want of grace which always follows want of freedom.

Why should clogs be despised? Much art has been expended on clogs. They have been made of lovely woods, and delicately inlaid with ivory, and with mother-of-pearl. A clog might be a dream of beauty, and, if not too high or too heavy, most comfortable also. But if there be any who do not like clogs, let them try some adaptation of the trouser of the Turkish lady, which is loose round the limb and tight at the ankle.

The "Girl Graduate," with a pathos to which I am not insensible, entreats me not to apotheosize "that awful, befringed, beflounced, and bekilted divided skirt." Well, I will acknowledge that the fringes, the flounces, and the kilting do certainly defeat the whole object of the dress, which is that of ease and liberty; but I regard these things as mere wicked superfluities, tragic proofs that the divided skirt is ashamed of its own division. The principle of the dress is good, and, though it is not by any means perfection, it is a step towards it.[4]

. . . . And now to the question of men's dress, or rather to Mr. Huyshe's claim of the superiority, in point of costume, of the last quarter of the eighteenth century over the second quarter of

4. The *divided skirt,* invented in 1881 by Viscountess Harberton, a cofounder of the Rational Dress Society (see headnote p. 93 above), was essentially a pair of trousers with very wide legs masquerading as a skirt. It was the object of much ridicule from conservatives. After her 1884 marriage to Oscar, Wilde's wife Constance became a member (and eventually an officer) of the Rational Dress Society and, like her husband, an outspoken proponent of "rational dress" for women. Constance both modeled and spoke up for the divided skirt.

the seventeenth. The broad-brimmed hat of 1640 kept the rain of winter and the glare of summer from the face; the same cannot be said of the hat of one hundred years ago, which, with its comparatively narrow brim and high crown, was the precursor of the modern "chimney-pot": a wide turned-down collar is a healthier thing than a strangling stock, and a short cloak much more comfortable than a sleeved overcoat, even though the latter may have had "three capes"; a cloak is easier to put on and off, lies lightly on the shoulder in summer, and wrapped round one in winter keeps one perfectly warm. A doublet, again, is simpler than a coat and waistcoat; instead of two garments we have one; by not being open, also, it protects the chest better.

Short loose trousers are in every way to be preferred to the tight knee-breeches which often impede the proper circulation of the blood; and finally, the soft leather boots, which could be worn above or below the knee, are more supple, and give consequently more freedom, than the stiff Hessian which Mr. Huyshe so praises. I say nothing about the question of grace and picturesqueness, for I suppose that no one, not even Mr. Huyshe, would prefer a macaroni to a cavalier, a Lawrence to a Vandyke, or the third George to the first Charles;[5] but for ease, warmth and comfort this seventeenth-

---

5. The *macaroni* was an eighteenth-century precursor of the Regency dandy. Named for the pasta dish that rich young Englishmen brought back from their grand tours in Europe, the term was applied in the 1770s to a young man who exceeded the perceived standards of good taste through his adoption of elite Continental dress and manners. According to Samuel Johnson, a *cavalier* is "a gay sprightly military man," while OED defines him more broadly as "a courtly gentleman, a gallant." Sir Thomas Lawrence (1769–1830) and the Dutchman Anthony Van Dyke (1599–1641) were both, in their respective days, among Europe's most

Photoportrait of Wilde, by Napoleon Sarony, 1882. Where men's dress is concerned, Wilde writes, "a cloak is easier to put on and off, lies lightly on the shoulder in summer, and wrapped round one in winter keeps one perfectly warm."

LETTERS TO THE PRESS

century dress is infinitely superior to anything that came after it, and I do not think it is excelled by any preceding form of costume. I sincerely trust that we may soon see in England some national revival of it.

---

fashionable court portrait painters. Britain's King George III famously became mad and despotic, eventually to be displaced ten years before his death by his son the Prince Regent (later George IV). By contrast, the artistic Charles I, deposed and eventually executed by the Puritan government of Oliver Cromwell, was a hero to Wilde and the aesthetes of the 1890s.

To Read, or Not to Read*

Books, I fancy, may be conveniently divided into three classes:

1. Books to read, such as Cicero's *Letters,* Suetonius, Vasari's *Lives of the Painters,* the *Autobiography* of Benvenuto Cellini, Sir John Mandeville, Marco Polo, St. Simon's *Memoirs,* Mommsen, and (till we get a better one) Grote's *History of Greece.*[1]

* So titled by the *Pall Mall Gazette,* which early in 1886 asked a number of leading figures to list their "Hundred Best Books." Wilde's response, treated here as a letter, appeared on February 8, 1886, and was prefaced by the following editor's note: "As we have published so many letters advising what to read, the following advice [about] 'what not to read' from so good an authority as Mr. Oscar Wilde may be of service."

1. Cicero, *Letters to Friends* and *Letters to Atticus* (c. 65–43 BCE); Suetonius, *Lives of the Caesars* (121 CE); Giorgio Vasari, *Lives of the Artists* (1550, enlarged 1568); Benvenuto Cellini, *The Autobiography of Benvenuto Cellini* (1558–1563); John Mandeville, *The Book of Marvels and Travels* (c. 1357); Marco Polo, *The Travels* (c. 1300); *Historical Memoirs of the Duc de Saint-Simon* (1691–1723); Theodor Mommsen, *The History of Rome* (1854–1856); and George Grote, *A History of Greece* (1846–1856). Although Wilde gives the titles of "books to read" in English, only Grote's *History of Greece* was composed in English. All but the last two titles are either memoirs or biographies. In "The Critic as Artist," Gilbert confesses early on that "I like all memoirs. I like them for their form, just as much as for their matter. In literature mere egotism is delightful. It is what fascinates

2. Books to re-read, such as Plato and Keats: in the sphere of
   poetry, the masters not the minstrels; in the sphere of
   philosophy, the seers not the savants.[2]

---

us in the letters of personalities so different as Cicero and Balzac, Flaubert and Berlioz, Byron and Madame de Sévigné." For Wilde's comment that in Cicero's "speeches," Suetonius's *Lives,* Cellini's *Autobiography,* and Marco Polo's *Travels,* "facts are either kept in their proper subordinate position, or else entirely excluded on the general ground of dulness," see p. 213 above; and for his suggestion that Mandeville's "fascinating book of travels" was penned by "some honest gentleman, who [had] never been farther than the yew-trees of his own garden," see p. 216 above. For the influence of Suetonius's *Lives* on Wilde's *Picture of Dorian Gray,* see *The Picture of Dorian Gray: An Annotated, Uncensored Edition,* ed. Nicholas Frankel (Cambridge, MA: The Belknap Press of Harvard Univ. Press, 2011), 206n54.

2. For the "artistic pleasure [of] re-reading," and for re-reading "as the best rough test of what is literature and what is not," see p. 206 above.

The profound influence of Plato and Keats on Wilde's thought and writing has long been noted by scholars. So too has these authors' importance for emerging concepts of homosexuality and masculinity. For Plato, see Linda Dowling, *Hellenism and Homosexuality in Victorian Oxford* (Ithaca, NY: Cornell Univ. Press, 1994); Stefano Evangelista, "'Lovers and Philosophers at Once': Aesthetic Platonism in the Fin de Siècle," *Yearbook of English Studies* 36, no. 2 (2006): 230–244; Marylu Hill, "Wilde's New Republic," in *Oscar Wilde and Classical Antiquity*, ed. Kathleen Riley et al. (Oxford: Oxford Univ. Press, 2018), 231–250; and headnote pp. 184–185 above. For Keats, see Sarah Wootton, *Consuming Keats: Nineteenth Century Representations in Art & Literature* (New York: Palgrave MacMillan, 2006); James Najarian, *Victorian Keats: Manliness, Sexuality, and Desire* (New York: Palgrave MacMillan, 2002); and Eleanor Fitzsimons, "In My Heaven He Walks Eternally with Shakespeare and the Greeks: Oscar Wilde and John Keats," *The Wildean* 53 (2018): 22–32.

Notably absent from Wilde's list of "books to re-read" are any works by Walter Pater, whose *The Renaissance* Wilde once called "the golden book of spirit and sense, the holy writ of beauty" (p. 86 above). Wilde's

3. Books not to read at all, such as Thomson's *Seasons,*
Rogers's *Italy,* Paley's *Evidences,* all the Fathers except
St. Augustine, all John Stuart Mill except the essay on
Liberty, all Voltaire's plays without any exception, Butler's
Analogy, Grant's *Aristotle,* Hume's *England,* Lewes's *History
of Philosophy,* all argumentative books and all books that try
to prove anything.[3]

The third class is by far the most important. To tell people what
to read is, as a rule, either useless or harmful; for, the appreciation
of literature is a question of temperament not of teaching; to Parnassus there is no primer and nothing that one can learn is ever
worth learning.[4] But to tell people what not to read is a very dif-

---

admiration for Pater is clear from "Mr. Pater's Last Volume," and Pater's
works were among the first books that Wilde was permitted to (re-)read
in prison in 1895. Ten months before his release from prison, Wilde was
also granted special permission to re-read Keats's poems. Keats was one
of just thirteen authors, including Flaubert, Baudelaire, and Dante,
whose works Wilde later asked to be made available to him immediately
upon his release, since Wilde had "a horror of going out into the world
without a single book of my own" (*The Complete Letters of Oscar Wilde,*
ed. Merlin Holland and Rupert Hart-Davis [New York: Henry Holt,
2000], 790–791).

3. James Thomson, *The Seasons* (1726–1730); Samuel Rogers, *Italy: A
Poem* (1822); William Paley, *Natural Theology, or Evidences of the Existence and Attributes of the Deity* (1802); John Stuart Mill, *On Liberty*
(1859); Joseph Butler, *Analogy of Religion, Natural and Revealed, to the
Constitution and Course of Nature* (1736); Alexander Grant, *Aristotle*
(1877); David Hume, *The History of England* (1754–1762); George Henry
Lewes, *The Biographical History of Philosophy* (1845–1846).

4. Literally a mountain in central Greece, adjacent to the site of the
ancient city of Delphi (in Greek mythology, sacred to Apollo and regarded

ferent matter, and I venture to recommend it as a mission to the University Extension Scheme.[5] Indeed, it is one that is eminently needed in this age of ours, an age that reads so much that it has no time to admire, and writes so much that it has no time to think. Whoever will select out of the chaos of our modern curricula "The Worst Hundred Books," and publish a list of them, will confer on the rising generation a real and lasting benefit.

After expressing these views I suppose I should not offer any suggestions at all with regard to "The Best Hundred Books," but I hope you will allow me the pleasure of being inconsistent, as I am anxious to put in a claim for a book that has been strangely omitted by most of the excellent judges who have contributed to your columns. I mean the *Greek Anthology*.[6] The beautiful poems contained

---

as the home of the Muses), Parnassus refers figuratively to the home or source of poetry and learning. For Wilde's adaptation of the aphorism "nothing that one can learn is ever worth learning" into the first of his "Maxims for the Instruction of the Over-Educated," see p. 358 below.

5. The University Extension Scheme, the progenitor of the modern university's "extramural" curriculum, was a loose association of programs developed in the final decades of the nineteenth century whereby the principal English universities offered free lectures to unenrolled students in the major industrial cities. It was of particular importance to women and the working classes, who, with few exceptions, had little formal access to higher education. See Alexandra Lawrie, "The University Extension Movement," chapter 3 of her *The Beginnings of University English: Extramural Study 1885–1910* (Basingstoke: Palgrave Macmillan, 2014), 56–85; and Stuart Marriott, *A Backstairs to a Degree: Demands for an Open University in Late-Victorian England* (Leeds: Univ. of Leeds, 1981).

6. The *Greek Anthology*, described by Wilde's contemporary John Addington Symonds as "the most valuable relic of antique literature that we possess," is the name generally given to an anthology of Greek epigrammatic poems that has descended from classical times. Translated

in this collection seem to me to hold the same position with regard to Greek dramatic literature as do the delicate little figurines of

---

selections from the anthology—some in prose, and many of them inadequate—appeared throughout the nineteenth century and grew more frequent following the publication of John Addington Symonds's bestselling *Studies of the Greek Poets* (1873, expanded 1876), whose longest and most important chapter was devoted to the *Anthology*. For the *Anthology's* reputation among the Victorians, see Gideon Nisbet, *Greek Epigram in Reception: J. A Symonds, Oscar Wilde, and the Invention of Desire, 1805–1929* (Oxford: Oxford Univ. Press, 2013). In late 1889, in the last of many short critical contributions to the magazine *Woman's World*, which he had edited for the past two years, Wilde published an enthusiastic, anonymous review of *Selections from the Greek Anthology*, edited by the poet "Graham R. Tomson" (pseud. of Rosamund Marriott Watson), whom he is known to have admired and whose previous book he had reviewed excitedly in *Woman's World* the previous June. After calling Marriott Watson's selection "a delightful little volume" ("New Books," *Woman's World* 3 [1889–1890]: 105), he writes that "[t]o the general reader whose acquaintance with Greek may be presumed to be limited, the 'Anthology' has always been a sealed book." But Marriott Watson has "performed her task with unusual judgment and good sense," he goes on to say, and "succeeded in bringing together within a small compass a large number of admirable translations." The Greek epigrams "possess a charm which is all their own," he explains: "[n]or are they marked by that severe beauty, that exquisiteness of restraint, which renders the masterpieces of Greek literature difficult of appreciation to the unlearned. Meleager, Leonidas, and the rest are frivolous enough in their view of life, in their treatment of love—the subject which ever engrosses them—to prove acceptable to the most modern reader. Here and there, it is true, we listen to the genuine note of pathos. But, as a rule, the poets of the 'Anthology' are no less and no more serious than were the English poets of the seventeenth century. They touch lightly on art, on love, on the beauties of nature; on all the topics, indeed, which might be expected to inspire the modern writer of *vers de société*." See too headnote p. 351 below.

Tanagra to the Phidian marbles, and to be quite as necessary for the complete understanding of the Greek spirit.[7]

I am also amazed to find that Edgar Allan Poe has been passed over. Surely this marvellous lord of rhythmic expression deserves a place? If, in order to make room for him, it be necessary to elbow out some one else, I should elbow out Southey, and I think that Baudelaire might be most advantageously substituted for Keble.

7. In the 1870s, a great quantity of small mold-cast terracotta figurines, dating from the fourth or third century BCE, were excavated around Tanagra in east-central Greece. Wilde revered them highly as embodiments of Greek spirit and beauty, remarking in a review of Ernst von Wildenbruch's *The Master of Tanagra* that it is "impossible to reproduce by any process the delicate and exquisite charm of the Tanagra figurines." Early in "The Critic as Artist," Ernest describes Tanagra figurines as "forms so exquisite that the people gave them to the dead as their playthings, and we find them still in the dusty tombs on the yellow hillside by Tanagra, with the faint gold and the fading crimson still lingering about hair and lips and raiment" (Wilde, *Criticism: Historical Criticism, Intentions, The Soul of Man,* ed. Josephine Guy, vol. 4 of *The Complete Works of Oscar Wilde* [Oxford: Oxford Univ. Press, 2007], 132).

Phidian marbles refers to the Elgin Marbles, also known as the Parthenon Marbles, a collection of Classical Greek marble sculptures made under the supervision of the architect and sculptor Phidias (c. 480–430 BCE) and his assistants. They are now controversially housed in the British Museum, but were originally part of the temple of the Parthenon and other buildings on the Acropolis of Athens. Phidias himself was one of the greatest ancient Greek sculptors—his statue of Zeus at Olympia was one of the seven wonders of the ancient world—but he was mainly celebrated for statuary in bronze or gold and ivory; and Plato, in his *Hippias Major,* claims that Phidias seldom, if ever, executed works in marble.

No doubt, both in *The Curse of Kehama* and in *The Christian Year* there are poetic qualities of a certain kind, but absolute catholicity of taste is not without its dangers. It is only an auctioneer who should admire all schools of art.[8]

8. *The Curse of Kehama* (1810) and *The Christian Year* (1827) are book-length works by the poets Robert Southey and John Keble respectively. The latter, a series of poems for Sundays and feastdays in the liturgical calendar of the Church of England, was the most popular book of poetry in Victorian England.

From "Fashions in Dress"*

. . . Allow me to point out that the costume worn now by Mr. Wyndham in *London Assurance* might be taken as the basis for a new departure, not in the style, but in the colour of modern evening dress. Freedom in . . . selection of colour is a necessary condition of variety and individualism of costume, and the uniform black that is worn now, though valuable at a dinner-party, where it serves to isolate and separate women's dresses, to frame them as it were, still is dull and tedious and depressing in itself, and makes the aspect of club-life and men's dinners monotonous and uninteresting.

* So titled by the *Daily Telegraph,* which published Wilde's signed letter under this title on February 3, 1891. The occasion for Wilde's letter was a recent revival at the Criterion Theatre of Dion Boucicault's comedy *London Assurance,* featuring the actor-manager Charles Wyndham, whom Wilde knew well. The production was widely noted for Wyndham's decision to have the cast "habited, with punctilious correctness, in the high-collared, wasp-waisted, tight-legged garments of 1841, so that the student of costume may find in every curly wig, stock, . . . turnover shirt-cuff, and satin waistcoat, a private ecstasy" (A. B. Walkley, signed rev. of *The London Assurance, The Speaker,* [December 6, 1890]: 628). Four years later, Wilde contracted with Wyndham to produce and star in *The Importance of Being Earnest,* also at the Criterion. However, shortly after this event, they both agreed to transfer the play to the actor-manager George Alexander, at the St. James's Theatre, where it received its debut, to help the latter out of a "hole." See *The Complete Letters of Oscar Wilde,* ed. Merlin Holland and Rupert Hart-Davis (New York: Henry Holt, 2000), 677n1.

The actor-manager Charles Wyndham in character, photographer unknown, c. 1890. "The costume worn now by
Mr. Wyndham in *London Assurance* might be taken as the
basis for a new departure," writes Wilde. Wilde later contracted with Wyndham, a personal friend, to stage and star in
the first production of *The Importance of Being Earnest,* although circumstances prevented this from coming about.

The little note of individualism that makes dress delightful can only be attained nowadays by the colour and treatment of the flower one wears.[1] This is a great pity. The colour of the coat should be entirely for the good taste of the wearer to decide. This would give pleasure, and produce charming variety of colour effects in modern life.

Another important point . . . is that the decorative value of buttons is recognised. At present we all have more than a dozen useless buttons on our evening coats, and by always keeping them black and of the same colour as the rest of the costume we prevent them being in any way beautiful. Now, when a thing is useless it should be made beautiful, otherwise it has no reason for existing at all. Buttons should be either gilt . . . or of paste, or enamel, or inlaid metals, or any other material that is capable of being artistically treated. The handsome effect produced by servants' liveries is almost entirely due to the buttons they wear.

Nor would these suggested changes be in any way violent, or abrupt, or revolutionary, or calculated to excite terror in the timid, or rage in the dull, or fury in the honest Philistine.[2] For the dress of 1840 is really the same in design and form as ours. Of course, the sleeves are tighter and the cuffs turn each over them, as sleeves should be and as cuffs should do. The trousers, also, are tighter than the present fashion, but the general cut of the dress is the same. . . .

Two other points may be noticed. The first is that the use of a frill to the shirt prevents the tediousness of a flat polished surface of stiff linen—breaks it up very pleasantly in fact. The second point

1. That is, the flower worn as a "buttonhole" in the jacket's lapel. "A really well-made buttonhole is the only link between Art and Nature," Wilde proclaims in "Phrases and Philosophies for the Use of the Young."
2. For *Philistine,* see p. 43, n.2 and p. 115, n.5 above.

is the beauty and utility of . . . cloaks [whose] folds are ample, picturesque, and comforting, [and whose] bright coloured linings are delightful, and fanciful and gay. Their capes give warmth and suggest dignity and serve to make the lines of the cloaks richer and more complex. A cloak is an admirable thing. Our nearest approach to it is the Inverness cape,[3] which, when its wings are lined with black satin, is very charming in its way. Still it has, though not sleeves, yet sleeve openings. A cloak can be put on, or thrown off, far more easily. A cloak is also warmer, and can be wrapped around one, if there is a chill wind. We must wear cloaks with lovely linings. Otherwise we shall be very incomplete.

The coat, then, of next season, will be an exquisite colour-note, and have also a great psychological value. It will emphasize the serious and thoughtful side of a man's character. One will be able to discern a man's views of life by the colour he selects. The colour of the coat will be symbolic. It will be part of the wonderful symbolist movement in modern art. The imagination will concentrate itself upon the waistcoat. Waistcoats will show whether a man can admire poetry or not. That will be very valuable. Over the shirtfront Fancy will preside. By a single glance one will be able to detect the tedious. How the change is to be brought about is not

---

3. A form of weatherproof outercoat, now firmly associated with the fictional Sherlock Holmes, notable for being sleeveless, the arms emerging from armholes beneath a cape. Originally a topcoat featuring "sleeves covered by a long cape, which reached the entire length of the sleeve," the *Inverness coat* "transformed into the *Inverness cape* in the 1880s, when the sleeves were completely removed and the armholes were cut away beneath the cape, leaving the topcoat and cape together as one" (Jessica Schwartz, "Inverness Coat," in *Ethnic Dress in the United States: A Cultural Encyclopedia,* ed. Annette Lynch and Mitchell D. Strauss [Lanham, MD: Rowman & Littlefield, 2015], 157).

Oscar Wilde, 1889. Photoportrait by W. & D. Downey. "The little note of individualism that makes dress delightful," Wilde writes, "can only be attained nowadays by the colour and treatment of the flower one wears."

difficult to see. . . . Nothing but a resolution on the subject passed by the House of Commons will do. . . . Surely there are some amongst our legislators who are capable of taking a serious interest in serious things? They cannot all be absorbed in the county-court collection of tithes. . . .

Of the moral value and influence of such a charming costume I think I had better say nothing. The fact is that when Mr. Wyndham and Mr. Arthur Bourchier appear in their delightful dresses they have been behaving very badly. . . . . But if one is to behave badly, it is better to be bad in a becoming dress than in one that is unbecoming, and it is only fair to add that at the end of the play Mr. Wyndham accepts his lecture with a dignity and courtesy of manner that can only result from the habit of wearing delightful clothes.

Puppets and Actors*

19 February, London

Sir, I have just been sent an article that seems to have appeared in your paper some days ago, in which it is stated that, in the course of some remarks addressed to the Playgoers' Club on the occasion of my taking the chair at their last meeting, I laid it down as an axiom that the stage is only "a frame furnished with a set of puppets."

Now, it is quite true that I hold that the stage is to a play no more than a picture-frame is to a painting, and that the actable value of a play has nothing whatsoever to do with its value as a work of art. In this century, in England, to take an obvious example, we have had only two great plays—one is Shelley's *Cenci,*

---

* So titled by the *Daily Telegraph,* which published Wilde's signed letter under this title on February 20, 1892. Wilde evidently composed the letter on the previous day, although the article to which he refers in opening had appeared one week before, on February 12. Founded in 1884, the Playgoers' Club met regularly in a variety of temporary locations during its roughly twenty-year existence, so that "kindred spirits could assemble and discuss at leisure the events of the dramatic world" (Benjamin W. Findon, *The Playgoers' Club, 1884 to 1905: Its History and Memories* [London: Ballantyne, 1905], 2). The meeting of the Playgoers' Club to which Wilde refers, at which the poet John Gray lectured on the modern actor (see n.4 below), had taken place on February 7.

the other Mr. Swinburne's *Atalanta in Calydon,* and neither of them is in any sense of the word an actable play. Indeed, the mere suggestion that stage representation is any test of a work of art is quite ridiculous. In the production of Browning's plays, for instance, in London and at Oxford, what was being tested was obviously the capacity of the modern stage to represent, in any adequate measure or degree, works of introspective method and strange or sterile psychology. But the artistic value of *Strafford* or *In a Balcony* was settled when Robert Browning wrote their last lines. It is not, Sir, by the mimes that the muses are to be judged.

So far, the writer of the article in question is right. Where he goes wrong is in saying that I describe this frame—the stage—as being furnished with a set of puppets. He admits that he speaks only by report, but he should have remembered, sir, that report is not merely a lying jade, which I personally would willingly forgive her, but a jade who lies without lovely invention—a thing that I, at any rate, can forgive her never.

What I really said was that the frame we call the stage was "peopled with either living actors or moving puppets," and I pointed out briefly, of necessity, that the personality of the actor is often a source of danger in the perfect presentation of a work of art. It may distort. It may lead astray. It may be a discord in the tone or symphony. For anybody can act. Most people in England do nothing else. To be conventional is to be a comedian. To act a particular part, however, is a very different thing, and a very difficult thing as well. The actor's aim is, or should be, to convert his own accidental personality into the real and essential personality of the character he is called upon to impersonate, whatever that character may be; or perhaps I should say that there are two schools of actors—the school of those who attain their effect by exaggeration of personality, and the school of those who attain it by suppression. It would be too long to discuss these schools, or to decide which of them the dramatist loves best. Let me note the danger of personality, and pass on to my puppets.

There are many advantages in puppets. They never argue. They have no crude views about art. They have no private lives. We are never bothered by accounts of their virtues, or bored by recitals of their vices; and when they are out of an engagement they never do good in public or save people from drowning; nor do they speak more than is set down for them. They recognise the presiding intellect of the dramatist, and have never been known to ask for their parts to be written up. They are admirably docile, and have no personalities at all. I saw lately, in Paris, a performance by certain puppets of Shakespeare's *Tempest,* in M. Maurice Bouchor's translation.[1] Miranda was the image of Miranda, because an artist had

1. The playwright, poet, translator, and puppeteer Maurice Bouchor (1855–1929) wrote and adapted plays for Henri Signoret's Petit Théâtre des Marionettes, in Paris's Galerie Vivienne, from 1889 to 1894. Here Bouchor and Signoret succeeded in making puppeteering an admired theatrical art form, in part through the adaptation of stage classics for performance by puppets. They began with a puppet production of Aristophanes's *Birds,* in June 1888, followed shortly after by *The Tempest.* Wilde evidently saw the latter production during his lengthy stay in Paris in the fall of 1891.

Wilde was not alone in seeing puppetry as a paradigm for theatrical performance. Heinrich von Kleist's "On the Marionette Theater" (1810) was well known in symbolist circles, and in 1890 Bouchor argued, in a lecture subsequently published in *La Revue Bleue,* that the great dramatic works of the past should be performed by puppets, not actors. For *fin de siècle* puppetry and its influence on stagecraft, see Frantisek Deak, *Symbolist Theater* (Baltimore: Johns Hopkins Univ. Press, 1993), 174–175; Harold B. Segel, *Pinocchio's Progeny: Puppets, Marionettes, Automatons, and Robots in Modernist and Avant-Garde Drama* (Baltimore: Johns Hopkins

so fashioned her; and Ariel was true Ariel, because so had she been made. Their gestures were quite sufficient, and the words that seemed to come from their little lips were spoken by poets who had beautiful voices.[2] It was a delightful performance, and I remember it still with delight, though Miranda took no notice of the flowers I sent her after the curtain fell. For modern plays, however, perhaps we had better have living players, for in modern plays actuality is everything. The charm—the ineffable charm—of the unreal is here denied us, and rightly.[3]

Univ. Press, 1995); and Olga Taxidou, "Gentlemen, The Marionette," chapter 6 of her *The Mask: A Periodical Performance by Edward Gordon Craig* (London: Routledge, 2013).

2. In early productions at the Petit Théâtre des Marionettes, according to both Maurice Bouchor and Anatole France, "poets instead of professional actors read the text, while some of the puppets were manipulated by artists" (Deak, *Symbolist Theater,* 174).

3. Wilde had not yet embraced the absurdism and farcicality that are pronounced features of his greatest play, *The Importance of Being Earnest* (composed 1894, first performed 1895). Nonetheless, Wilde's remark that "in modern plays actuality is everything" sits somewhat oddly with his recent biblical drama *Salomé (*composed in French in late 1891 and early 1892) which is steeped in the influence of French anti-naturalist and symbolist drama, and was adapted for the opera by Richard Strauss in 1905. However, *Salomé*— which was first perfomed in 1896 in Paris and was never performed in Britain in Wilde's lifetime—was something of an anomaly in Wilde's dramatic oeuvre at this time; and in his social comedies of the early 1890s, written expressly for London's West End stage, Wilde certainly strove to represent modern-day actuality, as his plays' stage directions alone indicate. For instance, Wilde's opening stage direction to *Lady Windermere's Fan*—which debuted at London's St. James's Theatre on the very day the present letter was published—insists that the play is set in "the present" and that "the action of the play takes place within twenty-four hours beginning on a Tuesday afternoon at

Suffer me one more correction. Your writer describes the author of the brilliant fantastic lecture on "The Modern Actor" as *"a protégé"* of mine. Allow me to state that my acquaintance with Mr. John Gray is, I regret to say, extremely recent, and that I sought it because he had already a perfected mode of expression both in prose and verse.[4] All artists in this vulgar age need protection certainly. Perhaps they have always needed it. But the nineteenth-century artist finds it not in Prince, or Pope, or patron, but in high indifference of temper, in the pleasure of the creation of beautiful things, and the long contemplation of them, in disdain of what in life is common and ignoble, and in such felicitous sense of humour as

---

five o'clock, and ending the next day at 1.30 p.m." In this concern with modern actuality, Wilde's social comedies reflect the influence of Henrik Ibsen, the so-called father of modern drama, the powerful realism and feminism of whose plays Wilde is known to have admired.

4. The poet and (later) Catholic priest John Gray (1866–1934) has often been described as Wilde's protégé at the time this letter was written, and although the exact nature of their relationship remains a mystery, it is commonly assumed that they were lovers. Wilde first met Gray in the summer of 1889, possibly through the artists Charles Ricketts and Charles Shannon, who had been friends with Gray for some time. Ricketts and Shannon published and illustrated Gray's story "The Great Worm" in the inaugural (1889) number of their self-produced periodical *The Dial,* a copy of which they sent to Wilde. Gray's poetry appeared in each succeeding number of *The Dial,* and he was unquestionably one of the best poets of the 1890s. Wilde admired both the poet and his poetry greatly, so much so that he subsidized and helped arrange the publication of Gray's important 1893 poetry collection *Silverpoints,* designed throughout (like Wilde's own books at this time) by Ricketts. Gray was no mean prose writer too: for his "brilliant fantastic lecture on 'The Modern Actor,'" first published in the monthly review *The Albermarle* in July 1892, see *The Selected Prose of John Gray* (Greensboro, NC: ELT Press, 1992). Wilde and Gray fell out abruptly in 1893.

Charles Haslewood Shannon, portrait of John Gray. Lithograph, 1896. "The nineteenth-century artist," Wilde wrote of Gray in 1892 at the height of their friendship, "finds [protection] not in Prince, or Pope, or patron, but in high indifference of temper, in the pleasure of the creation of beautiful things, and the long contemplation of them. . . . These qualities Mr. John Gray possesses in a marked degree." Purportedly the model for Wilde's Dorian Gray, Gray fell out with Wilde abruptly in 1893.

enables one to see how vain and foolish is all popular opinion, and popular judgment, upon the wonderful things of art. These qualities Mr. John Gray possesses in a marked degree. He needs no other protection, nor, indeed, would he accept it.—I remain, Sir, your obedient servant, OSCAR WILDE.

EPIGRAMS AND PARADOXES*

* "The epigram in its first intention may be described as a very short poem summing up as though in a memorial inscription what it is desired to make permanently memorable in any action or situation. It must have the compression and conciseness of a real inscription, and in proportion to the smallness of its bulk must be highly finished, evenly balanced, simple and lucid. In literature it holds something of the same place as is held in art by an engraved gem" (J. W. Mackail, introduction to *Select Epigrams from the Greek Anthology* [1890]). See also p. 294, n.282 above, and for Wilde's notion that "paradoxes are always dangerous things," see p. 219 above.

Preface to *The Picture of Dorian Gray**

The artist is the creator of beautiful things.

To reveal art and conceal the artist is art's aim.

The critic is he who can translate into another manner or a new material his impression of beautiful things.

The highest as the lowest form of criticism is a mode of autobiography.

* Wilde's epigrams on art, artistry, and criticism were originally titled "Dogmas for the Use of the Aged" in an early manuscript draft (British Library Add MS 81635). Frequently understood as Wilde's personal artistic manifesto, they were first published separately from *The Picture of Dorian Gray*, in March 1891, over Wilde's signature and under the title "A Preface to *Dorian Gray*," in the *Fortnightly Review*, edited by Wilde's friend and fellow Irishman Frank Harris (see headnote p. 358 below). They were republished one month later, again over Wilde's signature, under the title "The Preface" in the first book edition of *The Picture of Dorian Gray*, although now Wilde split the ninth epigram in two, added the further epigram "No artist is ever morbid. The artist can express everything" (used previously with slight variation in "The Soul of Man Under Socialism"), and made other light changes

Printed here in its later, revised version, the Preface incorporates a number of phrases Wilde had used the previous summer when defending the periodical version of *Dorian Gray* in the British press. For discussion of whether Wilde's Preface might be considered a "delayed preface" or a "preface-manifesto," see introduction, p. 31, n.17 above.

Those who find ugly meanings in beautiful things are corrupt without being charming. This is a fault.

Those who find beautiful meanings in beautiful things are the cultivated. For these there is hope.

They are the elect to whom beautiful things mean only Beauty.

There is no such thing as a moral or an immoral book.

Books are well written, or badly written. That is all.[1]

The nineteenth-century dislike of Realism is the rage of Caliban seeing his own face in a glass.[2]

1. In May 1895 Wilde was pressed about this aphorism—which echoes his statement of June 1890 to the editor of the *St. James's Gazette,* "I am quite incapable of understanding how any work of art can be criticized from a moral standpoint"—in court by the Marquess of Queensberry's lawyer, Edward Carson. Carson asked pointedly whether "a well written book putting forth sodomitical views might be a good book" (Merlin Holland, *The Real Trial of Oscar Wilde* [New York: Harper Collins, 2004], 80). Wilde replied that "no work of art ever puts forward views of any kind" and that "if a book is well written . . . the impression that it produces is a sense of beauty, which is the very highest sense that I think human beings are capable of" (80).

2. cf. "I have no sympathy at all with the moral indignation of our time against M. Zola. It is simply the rage of Caliban on seeing his own face in a glass" (Wilde, *Criticism: Historical Criticism, Intentions, The Soul of Man,* ed. Josephine Guy, vol. 4 of *The Complete Works of Oscar Wilde* [Oxford: Oxford Univ. Press, 2007], 79). Caliban, a bestial precivilized human driven by appetite and sensual gratification, is a character in Shakespeare's play *The Tempest.* When *The Picture of Dorian Gray* was savaged by the *St. James's Gazette* in June 1890, Wilde remarked that the paper's editor "employed Caliban as his art-critic" (*The Complete Letters of Oscar Wilde,* ed. Merlin Holland and Rupert Hart-Davis [New York: Henry Holt, 2000], 439); and in *De Profundis* Wilde remarks that although "my business as an artist was with Ariel, I set myself to wrestle

The nineteenth-century dislike of Romanticism is the rage of Caliban not seeing his own face in a glass.[3]

The moral life of man forms part of the subject-matter of the artist, but the morality of art consists in the perfect use of an imperfect medium.

No artist desires to prove anything. Even things that are true can be proved.

No artist has ethical sympathies. An ethical sympathy in an artist is an unpardonable mannerism of style.[4]

No artist is ever morbid. The artist can express everything.[5]

Thought and language are to the artist instruments of an art.

----

with Caliban" (*The Annotated Prison Writings of Oscar Wilde,* ed. Nicholas Frankel [Cambridge, MA: Harvard Univ. Press, 2018], 241).

Realism designates a movement among nineteenth-century writers and artists, who, rejecting the excesses of Romanticism, sought to depict reality or everyday life with truth and accuracy. *Romanticism,* by contrast, deriving etymologically from the French and Italian narrative *romances* of the Middle Ages, designates the Europe-wide movement in art and literature, flourishing roughly from the 1780s onwards, that emphasized subjective experience, imagination, and individual feeling rather than objective truth. In Wilde's early draft manuscript, "the nineteenth-century dislike of Romanticism" was "the rage of the nineteenth century against Idealism."

3. In the earlier published version of the Preface, this aphorism was continuous with the previous one, not separate as here.

4. "An artist . . . has no ethical sympathies at all," Wilde wrote to the *Scots Observer* in July 1890; similarly, "The sphere of art and the sphere of ethics are absolutely distinct and separate," Wilde wrote to the *St. James's Gazette* the previous month.

5. This aphorism was absent from the first published version of the Preface. Wilde had used it previously with slight variation in "The Soul of Man Under Socialism" (see p. 172 above).

Vice and virtue are to the artist materials for an art.[6]
From the point of view of form, the type of all the arts is the art of
the musician. From the point of view of feeling, the actor's craft is
the type.[7]
All art is at once surface and symbol.
Those who go beneath the surface do so at their peril.
Those who read the symbol do so at their peril.
It is the spectator, and not life, that art really mirrors.[8]
Diversity of opinion about a work of art shows that the
work is new, complex, and vital.[9]
When critics disagree the artist is in accord with himself.

6. The earlier published version of the Preface has "materials of his art," not "materials for an art."

7. Wilde's notion that "the type of all the arts is the art of the musician" is heavily indebted to Walter Pater, who had written that "all art constantly aspires towards the condition of music" and explained that the "constant effort" of art is to "obliterate" the distinction between matter and form, so that the latter becomes "an end in itself, . . . penetrat[ing] every part of the matter" (*The Renaissance*, ed. Donald L. Hill [Berkeley: Univ. of California Press, 1980], 106). However, in "The Decay of Lying" (p. 231 above), Vivian says that it is the fact that "Art never expresses anything but itself, . . . more than that vital connection between form and substance, on which Mr. Pater dwells, that makes music the type of all the arts." For Wilde's notion that the poet is "the real musician," see p. 48 above; and for Wilde's notion that the actor's craft or "aim" should be "to convert his own accidental personality into the real and essential personality of the character he is called upon to impersonate," see p. 344 above.

8. Wilde used this expression verbatim in a letter to the editor of the *Scots Observer* in July 1890.

9. "If a work of art is rich and vital and complete," Wilde wrote to the *Scots Observer* in July 1890, "those who have artistic instincts will see its beauty."

We can forgive a man for making a useful thing as long as he does not admire it. The only excuse for making a useless thing is that one admires it intensely.[10]

All art is quite useless.[11]

10. In the earlier published version of the Preface, "intensely" had been "inordinately."

11. Wilde's final two aphorisms reject the utilitarianism driving the aesthetic philosophy of William Morris and the Arts and Crafts movement. They are heavily influenced by Théophile Gautier's comment, in his 1834 Preface to *Mademoiselle de Maupin*, that "the only things that are really beautiful are those which have no use" (Gautier, *Mademoiselle de Maupin*, ed. and trans. Helen Constantine [London: Penguin Books, 2005], 23).

A Few Maxims for the Instruction
of the Over-Educated*

Education is an admirable thing. But it is well to remember from time to time that nothing that is worth knowing can be taught.[1]

Public opinion exists only where there are no ideas.[2]

* First published over Wilde's signature in *The Saturday Review* 78 (November 17, 1894): 533–534. *The Saturday Review* was at this date owned and edited by Wilde's friend, the iconoclastic Frank Harris, who had, in his capacity as editor of *The Fortnightly Review,* previously accepted for publication "Pen Pencil and Poison," "The Soul of Man Under Socialism," and "Preface to *The Picture of Dorian Gray.*" Later, during Wilde's imprisonment and final exile (1895–1900), when Wilde was shunned by many old friends as well as enemies, Harris would prove to be amongst the most loyal and steadfast of Wilde's supporters.

1. This maxim had been used previously in part one of "The Critic as Artist" (see Wilde, *Criticism: Historical Criticism, Intentions, The Soul of Man,* ed. Josephine Guy, vol. 4 of *The Complete Works of Oscar Wilde* [Oxford: Oxford Univ. Press, 2007], 136); for Wilde's earlier formulation "nothing that one can learn is ever worth learning," see p. 332 above.

2. cf. "The public dislike novelty because they are afraid of it" (p. 168 above).

The English are always degrading truths into facts. When a truth becomes a fact it loses all its intellectual value.[3]

It is a very sad thing that nowadays there is so little useless information.[4]

The only link between Literature and the Drama left to us in England at the present moment is the bill of the play.

In old days books were written by men of letters and read by the public. Nowadays books are written by the public and read by nobody.[5]

Most women are so artificial that they have no sense of Art. Most men are so natural that they have no sense of Beauty.

Friendship is far more tragic than love. It lasts longer.

What is abnormal in Life stands in normal relations to Art. It is the only thing in Life that stands in normal relations to Art.

---

3. cf. "the aesthetic value of Shakespeare's plays does not, in the slightest degree, depend on their facts, but on their Truth, and Truth is independent of facts always, inventing or selecting them at pleasure" (Wilde, *Criticism,* 220). For "our monstrous worship of facts," see "The Decay of Lying," pp. 195–198 above.

4. Another echo of "The Critic as Artist," in which Gilbert at one point tells Ernest: "Don't degrade me into the position of giving you useful information" (Wilde, *Criticism*, 136).

5. cf. "The public has always, and in every age, been badly brought up. They are continually asking Art to be popular" (p. 166 above)

A subject that is beautiful in itself gives no suggestion to the artist. It lacks imperfection.

The only thing that the artist cannot see is the obvious. The only thing that the public can see is the obvious. The result is the Criticism of the Journalist.

Art is the only serious thing in the world. And the artist is the only person who is never serious.

To be really mediæval one should have no body. To be really modern one should have no soul. To be really Greek one should have no clothes.[6]

Dandyism is the assertion of the absolute modernity of Beauty.[7]

The only thing that can console one for being poor is extravagance. The only thing that can console one for being rich is economy.

One should never listen. To listen is a sign of indifference to one's hearers.

6. For Wilde's notions that "Greek dress was in its essence inartistic" and that "Nothing should reveal the body but the body," see p. 366 below.

7. See *The Picture of Dorian Gray: An Annotated, Uncensored Edition*, ed. Nicholas Frankel (Cambridge, MA: The Belknap Press of Harvard Univ. Press, 2011), 190, for an earlier version of this maxim.

Even the disciple has his uses. He stands behind one's throne, and at the moment of one's triumph whispers in one's ear that, after all, one is immortal.[8]

The criminal classes are so close to us that even the policemen can see them. They are so far away from us that only the poet can understand them.

Those whom the gods love grow young.[9]

8. cf. "the true disciples of the great artist are not his studio-imitators, but those who become like his works of art" (p. 221 above).

9. "Youth is the one thing worth having," Lord Henry Wotton tells the eponymous protagonist of *The Picture of Dorian Gray:* "Realise your youth while you have it. Don't squander the gold of your days, listening to the tedious, trying to improve the hopeless failure, or giving away your life to the ignorant, the common, and the vulgar . . . Live! Live the wonderful life that is in you! Let nothing be lost upon you. . . . For there is such a little time that your youth will last, such a little time." For Wilde's notion that "the aim of perfection is youth," see p. 368 below.

Phrases and Philosophies for the
Use of the Young*

*The first duty in life is to be as artificial as possible. What the
second duty is no one has as yet discovered.*

*Wickedness is a myth invented by good people to account for
the curious attractiveness of others.*

*If the poor only had profiles there would be no difficulty in solving
the problem of poverty.*

* First published, signed, in December 1894, in Vol. 1, No. 1—the
only number ever published—of *The Chameleon*, an Oxford undergraduate magazine that was openly homosexual in orientation. Four months
later, in the course of his fateful, unsuccessful libel proceedings against
the Marquess of Queensberry, the father of his lover Lord Alfred Douglas,
Wilde was interrogated in court about these epigrams and about his association with *The Chameleon* generally. Queensberry's legal counsel,
Edward Carson, called the epigrams "immoral" (Merlin Holland, *The
Real Trial of Oscar Wilde* [New York: HarperCollins, 2004], 39), "likely to
tend to immorality amongst young men" (73), and questioned whether
any of them was "a good educational maxim for youth" (75). Wilde responded calmly "I should think the young had enough sense of humour
to see the beautiful nonsense" (76). Weeks later, during his criminal
trials, Wilde confessed: I am a lover of youth, I like to study the young
in everything. There is something fascinating in youthfulness" (quoted
in H. Montgomery Hyde, *The Trials of Oscar Wilde*, 2nd ed. [New York:
Dover Publications, 1973], 202–203).

No. 20

The Chameleon

'A Bazaar of Dangerous and Smiling Chances'
(R. L. STEVENSON)

Three Numbers } VOL. I. NUMBER 1. { Subscription, 15/ per
a Year } { Annum, Post Free
The Edition of each Number is limited to 100 numbered copies

CONTENTS

LONDON: GAY AND BIRD
5 CHANDOS STREET, STRAND

Front wrapper and table of contents for *The Chameleon* 1, no. 1 (December 1894). Subtitled "a bazaar of dangerous and smiling chances," *The Chameleon* was originally meant to appear three times per year, but only one number was ever published. Wilde's "Phrases and Philosophies for the Use of the Young" was the opening contribution; others included Lord Alfred Douglas's poem "Two Loves" and John Francis Bloxam's pederastic story "The Priest and The Acolyte." *The Chameleon* was unashamedly homosexual in orientation, but Bloxam's story went too far, as Wilde made clear during the first of his legal trials, in April 1895, when he called it "bad and indecent." Grilled on his association with the magazine, Wilde tried to distance himself from *The Chameleon* in court.

Those who see any difference between soul and body have neither.

A really well-made buttonhole is the only link between Art and Nature.[1]

Religions die when they are proved to be true. Science is the record of dead religions.[2]

The well-bred contradict other people. The wise contradict themselves.

Nothing that actually occurs is of the smallest importance.[3]

Dullness is the coming of age of seriousness.

In all unimportant matters, style, not sincerity, is the essential. In all important matters, style, not sincerity, is the essential.[4]

1. For Wilde's notion that "the little note of individualism that makes dress delightful can only be attained nowadays by the colour and treatment of the flower one wears," see p. 339 above; and for his notion that "Art is our spirited protest, our gallant attempt to teach Nature her proper place," see p. 187 above.

2. On being cross-examined in court about this epigram, Wilde called it "a suggestion towards the philosophy of the absorption of religion into science" (Holland, *The Real Trial,* 75). Years earlier, in his undergraduate thesis, "The Rise of Historical Criticism," Wilde had written "religions may be absorbed, but they are never disproved."

3. For Wilde's notion that action is "the last resource of those who know not how to dream," see p. 298 above. Also p. 80 above.

4. cf. "In matters of grave importance, style, not sincerity, is the vital thing" (*The Importance of Being Earnest*).

If one tells the truth one is sure, sooner or later, to be found out.[5]

Pleasure is the only thing one should live for. Nothing ages like happiness.[6]

It is only by not paying one's bills that one can hope to live in the memory of the commercial classes.

No crime is vulgar, but all vulgarity is crime. Vulgarity is the conduct of others.

Only the shallow know themselves.

Time is waste of money.

One should always be a little improbable.

There is a fatality about all good resolutions. They are invariably made too soon.

The only way to atone for being occasionally a little overdressed is by being always absolutely overeducated.[7]

5. cf. "the truth isn't quite the sort of thing one tells to a nice, sweet, refined girl" (*The Importance of Being Earnest*).

6. On being cross-examined about this aphorism, Wilde explained that "self-realisation—realisation of one's self—is the primal aim of life. I think that to realise one's self through pleasure is finer than to realise one's self through pain" (Holland, *The Real Trial*, 75). In the opening scene of *The Importance of Being Earnest,* Jack answers Algernon's question "What brings you up to town?," "Oh, pleasure, pleasure! What else should bring one anywhere?"

7. cf. "If I am occasionally a little over-dressed, I make up for it by being always immensely over-educated" (*The Importance of Being Earnest*).

To be premature is to be perfect.

Any preoccupation with ideas of what is right and wrong in conduct shows an arrested intellectual development.

Ambition is the last refuge of the failure.

A truth ceases to be true when more than one person believes in it.[8]

In examinations the foolish ask questions that the wise cannot answer.

Greek dress was in its essence inartistic. Nothing should reveal the body but the body.[9]

One should either be a work of art, or wear a work of art.

It is only the superficial qualities that last. Man's deeper nature is soon found out.

Industry is the root of all ugliness.

The ages live in history through their anachronisms.

8. On being cross-examined in court, Wilde described this aphorism as "my philosophical definition of truth—something so personal that when another person holds the same—that in fact the same truth can never be apprehended by two minds . . . to each mind there is its own truth; it is an important physical condition entirely" (Holland, *The Real Trial*, 76).

9. cf. "To be really Greek one should have no clothes" (p. 360 above).

It is only the gods who taste of death. Apollo has passed away,
but Hyacinth, whom men say he slew, lives on. Nero and
Narcissus are always with us.[10]

The old believe everything: the middle-aged suspect everything:
the young know everything.[11]

10. For Apollo, see p. 206, n.69 above. Hyacinth was a beautiful young man and the lover of Apollo. Apollo and Hyacinth took turns throwing the discus. Hyacinth ran to catch it to impress Apollo, was struck by the discus as it fell to the ground, and died, whereupon Apollo made a flower, the hyacinth, from the boy's spilled blood. Nero (38–68 CE), who ruled Rome for the last fourteen years of his life, was one of the most depraved and excessive of Roman emperors. The Narcissus myth preoccupied Wilde: it forms the basis of his prose-poem "The Disciple" and informs the central moment of *The Picture of Dorian Gray*, in which "the sense of his own beauty came on [Dorian] like a revelation" (*The Picture of Dorian Gray: An Annotated, Uncensored Edition,* ed. Nicholas Frankel [Cambridge, MA: The Belknap Press of Harvard Univ. Press, 2011], 102). According to classical legend, Narcissus was a beautiful youth of awesome vanity, beloved by suitors of both sexes, all of whom he rejected or ignored. Upon being rejected by Narcissus, one of his lovesick victims uttered a curse dooming him to experience the same intensity of passion for an unattainable object. Thereafter Narcissus came upon a clear, silvery mountain pool, and upon stooping down to drink from its waters, he fell in love with his own reflection. Unable to possess the beautiful youth that he had found in the water, whose image dissipated with the falling of his tears, Narcissus pined away until his body was no more and all that remained was the flower that bears his name.

11. "It's absurd to talk of the ignorance of youth," says Lord Henry Wotton in *The Picture of Dorian Gray*: "The only people whose opinions I listen to now with any respect are people much younger than myself. . . . As for the aged, I always contradict the aged."

The condition of perfection is idleness: the aim of perfection is youth.[12]

Only the great masters of style ever succeed in being obscure.

There is something tragic about the enormous number of young men there are in England at the present moment who start life with perfect profiles, and end by adopting some useful profession.

To love oneself is the beginning of a life-long romance.

12. Wilde defended the first half of this aphorism in court by explaining "I think the life of contemplation is the highest life, and I think [it is] so recognised by the philosopher and the saint." Compare the second half with his notion that "Those whom the gods love grow young" (p. 361 above).

FURTHER READING

Editions

The Annotated Prison Writings of Oscar Wilde. Edited by Nicholas Frankel. Cambridge, MA: Harvard University Press, 2018.

The Complete Letters of Oscar Wilde. Edited by Merlin Holland and Rupert Hart-Davis. New York: Henry Holt, 2000.

Criticism: Historical Criticism, Intentions, The Soul of Man. Edited by Josephine M. Guy. Vol. 4 of *The Complete Works of Oscar Wilde*. Oxford: Oxford University Press, 2007.

Journalism. Edited by John Stokes and Mark Turner. Vols. 6 and 7 of *The Complete Works of Oscar Wilde*. Oxford: Oxford University Press, 2013.

The Picture of Dorian Gray: An Annotated, Uncensored Edition. Edited by Nicholas Frankel. Cambridge, MA: The Belknap Press of Harvard University Press, 2011.

Biographical

Bristow, Joseph. *Oscar Wilde on Trial: The Criminal Proceedings*. New Haven, CT: Yale University Press, forthcoming.

Coakley, Davis. *Oscar Wilde: The Importance of Being Irish*. Dublin: Town House, 1994.

Ellmann, Richard. *Oscar Wilde.* New York: Knopf, 1988.

Frankel, Nicholas. *Oscar Wilde: The Unrepentant Years.* Cambridge, MA: Harvard University Press, 2017.

———. *The Invention of Oscar Wilde.* London: Reaktion Books, 2021.

Holland, Merlin. *The Wilde Album.* New York: Henry Holt, 1998.

———. *The Real Trial of Oscar Wilde.* New York: Harper Perennial, 2004. Published in the United Kingdom as *The Irish Peacock and The Scarlet Marquess.* London: Fourth Estate, 2003.

Holland, Vyvyan. *Son of Oscar Wilde.* 1954. Rev. ed., New York: Carroll & Graf, 1999.

McKenna, Neil. *The Secret Life of Oscar Wilde.* New York: Basic Books, 2005.

Mendelssohn, Michèle. *Making Oscar Wilde.* Oxford: Oxford University Press, 2018.

Mikhail, E. H., ed. *Oscar Wilde: Interviews and Recollections.* 2 vols. London: Macmillan, 1979.

Stern, Kimberley J., *Oscar Wilde: A Literary Life.* Cham, Switzerland: Palgrave Macmillan, 2019.

Sturgis, Matthew. *Oscar: A Life.* London: Head of Zeus, 2018.

Bibliographical

Beckson, Karl, ed. *Oscar Wilde: The Critical Heritage.* London: Routledge & Kegan Paul, 1970.

Fletcher, Ian, and John Stokes. "Oscar Wilde." In *Anglo-Irish Literature: A Review of Research*, edited by Richard Finneran. New York: MLA, 1976.

———. "Oscar Wilde." In *Recent Research on Anglo-Irish Writers*, edited by Richard Finneran. New York: MLA, 1983.

Mason, Stuart [Christopher Millard]. *Bibliography of Oscar Wilde.* London: T. Werner Laurie, 1914.

Mikhail, E. H., ed. *Oscar Wilde: An Annotated Bibliography of Criticism.* London: Macmillan, 1978.

Mikolyzk, Thomas A. *Oscar Wilde: An Annotated Bibliography.* Westport, CT: Greenwood Press, 1993.

Small, Ian. *Oscar Wilde Revalued: An Essay on New Materials & Methods of Research.* Greensboro, NC: ELT Press, 1993.

———. *Oscar Wilde, Recent Research: A Supplement to "Oscar Wilde Revalued."* Greensboro, NC: ELT Press, 2000.

Small, Ian, and Josephine Guy. *Studying Oscar Wilde: History, Criticism, and Myth.* Greensboro, NC: ELT Press, 2006.

Critical and Contextual Studies

Bashford, Bruce. *Oscar Wilde: The Critic as Humanist.* Vancouver, BC: Fairleigh Dickinson University Press, 1999.

Bendz, Ernst. *The Influence of Pater and Matthew Arnold in the Prose Writings of Oscar Wilde.* London: Grevel, 1914.

Bennet, Michael Y., ed. *Philosophy and Oscar Wilde.* New York: Palgrave Macmillan, 2017.

Borelius, Birgit. "Oscar Wilde, Whistler and Colours." *Scripta Minora* 3 (1966–1967): 1–65.

Bristow, Joseph, ed. *Oscar Wilde and Modern Culture: The Making of a Legend.* Athens: Ohio University Press, 2008.

———, ed. *Wilde Discoveries: Traditions, Histories, Archives.* Toronto: University of Toronto Press, 2013.

Bristow, Joseph, and Rebecca N. Mitchell. "Oscar Wilde's 'Cultivated Blindness': Reassessing the Textual and Intellectual History of 'The Decay of Lying.'" *Review of English Studies* n.s. 69, no. 288 (2018): 94–156.

Brown, Julia Prewitt. *Cosmopolitan Criticism: Oscar Wilde's Philosophy of Art.* Charlottesville: University of Virginia Press, 1997.

Bruder, Anne. "Constructing Artist and Critic Between J. M. Whistler and Oscar Wilde: 'In The Best Days Of Art There Were No Art-Critics.'" *English Literature in Transition, 1880–1920* 47 (2004): 161–180.

Cavendish-Jones, Colin. "Oscar Wilde and The Philosophy of Fashion." In *Transglobal Fashion Narratives*, edited by Ann Pierson-Jones and Joseph Hancock, 79–90. Bristol, UK: Intellect, 2015.

Chen, Qi. "Activism Via Inaction (*Wu Wei*): Oscar Wilde's Interpretation and Appropriation of *Chuang Tzu*." *Philosophy and Literature* 45 (2021): 103–120.

Clayton, Loretta. "Oscar Wilde, Aesthetic Dress, and the Modern Woman." In *Wilde Discoveries*, edited by Joseph Bristow, 143–166.

Cooper, John. *Oscar Wilde on Dress, including "The Philosophy of Dress" by Oscar Wilde.* Philadelphia: CSM Press, 2013.

Danson, Lawrence. *Wilde's Intentions: The Artist in his Criticism.* Oxford: Clarendon Press, 1997.

Davis, Michael F., and Petra Dierkes-Thrun, eds. *Wilde's Other Worlds.* New York: Routledge, 2018.

Dellamora, Richard. *Masculine Desire: The Sexual Politics of Victorian Aestheticism.* Chapel Hill: University of North Carolina Press, 1990.

Dollimore, Jonathan. *Sexual Dissidence: Augustine to Wilde, Freud to Foucault.* Oxford: Clarendon Press, 1991.

Dowling, Linda. *Hellenism and Homosexuality in Victorian Oxford*. Ithaca, NY: Cornell University Press, 1994.

———. *Language and Decadence in the Victorian Fin-de-Siècle*. Princeton, NJ: Princeton University Press, 1986.

———. *The Vulgarization of Art: The Victorians and Aesthetic Democracy*. Charlottesville: University of Virginia Press, 1996.

Ellmann, Richard. "The Critic as Artist as Wilde." Introduction to *The Artist as Critic: Critical Writings of Oscar Wilde*, edited by Richard Ellmann, ix–xxviii. New York: Random House, 1969.

Frankel, Nicholas. "Wilde's *Intentions* and the Simulation of Meaning." In *Oscar Wilde's Decorated Books*, 79–108. Ann Arbor: University of Michigan Press, 2000.

Friedman, Dustin. *Before Queer Theory: Victorian Aestheticism and The Self*. Baltimore: Johns Hopkins University Press, 2019.

Gagnier, Regenia. *Idylls of the Marketplace: Oscar Wilde and the Victorian Public*. Stanford, CA: Stanford University Press, 1986.

Harris, Wendell V. "Arnold, Pater, Wilde, and the Object as in Themselves They See It." *Studies in English Literature, 1500–1900* 11 (1971): 733–747.

Horrocks, Jamie. "Vernon Lee, Oscar Wilde, and the Dialogue of 'New Aesthetics.'" *Nineteenth Century Prose* 40, no.1 (2013): 201–238.

Johnson, R. V. *Aestheticism*. London: Methuen, 1969.

Kohl, Norbert. *Oscar Wilde: The Works of a Conformist Rebel*. Translated by David. H. Wilson. Cambridge: Cambridge University Press, 1989.

Livesey, Ruth. *Socialism, Sex, and the Culture of Aestheticism in Britain, 1880–1914*. Oxford: Oxford University Press, 2007.

Longxi, Zhuang. "The Critical Legacy of Oscar Wilde." *Texas Studies in Literature and Language* 30 (1988).

McCormack, Jerusha, ed. *Wilde the Irishman*. New Haven, CT: Yale University Press, 1998.

———. "From Chinese Wisdom to Irish Wit: Zhuangzi and Oscar Wilde." *Irish University Review* 37, no. 2 (2007): 302–321.

———. "Oscar Wilde as Daoist Sage." In *Philosophy and Oscar Wilde*, edited by Michael Bennett, 73–104.

Nunokawa, Jeff. *Tame Passions of Wilde: The Styles of Manageable Desire*. Princeton, NJ: Princeton University Press, 2003.

Parveen, Nazia. "The Body-Mind of Oscar Wilde's Reviews for the *Pall Mall Gazette*." *European Review of History* 17, no. 2 (2010): 303–315.

Pine, Richard. *The Thief of Reason: Oscar Wilde and Modern Ireland*. Dublin: Gill & Macmillan, 1995.

Potolsky, Matthew. "Decadence and Realism." *Victorian Literature and Culture* 49 (2021): 563–582.

Raby, Peter, and Kerry Powell, eds. *Oscar Wilde in Context*. Cambridge: Cambridge University Press, 2013.

Raby, Peter, ed. *The Cambridge Companion to Oscar Wilde*. Cambridge: Cambridge University Press, 1997.

Roden, Frederick S., ed. *Palgrave Advances in Oscar Wilde Studies*. Basingstoke: Palgrave Macmillan, 2004.

Roditi, Edouard. *Oscar Wilde*. rev. ed. New York: New Directions, 1986.

Rose, Clare, ed. *Clothing, Society and Culture in Nineteenth-Century Britain: Abuses and Reforms*. Abingdon: Routledge, 2016.

Sammells, Neil. "Theorizing Style: The Essays." In *Wilde Style: The Plays and Prose of Oscar Wilde,* 28–52. London: Pearson Education, 2000.

Schaffer, Talia. "Fashioning Aestheticism by Aestheticizing Fashion: Wilde, Beerbohm, and the Male Aesthetes' Sartorial Codes." *Victorian Literature and Culture* 28 (2000): 39–54.

Schiff, Hilda. "Nature and Art in Oscar Wilde's 'The Decay of Lying.'" *Essays and Studies* 18 (1965): 83–102

Schroeder, Horst. "The OET *Complete Works* Vol. IV. II 'The Truth of Masks.'" *The Wildean* 35 (July 2009): 20–51

———. "The OET *Complete Works* Vol. IV. III 'Pen, Pencil, and Poison.'" *The Wildean* 36 (Jan. 2010): 28–60.

———. "The OET *Complete Works* Vol. IV. IV 'The Decay of Lying.'" *The Wildean* 37 (July 2010): 16–64.

———. "The OET *Complete Works* Vol. IV. V 'The Critic as Artist. Part I.'" *The Wildean* 38 (Jan. 2011): 54–110.

———. "The OET *Complete Works* Vol. IV. VI 'The Critic as Artist. Part II.'" *The Wildean* 39 (July 2011): 59–110.

Selleri, Andrea. "Oscar Wilde on the Theory of the Author." *Philosophy and Literature* 42, no. 1 (April 2018): 49–66.

Shewan, Rodney. *Oscar Wilde: Art and Egotism*. London: Macmillan, 1977.

Small, Ian. "Semiotics and Oscar Wilde's Accounts of Art." *British Journal of Aesthetics* 25 (1985): 50–56.

Small, Ian, and Josephine M. Guy. *Oscar Wilde's Profession*. Oxford: Oxford University Press, 2000.

Smith II, Phillip E., ed. *Approaches to Teaching the Works of Oscar Wilde*. New York: MLA, 2008.

Smith II, Phillip E., and Michael S. Helfand. *Oscar Wilde's Oxford Notebooks: A Portrait of Mind in The Making*. Oxford: Oxford University Press, 1989.

Stokes, John, and Mark W. Turner. "Oscar Wilde: New Journalist." In *Journalism and the Periodical Press in Nineteenth-Century Britain*, edited by Joanne Shattock, 370–382. Cambridge: Cambridge University Press, 2017.

Sumpter, Caroline. "'No Artist has Ethical Sympathies': Oscar Wilde, Aesthetics, and Moral Evolution." *Victorian Literature and Culture* 44 (2016): 623–640

Sussman, Herbert. "Criticism as Art: Form in Oscar Wilde's Critical Writings." *Studies in Philology* 70 (1973).

Watson, Edward E. "Wilde's Iconoclastic Classicism: The Critic as Artist." *English Literature in Transition, 1880–1920* 27 (1988): 225–235.

Whitely, Giles. *Oscar Wilde and the Simulacrum: The Truth of Masks*. London: Legenda, 2015.

Williams, Kristian. *Resist Everything Except Temptation: The Anarchist Philosophy of Oscar Wilde*. With a foreword by Alan Moore. Chico, CA: AK Press, 2020.

Willoughby, Guy. *Art and Christhood: The Aesthetics of Oscar Wilde*. Vancouver, BC: Fairleigh Dickinson University Press, 1993.

Woodcock, George. *Oscar Wilde: The Double Image*. Montreal: Black Rose, 1986.

Wright, Thomas. *Built of Books: How Reading Defined the Life of Oscar Wilde*. New York: Henry Holt, 2009.

ILLUSTRATION CREDITS

Page viii: Photoportrait of Wilde, by Napoleon Sarony, 1882. Library of Congress.

Page 9: Oil portrait of James McNeill Whistler, by William Merritt Chase, 1885. The Metropolitan Museum, New York.

Page 10: James McNeill Whistler, *Nocturne in Black and Gold: The Falling Rocket,* c. 1875. Wikimedia Commons.

Page 40: Self-designed, engraved invitation for Whistler's "Ten O'Clock," Prince's Hall, Piccadilly, February 1885. Library of Congress.

Page 49: William Powell Frith, *A Private View at the Royal Academy, 1881.* Photogravure engraving. The Furió Collection.

Page 75: Portrait of Zhuang Zhou (Chuang Tzǔ), artist and date unknown. Wikimedia Commons.

Page 96: Dress, by Charles Frederick Worth, 1880s. Metropolitan Museum.

Page 101: "The Latest Paris Bonnet." Reprinted from *Woman's World* 2 (1888–1889): 139.

Page 105: Photoportrait of the American actress Cora Brown-Potter (1859–1936), by B. J. Falk, 1895. Library of Congress.

Page 109: James McNeill Whistler, *Arrangement in Grey and Black No. 1: Portrait of the Artist's Mother.* Lithographic print by Thomas R. Way, 1892. The Metropolitan Museum.

Page 130: "Do you want a model?" engraved illustration, by R. G. Harper Pennington. Reprinted from *The English Illustrated Magazine* 6, no. 64 (January 1889): 317.

Page 137: Pyotr Alexeyevich Kropotkin (1842–1921), photographer and date unknown. Library of Congress.

Page 183: Oscar Wilde, *Intentions* (London: Osgood McIlvaine & Co., 1891). Title page.

Page 188: William Morris and Company, London. "Sussex" armchair, c. 1865. Wikimedia Commons.

Page 228: James McNeill Whistler, *Nocturne: The Thames at Battersea*. Lithotint print, 1878. The Metropolitan Museum.

Page 247: Thomas Griffiths Wainewright, *Portrait of a Young Man (Self-Portrait)*. c. 1825. Pencil and watercolor on paper. Wikimedia Commons.

Page 273: Thomas Griffiths Wainewright, chalk portrait of his sister-in-law Helen Abercromby. Reprinted from *Essays and Criticisms of Thomas Griffiths Wainewright,* edited and introduced by W. Carew Hazlitt (London: Reeves and Turner, 1880), interleaved between pages xxviii and xxix.

Page 286: James McNeill Whistler, *Whistler v. Ruskin, Art and Art Critics* (London: Chatto and Windus, 1878), front paper wrapper. Mark Samuels Lasner Collection, University of Delaware Library, Museums and Press.

Page 325: Frontispiece to Mrs. H. R. Haweis, *The Art of Beauty*, 2nd ed. (London: Chatto and Windus, 1883). The Wellcome Collection.

Page 328: Photoportrait of Wilde, by Napoleon Sarony, 1882. Library of Congress.

Page 338: The actor-manager Charles Wyndham in character, photographer unknown, c. 1890. Library of Congress.

Page 341: Oscar Wilde, 1889. Photoportrait by W. & D. Downey. Mark Samuels Lasner Collection, University of Delaware Library, Museums and Press.

Page 348: Charles Haslewood Shannon, portrait of John Gray. Lithograph, 1896. Mark Samuels Lasner Collection, University of Delaware Library, Museums and Press.

Page 363: Front wrapper and table of contents for *The Chameleon* 1, no. 1 (December 1894). Mark Samuels Lasner Collection, University of Delaware Library, Museums and Press.

ACKNOWLEDGMENTS

This is the fifth book in Harvard University Press's series of annotated Wilde editions, and I remain deeply grateful to John Kulka, my then-editor, who commissioned the series over a decade ago. Working on the series has been one of the great pleasures and privileges of my academic life. I am deeply grateful as well to Andrew Kinney, who five years ago generously took over as editor and who expertly saw the current (as well as the previous) book into production; also Katrina Vassallo, who skillfully steered it through production; and Mary Ribesky, of Westchester Publishing Services, who prepared the book for printing. I owe much as well to the care and expertise with which the Press's three external readers reviewed the book in manuscript: their comments proved invaluable, not least in helping me avoid embarrassing and unnecessary errors.

Closer to home, the English Department at Virginia Commonwealth University has always proved a conducive environment, and I am grateful to its Chair and Associate Chair, Catherine

Ingrassia and Sachi Shimomura respectively, for consistently supporting my work on Wilde. My scholarship has benefited from the regularity with which I am invited to try out my ideas in the classroom, where the enthusiasm and insights of my students are always exciting.

My scholarly debts, especially to the work of previous Wilde editors and commentators—Josephine Guy, John Stokes and Mark Turner, Horst Schroeder, John Cooper (on Wilde's writings on dress)—will be clear from my annotations. My greatest debt is to my family—to my wife Susan and our boys Max, Theo, and Oliver—who have had to live and breathe Oscar Wilde for many years now. Without their love and support, my work would be impossible.

INDEX

Page numbers in italics refer to illustrations.

INDEX

INDEX